PHP and MongoDB
Web Development
Beginner's Guide

Combine the power of PHP and MongoDB to build
dynamic web 2.0 applications

Rubayeet Islam

BIRMINGHAM - MUMBAI

PHP and MongoDB Web Development
Beginner's Guide

First published: November 2011

Production Reference: 1181111

Published by Packt Publishing Ltd.
Livery Place
35 Livery Street
Birmingham B3 2PB, UK.

ISBN 978-1-84951-362-3

www.packtpub.com

Cover Image by Charwak A (charwak86@gmail.com)

Credits

Author
Rubayeet Islam

Reviewers
Sam Millman
Sigert de Vries
Nurul Ferdous
Vidyasagar N V

Acquisition Editor
Usha Iyer

Development Editor
Susmita Panda

Technical Editors
Joyslita D'Souza
Veronica Fernandes
Lubna Shaikh

Copy Editor
Laxmi Subramanian

Project Coordinator
Kushal Bhardwaj

Proofreader
Matthew Humphries

Indexer
Tejal Daruwale

Graphics
Valentina D'silva

Production Coordinator
Prachali Bhiwandkar

Cover Work
Prachali Bhiwandkar

About the Author

Rubayeet Islam is a Software Developer with over 4 years of experience in large-scale web application development on open source technology stacks (LAMP, Python/Django, Ruby on Rails). He is currently involved in developing cloud-based distributed software that use MongoDB as their analytics and metadata backend. He has also spoken in seminars to promote the use of MongoDB and NoSQL databases in general. He graduated from the University of Dhaka with a B.S. in Computer Science and Engineering.

I thank the Almighty for giving me such a blessed life and my parents for letting me follow my passion. My friend and colleague, Nurul Ferdous, for inspiring me to be an author in the first place. Finally, the amazing people at Packt – Usha Iyer, Kushal Bhardwaj, Priya Mukherji, and Susmita Panda, without your help and guidance this book would not have been possible to write.

About the Reviewers

Sam Millman, after achieving a B.Sc. in Computing from the University of Plymouth, immediately moved to advance his knowledge within Web development, specifically PHP. He is a fully self-taught professional Web Developer and IT Administrator working for a company in the south of England.

He first started to show an interest in MongoDB when he went in search of something new to learn. Now he is an active user of the MongoDB Google User Group and is about to release a new site written in PHP with MongoDB as the primary data store.

Sigert de Vries (1983) is a professional Web Developer working in The Netherlands. He has worked in several companies as a System Administrator and Web Developer. He is a specialist in high performance websites and is an open source enthusiast. With his communicative skills, he translates advanced technical issues to "normal" human language.

Sigert is currently working at `Worldticketshop.com`, helping them to be one of the largest ticket marketplaces in Europe. Within the company, there's plenty of room to use NoSQL solutions such as MongoDB.

I would like to thank Packt publishing for asking me to review this book, it has been a pleasure!

Vidyasagar N V was interested in Computer Science since an early age. Some of his serious work in computers and computer networks began during his high school days. Later, he went to the prestigious Institute Of Technology, Banaras Hindu University for his B.Tech. He has been working as a Software Developer and Data Expert, developing and building scalable systems. He has worked with a variety of 2nd, 3rd, and 4th generation languages. He has worked with flat files, indexed files, hierarchical databases, network databases, relational databases, NoSQL databases, Hadoop, and related technologies. Currently, he is working as a Senior Developer at Ziva Software Pvt. Ltd., developing big database-structured data-extraction techniques for the Web and local information. He enjoys producing high-quality software, web-based solutions, and designing secure and scalable data systems.

I would like to thank my parents, Mr. N Srinivasa Rao and Mrs.Latha Rao, and my family who supported and backed me throughout my life. My friends for being friends, and all those people willing to donate their time, effort, and expertise by participating in open source software projects. Thank you Packt Publishing for selecting me as one of the technical reviewers on this wonderful book. It is my honor to be a part of this book. You can contact me at `vidyasagar1729@gmail.com`.

www.PacktPub.com

Support files, eBooks, discount offers and more

You might want to visit www.PacktPub.com for support files and downloads related to your book.

Did you know that Packt offers eBook versions of every book published, with PDF and ePub files available? You can upgrade to the eBook version at www.PacktPub.com and as a print book customer, you are entitled to a discount on the eBook copy. Get in touch with us at service@packtpub.com for more details.

At www.PacktPub.com, you can also read a collection of free technical articles, sign up for a range of free newsletters and receive exclusive discounts and offers on Packt books and eBooks.

http://PacktLib.PacktPub.com

Do you need instant solutions to your IT questions? PacktLib is Packt's online digital book library. Here, you can access, read and search across Packt's entire library of books.

Why Subscribe?

- Fully searchable across every book published by Packt
- Copy and paste, print and bookmark content
- On demand and accessible via web browser

Free Access for Packt account holders

If you have an account with Packt at www.PacktPub.com, you can use this to access PacktLib today and view nine entirely free books. Simply use your login credentials for immediate access.

Table of Contents

Preface

MongoDB is an open source, non-relational database system designed to meet the needs of modern Web 2.0 applications. It is currently being used by some of the most popular websites in the world. This book introduces MongoDB to the web developer who has some background building web applications using PHP. This book teaches what MongoDB is, how it is different from relational database management systems, and when and why developers should use it instead of a relational database for storing data.

You will learn how to build PHP applications that use MongoDB as the data backend; solve common problems, such as HTTP session handling, user authentication, and so on.

You will also learn to solve interesting problems with MongoDB, such as web analytics with MapReduce, storing large files in GridFS, and building location-aware applications using Geospatial indexing.

Finally, you will learn how to optimize MongoDB to boost performance, improve security, and ensure data durability. The book will demonstrate the use of some handy GUI tools that makes database management easier.

What this book covers

Chapter 1, Getting Started with MongoDB introduces the underlying concepts of MongoDB, provides a step-by-step guide on how to install and run a MongoDB server on a computer, and make PHP and MongoDB talk to each other.

Chapter 2, Building your First MongoDB Powered Web App shows you how to build a simple blogging web application using PHP and MongoDB. Through the examples in this chapter, you will learn how to create/read/update/delete data in MongoDB using PHP.

Chapter 3, Building a Session Manager shows you how PHP and MongoDB can be used to handle HTTP sessions. You will build a stand-alone session manager module and learn how to perform user authentication/authorization using the module.

Chapter 4, Aggregation Queries introduces MapReduce, a powerful functional programming paradigm and shows you how it can be used to perform aggregation queries in MongoDB.

Chapter 5, Web Analytics using MongoDB shows you how you can store website traffic data in MongoDB in real time and use MapReduce to extract important analytics.

Chapter 6, Using MongoDB with Relational Databases explores use cases where MongoDB can be used alongside a relational database. You will learn how to archive data in MongoDB, use it for caching expensive query results, and store non-structured metadata about different objects in the domain.

Chapter 7, Handling Large Files with GridFS introduces GridFS, a specification in MongoDB that allows us to store large files in the database.

Chapter 8, Building Location-aware Web Applications with MongoDB and PHP, uses PHP, HTML5, JavaScript, and the Geospatial Indexing feature of MongoDB to build a web application that helps you find restaurants close to your current location.

Chapter 9, Improving Security and Performance shows you how to boost query performance using indexes, use built-in tools for analyzing and fine-tuning queries, improve database security, and ensure data durability.

Chapter 10, Easy MongoDB Administration with RockMongo and phpMoAdmin demonstrates the use of a couple of PHP-based GUI tools for managing MongoDB server—RockMongo and phpMoAdmin.

What you need for this book

Apache web server (or IIS if you are on Windows) running PHP 5.2.6 or higher.

A web browser that supports the W3C Geolocation API (Internet Explorer 9.0+, Google Chrome 5.0+, Firefox 3.5+ or Safari 5.0+).

Chapter 6, Using MongoDB with Relational Databases requires that you have MySQL installed on your machine.

Who this book is for

This book assumes that you have some background in web application development using PHP, HTML, and CSS. Some of the chapters require that you know JavaScript and are familiar with AJAX. Having a working knowledge of using a relational database system, such as MySQL will help you grasp some of the concepts quicker, but it is not strictly mandatory. No prior knowledge of MongoDB is required.

Conventions

In this book, you will find several headings appearing frequently.

To give clear instructions of how to complete a procedure or task, we use:

Time for action – heading

1. Action 1

2. Action 2

3. Action 3

Instructions often need some extra explanation so that they make sense, so they are followed with:

What just happened?

This heading explains the working of tasks or instructions that you have just completed.

You will also find some other learning aids in the book, including:

Pop quiz – heading

These are short multiple choice questions intended to help you test your own understanding.

Have a go hero – heading

These set practical challenges and give you ideas for experimenting with what you have learned.

You will also find a number of styles of text that distinguish between different kinds of information. Here are some examples of these styles, and an explanation of their meaning.

Code words in text are shown as follows: "The value for the first field, _id, is autogenerated."

A block of code is set as follows:

```
try {
  $mongo = new Mongo($options=array('timeout'=> 100))
} catch(MongoConnectionException $e) {
  die("Failed to connect to database ".$e->getMessage());
}
```

When we wish to draw your attention to a particular part of a code block, the relevant lines or items are set in bold:

```
{
    _id        : ObjectId("4dcd2abe5981aec801010000"),
    title      : "The only perfect site is hind-site",
    content    : "Loren ipsum dolor sit amet…",
    saved_at   : ISODate('2011-05-16T18:42:57.949Z'),
    author_id  : ObjectId("4dd491695072aefc456c9aca")
}
```

Any command-line input or output is written as follows:

```
>db.movies.find({"genre":"sci-fi"})
{ "_id" : ObjectId("4db439153ec7b6fd1c9093ec"), "name" : "Source Code",
"genre" : "sci-fi", "year" : 2011 }
```

New terms and **important words** are shown in bold. Words that you see on the screen, in menus or dialog boxes for example, appear in the text like this: "Click on the **Delete** link on any one article."

Warnings or important notes appear in a box like this.

Tips and tricks appear like this.

Reader feedback

Feedback from our readers is always welcome. Let us know what you think about this book—what you liked or may have disliked. Reader feedback is important for us to develop titles that you really get the most out of.

To send us general feedback, simply send an e-mail to feedback@packtpub.com, and mention the book title via the subject of your message.

If there is a book that you need and would like to see us publish, please send us a note in the **SUGGEST A TITLE** form on www.packtpub.com or e-mail suggest@packtpub.com.

If there is a topic that you have expertise in and you are interested in either writing or contributing to a book, see our author guide on www.packtpub.com/authors.

Customer support

Now that you are the proud owner of a Packt book, we have a number of things to help you to get the most from your purchase.

Downloading the example code

You can download the example code files for all Packt books you have purchased from your account at `http://www.PacktPub.com`. If you purchased this book elsewhere, you can visit `http://www.PacktPub.com/support` and register to have the files e-mailed directly to you.

Errata

Although we have taken every care to ensure the accuracy of our content, mistakes do happen. If you find a mistake in one of our books—maybe a mistake in the text or the code—we would be grateful if you would report this to us. By doing so, you can save other readers from frustration and help us improve subsequent versions of this book. If you find any errata, please report them by visiting `http://www.packtpub.com/support`, selecting your book, clicking on the **errata submission form** link, and entering the details of your errata. Once your errata are verified, your submission will be accepted and the errata will be uploaded on our website, or added to any list of existing errata, under the Errata section of that title. Any existing errata can be viewed by selecting your title from `http://www.packtpub.com/support`.

Piracy

Piracy of copyright material on the Internet is an ongoing problem across all media. At Packt, we take the protection of our copyright and licenses very seriously. If you come across any illegal copies of our works, in any form, on the Internet, please provide us with the location address or website name immediately so that we can pursue a remedy.

Please contact us at `copyright@packtpub.com` with a link to the suspected pirated material.

We appreciate your help in protecting our authors, and our ability to bring you valuable content.

Questions

You can contact us at `questions@packtpub.com` if you are having a problem with any aspect of the book, and we will do our best to address it.

1

Getting Started with MongoDB

We are about to begin our journey in PHP and MongoDB web development. Since you picked up this book, I assume you have some background building web apps using PHP, and you are interested in learning to develop PHP applications with MongoDB as data backend. In case you have never heard of MongoDB before, it is an open source, document-oriented database that supports the concept of flexible schema. In this chapter, we will learn what MongoDB is, and what do we gain from using MongoDB instead of trusted old SQL databases. We will start by learning briefly about the NoSQL databases (a set of database technologies that are considered alternative to RDBM systems), the basics of MongoDB, and what distinguishes it from relational databases. Then we will move on to installing and running MongoDB and hooking it up with PHP.

To sum it up, in this chapter we will:

- Learn about the NoSQL movement
- Learn the basic concepts behind MongoDB
- Learn how to download, install, and run MongoDB on a computer
- Learn to use the mongo Interactive Shell
- Learn how to make PHP and MongoDB talk to each other

So let's get on with it...

The NoSQL movement

You probably have heard about NoSQL before. You may have seen it in the RSS feed headlines of your favorite tech blogs, or you overheard a conversation between developers in your favorite restaurant during lunch. NoSQL (elaborated "Not only SQL"), is a data storage technology. It is a term used to collectively identify a number of database systems, which are fundamentally different from relational databases. NoSQL databases are increasingly being used in web 2.0 applications, social networking sites where the data is mostly user generated. Because of their diverse nature, it is difficult to map user-generated content to a relational data model, the schema has to be kept as flexible as possible to reflect the changes in the content. As the popularity of such a website grows, so does the amount of data and the read-write operations on the data. With a relational database system, dealing with these problems is very hard. The developers of the application and administrators of the database have to deal with the added complexity of scaling the database operations, while keeping its performance optimum. This is why popular websites—Facebook, Twitter to name a few—have adopted NoSQL databases to store part or all of their data. These database systems have been developed (in many cases built from scratch by developers of the web applications in question!) with the goal of addressing such problems, and therefore are more suitable for such use cases. They are open source, freely available on the Internet, and their use is increasingly gaining momentum in consumer and enterprise applications.

Types of NoSQL databases

The NoSQL databases currently being used can be grouped into four broad categories:

- **Key-value data stores**: Data is stored as key-value pairs. Values are retrieved by keys. Redis, Dynomite, and Voldemort are examples of such databases.

- **Column-based databases**: These databases organize the data in tables, similar to an RDBMS, however, they store the content by columns instead of rows. They are good for data warehousing applications. Examples of column-based databases are Hbase, Cassandra, Hypertable, and so on.

- **Document-based databases**: Data is stored and organized as a collection of documents. The documents are flexible; each document can have any number of fields. Apache CouchDB and MongoDB are prominent document databases.

- **Graph-based data-stores**: These databases apply the computer science graph theory for storing and retrieving data. They focus on interconnectivity of different parts of data. Units of data are visualized as nodes and relationships among them are defined by edges connecting the nodes. Neo4j is an example of such a database.

MongoDB – A document-based NoSQL database

MongoDB falls into the group of document-oriented NoSQL databases. It is developed and maintained by 10gen (http://www.10gen.com). It is an open source database, written in the programming language C. The source code is licensed under AGPL and freely available at GitHub, anyone can download it from the repo https://github.com/mongodb/mongo and customize it to suit his/her needs. It is increasingly being used as a data storage layer in different kinds of applications, both web-based and nonweb-based.

Why MongoDB?

Features that make learning and using MongoDB a win, include:

- Easy to learn, at least easier than learning other NoSQL systems, if I dare say. Column-oriented or graph-based databases introduce radical ideas that many developers struggle to grasp. However, there is a lot of similarity in the basic concepts of MongoDB and a relational database. Developers coming from an RDBMS background, find little trouble adapting to MongoDB.

- It implements the idea of flexible schema. You don't have to define the structure of the data before you start storing it, which makes it very suitable for storing non-structured data.

- It is highly scalable. It comes with great features to help keep performance optimum, while the size and traffic of data grows, with little or no change in the application layer.

It is free, it can be downloaded and used without charge. It has excellent documentation and an active and co-operative online community who participate in mailing lists, forums, and IRC chat rooms.

Who is using MongoDB?

Let's take a look at some real world use cases of MongoDB:

- **Craigslist**: Craigslist is the world's most popular website for featuring free classified advertisements. It uses MongoDB to archive billions of records. They had been using a MySQL based solution for achieving that. Replacing them with MongoDB has allowed them to add schema changes without delay, and scale much more easily.

- **Foursquare**: Foursquare is a popular location-based social networking application. It stores the geographical location of interesting venues (restaurants, cafes, and so on) and records when users visit these venues. It uses MongoDB for storing venue and user information.

- **CERN**: The renowned particle physics laboratory based in Geneva, uses MongoDB as an aggregation cache for its Large Hadron Collider experiment. The results for expensive aggregation queries, performed on massive amounts of data, are stored in MongoDB for future use.

MongoDB concepts—Databases, collections, and documents

A MongoDB server hosts a number of databases. The databases act as containers of data and they are independent of each other. A MongoDB database contains one or more collections. For example, a database for a blogging application named myblogsite may typically have the collections articles, authors, comments, categories, and so on.

A **collection** is a set of documents. It is logically analogous to the concept of a table in a relational database. But unlike tables, you don't have to define the structure of the data that is going to be stored in the collection beforehand.

A **document** stored in a collection is a unit of data. A document contains a set of fields or key-value pairs. The keys are strings, the values can be of various types: strings, integers, floats, timestamps, and so on. You can even store a document as the value of a field in another document.

Anatomy of document

Let's take a closer look at a MongoDB document. The following is an example of a document that stores certain information about a user in a web application:

```
{
  _id : ObjectId("4db31fa0ba3aba54146d851a")
  username : "joegunchy"
  email : "joe@mysite.org"
  age : 26
  is_admin : true
  created : "Sun Apr 24 2011 01:52:58 GMT+0700 (BDST)"
}
```

The previous document has six fields. If you have some JavaScript experience, you would recognize the structure as **JSON** or **JavaScript Object Notation**. The value for the first field, _id, is autogenerated. MongoDB automatically generates an ObjectId for each document you create in a collection and assigns it as _id for that document. This is also unique; that means no two documents in the same collection will have the same values for ID, just like a primary key of a table in a relational database. The next two fields, username and email are strings, age is an integer, and is_admin is boolean. Finally, created is a JavaScript DateTime object, represented as a string.

BSON—The data exchange format for MongoDB

We have already seen that the structure of a document imitates a JSON object. When you store this document in the database, it is serialized into a special binary encoded format, known as **BSON,** short for **binary JSON**. BSON is the default data exchange format for MongoDB. The key advantage of BSON is that it is more efficient than conventional formats such as XML and JSON, both in terms of memory consumption and processing time. Also, BSON supports all the data types supported by JSON (string, integer, double, Boolean, array, object, null) plus some special data types such as regular expression, object ID, date, binary data, and code. Programming languages such as PHP, Python, Java, and so on have libraries that manage conversion of language-specific data structures (for example, the associative array in PHP) to and from BSON. This enables the languages to easily communicate with MongoDB and manipulate the data in it.

 If you are interested to learn more about BSON format, you may try visiting http://bsonspec.org/.

Similarity with relational databases

Developers with a background on working with relational database systems will quickly recognize the similarities between the logical abstractions of the relational data model and the Mongo data model. The next figure compares components of a relational data model with those of the Mongo data model:

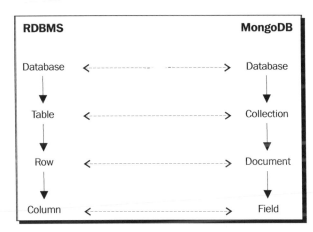

The next figure shows how a single row of a hypothetical table named `users` is mapped into a document in a collection:

Table: *users*

id	username	email	created at
256	joegunchy	joe@mysite.com	2011-04-24 01:52:58

Collection: *users*

```
{
    _id        : ObjectId("4db31fa0ba3aba54146d851a")
    username   : "joegunchy"
    email      : "joe@mysite.org"
    created_at : "Sun Apr 24 2011 01:52:58 GMT+0700 (BDST)"
}
```

Also just like columns of a RDBMS table, fields of a collection can be indexed, although implementations of indexing are different.

So much for the similarities: now let's talk briefly about the differences. The key thing that distinguishes MongoDB from a relational model is the absence of relationship constraints. There are no foreign keys in a collection and as a result there are no JOIN queries. Constraint management is typically handled in the application layer. Also, because of its flexible schema property, there is no expensive ALTER TABLE statement in MongoDB.

Downloading, installing, and running MongoDB

We are done with the theoretical part, at least for now. It is time for us to download, install, and start playing with MongoDB on the computer.

System requirements

MongoDB supports a wide variety of platforms. It can run on Windows (XP, Vista, and 7), various flavors of Linux (Debian/Ubuntu, Fedora, CentOS, and so on), and OS X running on Intel-based Macs. In this section, we are going to see step-by-step instructions for having a MongoDB system up and running in a computer, running on Windows, Linux, or OS X.

Time for action – downloading and running MongoDB on Windows

We are going to learn how to download, install, and run MongoDB on a computer running on Windows:

1. Head on over to the downloads page on the MongoDB official website, `http://www.mongodb.org/downloads`.

2. Click on the **download** link for the latest stable release under Windows 32-bit. This will start downloading a ZIP archive:

MongoDB Downloads

This table lists MongoDB distributions by platform and version. There are also packages available for various package managers.

	OS X 32-bit note	OS X 64-bit	Linux 32-bit note	Linux 64-bit	Windows 32-bit note	Windows 64-bit	Solaris i86pc note	Solaris 64	Source
Production Release (Recommended)									
1.8.1 4/6/2011 Changelog Release Notes	download	download	download *legacy-static	download *legacy-static	download	download	download	download	tgz zip
Nightly Changelog	download	download	download *legacy-static	download *legacy-static	download	download	download	download	tgz zip

3. Once the download is finished, move the ZIP archive to the `C:\` drive and extract it. Rename the extracted folder (`mongodb-win32-i386-x.y.z` where `x.y.z` is the version number) to `mongodb`.

4. Create the folder `C:\data\db`. Open a CMD prompt window, and enter the following commands:

```
C:\> cd \mongodb\bin

C:\mongodb\bin> mongod
```

```
Command Prompt - C:\mongodb\bin\mongod
Microsoft Windows XP [Version 5.1.2600]
(C) Copyright 1985-2001 Microsoft Corp.

C:\Documents and Settings\Rubayeet>C:\mongodb\bin\mongod
C:\mongodb\bin\mongod --help for help and startup options
Thu Apr 28 16:21:47 [initandlisten] MongoDB starting : pid=1812 port=27017 dbpath=/data/db/ 32-bit

** NOTE: when using MongoDB 32 bit, you are limited to about 2 gigabytes of data
**       see http://blog.mongodb.org/post/137788967/32-bit-limitations
**       with --dur, the limit is lower

Thu Apr 28 16:21:47 [initandlisten] db version v1.8.1, pdfile version 4.5
Thu Apr 28 16:21:47 [initandlisten] git version: a429cd4f535b2499cc4130b06ff7c26f41c00f04
Thu Apr 28 16:21:47 [initandlisten] build sys info: windows (5, 1, 2600, 2, 'Service Pack 3') BOOST_LIB_V
Thu Apr 28 16:21:47 [initandlisten] waiting for connections on port 27017
Thu Apr 28 16:21:47 [websvr] web admin interface listening on port 28017
```

5. Open another CMD prompt window and enter the following commands:

```
C:\> cd \mongodb\bin
C:\mongodb\bin> mongo
```

6. Type `show dbs` into the shell and hit *Enter*.

What just happened?

In steps 1 to 3, we downloaded and extracted a ZIP archive that contains binary files for running MongoDB on Windows, moved and extracted it under the `C:\` drive, and renamed the folder to `mongodb` for convenience. In step 4, we created the data directory (`C:\data\db`). This is the location where MongoDB will store its data files. In step 5, we execute the `C:\mongodb\bin\mongod.exe` program in the CMD prompt to launch the MongoDB server; this is the server that hosts multiple databases (you can also do this by double-clicking on the file in Windows Explorer). In step 6, after the server program is booted up, we invoke the `C:\mongodb\bin\mongo.exe` program to start the **mongo** interactive shell, which is a command-line interface to the MongoDB server:

```
C:\mongodb\bin\mongo
MongoDB shell version: 1.8.1
connection to test
type "help" for help
>
```

Once the shell has started, we issue the command `show dbs` to list all the pre-loaded databases in the server:

```
>show dbs
admin (empty)
local (empty)
>
```

Installing the 64-bit version

The documentation at the MongoDB website recommends that you run the 64-bit version of the system. This is because the 32-bit version cannot store more than 2 gigabytes of data. If you think it is likely that the data in your database will exceed the 2 GB limit, then you should obviously download and install the 64-bit version instead. You will also need an operating system that supports running applications in the 64-bit mode. For the purpose of the practical examples shown in this book, we are just fine with the 32-bit version, you should not worry about that too much.

Time for action – downloading and running MongoDB on Linux

Now, we are going to learn how to download and run the MongoDB server on a Linux box:

1. Fire up the terminal program. Type in the following command and hit *Enter*

   ```
   wget http://fastdl.mongodb.org/linux/mongodb-linux-i686-1.8.3.tgz
   > mongo.tgz
   ```

2. Extract the downloaded archive by using the following command:

   ```
   tar xzf mongo.tgz
   ```

3. Rename the extracted directory by using the following command:

   ```
   mv mongodb-linux-i686-1.8.3 mongodb
   ```

4. Create the data directory /data/db by using the following command:

   ```
   sudo mkdir -p /data/db
   sudo chown `id -u` /data/db
   ```

5. Startup the server by running the following command:

   ```
   ./mongodb/bin/mongod
   ```

6. Open another tab in the terminal and run the next command:

   ```
   ./mongodb/bin/mongo
   ```

7. Type show dbs into the shell and hit *Enter*.

What just happened?

In step 1, we downloaded the latest stable release of MongoDB 32-bit version for Linux using the wget program, and stored it as a GZIP tarball named mongo.tgz on your machine.

At the time of this writing, the latest production release for MongoDB is 1.8.3. So when you try this, if a newer production release is available, you should download that version instead.

In steps 2 and 3, we extracted the tarball and renamed the extracted directory to `mongodb` for convenience. In step 4, we created the data directory `/data/db` for MongoDB, and gave it permission to read from and write to that directory. In step 5, we startup the MongoDB server by executing the `mongodb/bin/mongod` script.

In step 6, after we have successfully launched the server, we start the **mongo** interactive shell:

```
$ ./mongodb/bin/mongo
MongoDB shell version: 1.8.1
url: test
connection to test
type "help" for help
>
```

Once the shell has started, we issue the command `show dbs` to list all the pre-loaded databases in the server:

```
>show dbs
local (empty)
admin (empty)
>
```

The databases listed here are special databases pre-built within the server. They are used for administration and authentication purposes. We do not need to concern ourselves with them right now.

Installing MongoDB using package managers

You can use the package manager of your Linux distribution (**apt** for Debian/Ubuntu, **yum** for Fedora/CentOS) to install MongoDB. To get distro-specific instructions, Ubuntu/Debian users should visit `http://www.mongodb.org/display/DOCS/Ubuntu+and+Debian+packages`. Users of CentOS and Fedora should visit `http://www.mongodb.org/display/DOCS/CentOS+and+Fedora+Packages`. The advantage of using a package manager, other than being able to install with fewer commands, is that you can launch the Mongo server and the client just by typing `mongod` and `mongo` respectively in the shell.

Installing MongoDB on OS X

The instructions for installing MongoDB on an OS X powered Mac machine are the same as those for Linux. You have to download the OS X specific binaries for Mongo (available at `http://www.mongodb.org/downloads`), and follow the same steps to execute them.

Alternatively, if you have package managers installed on your OS X (**Homebrew** or **MacPorts**), you can use them to install MongoDB.

To install MongoDB with HomeBrew use the following command:

```
$ brew update
$ brew install mongodb
```

To use MacPorts to install MongoDB use the following command:

```
$ sudo port install mongodb
```

Configuring MongoDB

When we launched the `mongod` program, it booted up with some default configuration settings, such as the path to the data directory (`C:\data\db` on Windows or `/data/db` on Unix). In real world deployments, we want to be able to specify these settings ourselves. There are two ways to achieve that. We can either modify them by supplying command-line parameters to the `mongod` program at invocation, or by using file-based configurations.

Command-line parameters

We can override the default MongoDB settings by passing command-line parameters to the `mongod` program. For example, the next command tells MongoDB to use `C:\mongodb_data` as data directory by sending it as a `--dbpath` argument:

```
C:\>mongodb\bin\mongod --dbpath C:\mongodb_data
```

The following table lists some useful command-line parameters and their functions:

Parameter	What it does
`--dbpath`	Path to the directory for storing data files.
`--bind_ip`	IP address that the `mongod` server will listen on, default is `127.0.0.1`.
`--port`	Port address that `mongod` will listen on, default is `27017`.
`--logpath`	Full file path to the log file where the MongoDB messages will be written. By default all messages are written to standard output.
`--logappend`	Setting this option to true appends the messages at the end of the log file. Setting it to `false` overwrites the log.

We can see the full list of command-line options by running `mongod` with the `--help` option:

```
C:\>mongodb\bin\mongod --help
```

File-based configuration

An alternative to sending all those command-line parameters to `mongod` manually is to put the required configuration settings in a file and then pass the path of the file as a `--config` option. For example, consider the following sample configuration file:

```
dbpath     = D:\mongodb_data
logpath    = D:\mongodb.log
logappend  = true
```

We store this file to a location, say `C:\mongodb.conf`. Now, to start MongoDB with the these settings, we have to enter the next command in the CMD prompt:

```
C:\>mongodb\bin\mongod --config C:\mongodb.conf
```

`mongod` will be loaded with these configuration settings. Note that file-based parameters are the same as those for command-line options.

If you are on a Linux machine, and you have installed Mongo using a package manager, such a configuration file may already exist in your system, typically at the location `/etc/mongo.conf`. You can modify that file to boot Mongo server with the configuration of your choice.

Have a go hero – configure MongoDB to run with non-default settings

Start MongoDB with the following settings, using a file-based configuration:

- Default data directory at `/usr/bin/mongo`.
- Default port address at `8888`.
- Messages will be logged at `/var/logs/mongodb.log`. The log file should be overwritten over time.

Stopping MongoDB

There are several ways you can shutdown a running MongoDB server.

Hitting Control + C

In the terminal window (or CMD prompt window in case you are on Windows) running the `mongod` process, hit *Ctrl + C*. This will signal the server to do a clean shutdown, flush, and close its data files.

From the mongo shell

From the mongo interactive shell, you can issue a shutdownServer() command, causing mongod to terminate:

```
>use admin
switched to db admin
>db.shutdownServer()
```

Sending INT or TERM signal in UNIX

In Linux/OS X, you can send a kill -2 <PID> signal to the process running mongod, which will cause the server to shutdown cleanly. You can get the PID by running the following command:

```
ps -aef | grep mongod
```

Creating databases, collections, and documents

Now that you have MongoDB up and running on your computer, it is time for us to create some databases, collections, and documents.

Time for Action – creating databases, collections, and documents

The next example will demonstrate how to create a database, and insert a document in a collection using the mongo shell program:

1. In the mongo shell, enter the following command:

    ```
    >use myfirstdb
    ```

2. When the prompt returns, enter the following commands to create documents in a collection named movies:

    ```
    >db.movies.insert({name:"Source Code", genre:"sci-fi", year:2011})
    >db.movies.insert({name:"The Dark Knight", genre:"action",
    year:2008})
    >db.movies.insert({name:"Megamind", genre:"animation", year:2010})
    >db.movies.insert({name:"Paranormal Activity", genre:"horror",
    year:2009})
    >db.movies.insert({name:"Hangover", genre:"comedy", year:2010})
    ```

3. The following command returns all documents from the movies collection:

    ```
    >db.movies.find()
    ```

What just happened?

In step 1, we applied the use `myfirstdb` command to switch to a new database namespace. Any collection/document we create now is going to be stored under this database. Next we create a collection named movies and insert some documents in it:

```
>db.movies.insert({name:"Source Code",genre:"sci-fi",year:2011})
```

The `db` part of the command always refers to the current database, which is "`myfirstdb`" in this case. The next part is the name of the collection (movies), if it does not already exist in the database, it gets created automatically when you invoke the `insert()` method on it. The argument to `insert` is a JSON object, a set of key-value pairs. After invoking the first `insert`, the database `myfirstdb` comes into physical existence. You can look into the data directory at this point, where you will find the files `myfirstdb.0`, `myfirstdb.1`, and so on that are storing the data for this database.

The `find()` command, invoked on the collection, returns all the documents in it:

```
>db.movies.find()
{ "_id" : ObjectId("4db439153ec7b6fd1c9093ec"), "name" : "Source Code",
"genre" : "sci-fi", "year" : 2011 }
{ "_id" : ObjectId("4db439df3ec7b6fd1c9093ed"), "name" : "The Dark
Knight", "genre" : "action", "year" : 2008 }
{ "_id" : ObjectId("4db439f33ec7b6fd1c9093ee"), "name" : "Megamind",
"genre" : "animation", "year" : 2010 }
{ "_id" : ObjectId("4db439f33ec7b6fd1c9093ef"), "name" : "Paranormal
Activity", "genre" : "horror", "year" : 2009 }
{ "_id" : ObjectId("4db439f43ec7b6fd1c9093f0"), "name" : "Hangover",
"genre" : "comedy", "year" : 2010 }
```

Pop quiz – configuring MongoDB

1. What is the default port address of MongoDB?

    a. 27107

    b. 27017

    c. 27170

2. How does a new database get created in MongoDB?

    a. By the command `create database <databasename>`

    b. By the command `use <databasename>`

    c. By doing `use <databasename>` first and then doing `db.<collectionname>.insert(<jsondocument>)`

Installing the PHP driver for MongoDB

To make PHP talk to the MongoDB server, we are going to need the PHP-MongoDB driver. It is a PHP extension library that manages connection to the MongoDB server and enables you to perform all kinds of operations on a database through PHP. Since you are a PHP programmer, I am going to assume you already have a functional PHP environment installed on your machine, running on top of an Apache web server. The driver officially supports PHP versions 5.1, 5.2, and 5.3. So if you are using an older version of PHP, I suggest you upgrade it.

Time for Action – installing PHP driver for MongoDB on Windows

Let's try installing the driver on a Windows machine running PHP 5.2 on Apache:

1. Download the ZIP archive `http://downloads.mongodb.org/mongo-latest-php5.2vc6ts.zip` on your machine and extract it.

2. Copy the `php_mongo.dll` file from the extracted folder to the PHP extension directory; this is usually the folder name `ext` inside your PHP installation.

3. Open the `php.ini` file inside your PHP installation and add the following line:

```
extension=php_mongo.dll
```

4. Save the file and close it. Restart the Apache web server.

5. Open up your text editor and add the following code to a new file:

```
<?php
phpinfo();
```

6. Save the file as `phpinfo.php` inside the **DocumentRoot** of the Apache web server (the `htdocs` folder).

7. Execute the `phpinfo.php` script in your browser
(`http://localhost/phpinfo.php`). Scroll down to find the
section **mongo** to see all the MongoDB driver-specific information.

mongo

MongoDB Support		enabled	
Version		1.0.11	

Directive	Local Value	Master Value
mongo.allow_empty_keys	0	0
mongo.allow_persistent	1	1
mongo.auto_reconnect	1	1
mongo.chunk_size	262144	262144
mongo.cmd	$	$
mongo.default_host	localhost	localhost
mongo.default_port	27017	27017
mongo.long_as_object	0	0
mongo.native_long	0	0
mongo.utf8	1	1

Congratulations! You have successfully installed the PHP driver for MongoDB.

What just happened?

In step 1, we download the ZIP file containing the DLL file `php_mongo.dll` for
the PHP-MongoDB driver for PHP 5.2 (for the PHP 5.3 specific version, download
`http://downloads.mongodb.org/mongo-latest-php5.3vc6ts.zip` instead).
In step 2, we copy the `php_mongo.dll` file to the PHP extensions directory. If the
installation directory of PHP on your machine is `C:\php`, the extension directory should
be `C:\php\ext`. Then we edit the `php.ini` file (located under `C:\php` as well) to add
the line `extension=php_mongo.dll` to it and restart Apache for the changes to take
effect. Next we create and execute a one-line PHP script to invoke the `phpinfo()`
method. If we are able to see the MongoDB driver specific information in the `phpinfo()`
output, listed under section **mongo**, this means the driver was installed without a glitch.

 If you are running PHP on IIS, you should download the
thread-safe VC9 version of the driver instead. Get it from the URL
`http://downloads.mongodb.org/mongo-latest-`
`php5.3vc9ts.zip`.

Installing the PHP-MongoDB driver on Unix

In a Unix-based system, the PHP driver for MongoDB can be installed using the **pecl** (PECL - PHP Extension Community Islam) program. You need to have it installed on your machine, which can be done by using the following command:

```
sudo pecl install mongo
```

When the installation is finished, edit the `php.ini` file (usually found at `/etc/php.ini`) to add the line:

```
extension=mongo.so
```

and then restart Apache.

In case you don't have **pecl** installed on your machine, you can download the driver source code from GitHub, build it, and install it manually:

```
$ tar zxvf mongodb-mongdb-php-driver-<commit_id>.tar.gz
$ cd mongodb-mongodb-php-driver-<commit_id>
$ phpize
$ ./configure
$ sudo make install
```

Check out the Mongo driver installation page `http://www.php.net/manual/en/mongo.installation.php` on the PHP official website to get operating system specific detailed information.

Connecting to the MongoDB server from PHP

In this section, we will learn how to use the API provided by the PHP-MongoDB driver to create a connection to the Mongo server from a PHP script.

Creating a PHP-Mongo connection

Let's write a very simple PHP program that creates a connection to the MongoDB server and shows all the available databases on that server.

Time for action – creating a connection to the MongoDB server from PHP

1. Open up your text editor and add the following code in a new file:

```php
<?php
  try{
      $mongo       = new Mongo(); //create a connection to MongoDB
      $databases = $mongo->listDBs(); //List all databases
      echo '<pre>';
      print_r($databases);
      $mongo->close();
  } catch(MongoConnectionException $e) {
      //handle connection error
      die($e->getMessage());
  }
```

2. Save the file as `test_connection.php` under the DocumentRoot of your web server.

3. Open up your browser, and execute the script by going to the location `http://localhost/test_connection.php`:

```
localhost:8888/mongodb/test_connection.php

Array
(
    [databases] => Array
        (
            [0] => Array
                (
                    [name] => myfirstdb
                    [sizeOnDisk] => 67108864
                    [empty] =>
                )

            [1] => Array
                (
                    [name] => admin
                    [sizeOnDisk] => 1
                    [empty] => 1
                )

            [2] => Array
                (
                    [name] => local
                    [sizeOnDisk] => 1
                    [empty] => 1
                )

            [3] => Array
                (
                    [name] => test
                    [sizeOnDisk] => 1
                    [empty] => 1
                )

        )

    [totalSize] => 67108864
```

What just happened?

We just wrote a simple PHP program to test if the PHP-MongoDB driver we installed works correctly. The program does two simple things. First, it creates a connection to the Mongo server, then it lists all the databases in the server.

Let's examine the code. We created a connection from PHP to MongoDB by instantiating a Mongo object:

```php
try{
    $mongo = new Mongo();
    ..............................................
} catch(MongoConnectionException $e) {
    die($e->getMessage());
}
```

We instantiated the object within a try/catch block to handle the exception named `MongoConnectionException` in case PHP fails to connect. Once the connection was made, we invoked the `listDBs()` method on the Mongo object. It returned an associative array, containing three fields. The first field—databases—is an array of associative arrays, each one corresponding to a database in the server, giving us the name of the database, its size in bytes, and a flag specifying if the database is empty or not.

```
Array
(
    [databases] => Array
    (
        [0] => Array
        (
            [name] => myfirstdb
            [sizeOnDisk] => 67108864
            [empty] =>
        )
        [1] => Array
        (
            [name] => adming
            [sizeOnDisk] => 1
            [empty] => 1
        )

    )
    [totalSize] => 67108864
    [ok] => 1
)
```

The `totalSize` field corresponds to the total size of data in the server (in bytes) and the `ok` flag specifies if the method ran successfully. Finally, we closed the connection by invoking the `close()` method on the Mongo object.

Configuring the PHP-MongoDB connection

When no parameter is passed to the constructor of the `Mongo` class, it connects to the Mongo server running on localhost, on port 27107 (or whatever value is specified for `mongo.default_host` and `mongo.default_port` in `php.ini`). If we want to connect to a server running on a different host and/or port, we can pass the connection string (`mongodb://<hostname>:<port_number>`) as the `$server` parameter to the `Mongo` constructor. For example, to connect to a Mongo server listening on port 8888, we will type the following command:

```
$mongo = new Mongo($server="mongodb://localhost:8888");
```

Specifying timeout for the connection attempt

We can specify for how long (in milliseconds) the driver should attempt to connect to the MongoDB server:

```
try {
  $mongo = new Mongo($options=array('timeout'=> 100))
} catch(MongoConnectionException $e) {
  die("Failed to connect to database ".$e->getMessage());
}
```

We supplied an array `{ 'timeout' => 100 }` as the `$option` argument to the `Mongo` constructor. In case PHP fails to connect within 100 milliseconds, it will throw an exception named `MongoConnectionException`.

Have a go hero – connect to a MongoDB server on a networked computer

Suppose your computer is connected to a local area network. There is another computer in the network, running on the IP address 192.168.1.101. It is hosting a MongoDB server that is listening on port 8000. Write a PHP script that connects to that MongoDB server, in under one second, and lists all the databases hosted there.

Summary

We covered a lot of things in this chapter.

Specifically, we covered:

- What the NoSQL movement is
- What MongoDB is, what is it good for, and who is using it
- The MongoDB data model (databases, collections, and documents)
- How to install and run MongoDB on a computer
- How to create databases, collections, and documents using the mongo interactive shell.
- How to install the MongoDB-PHP driver on a computer
- How to create a connection to MongoDB from PHP

We also discussed how to configure the MongoDB server using command-line parameters or configuration files.

By now you should have a PHP-MongoDB development environment up and running on your system. In the next chapter, we will learn to create a simple web application using MongoDB as data backend.

2

Building your First MongoDB Powered Web App

We know what MongoDB is, and what it is good for. We also have a PHP and MongoDB development environment set up. It is time for us to dive into some coding. In this chapter, we are going to build a very simple web application using PHP and HTML/CSS, with MongoDB as the data store. Through the practical examples of building components of this web app, we are going to learn how we store, retrieve, and manipulate data in Mongo.

In this chapter, we will learn how to use PHP to:

- Connect to a MongoDB database
- Save documents in a collection
- Querying documents in a collection
- Performing range queries
- Sorting documents
- Updating a document
- Deleting one or more documents from a collection
- Embedded and referenced documents

A MongoDB powered blog

For our first MongoDB powered web application, we are going to build a very simple blogging website. The reason I chose to build a blog as our first example application is because it is a CRUD (Create, Read, Update, Delete) application and it is very suitable in our case to ease into PHP and MongoDB web development. We will build plain user interfaces using HTML/CSS with simple textboxes and buttons. A MongoDB database will store all the content. PHP will take care of moving the data back and forth between the frontend and the database. By building tools to create/read/update/delete articles in the blog site, we will learn how to save, read, or remove documents in MongoDB.

Have the MongoDB server running

Since we are going to store data in MongoDB with PHP in the next examples, you should have the mongod process up and running on your machine. Take a look at the tutorials in *Chapter 1, Getting Started with MongoDB* to see how to run the MongoDB server. It is also a good idea to have the MongoDB interactive shell client (mongo) running as well, you may need it to explore the data in collections.

Inserting documents in MongoDB

In Chapter 1, *Getting Started with MongoDB* we learned how to insert documents to a collection on the fly, using the `insert()` method in the `mongo` interactive shell. In this section, we are going to do the same thing, but we are going to use PHP to achieve it. So as the first part of the blog site, we are going to build the blog post creator. It displays a web interface where a user can enter the title and contents of his blog post and save it to MongoDB.

Time for action – building the Blog Post Creator

Although it sounds fancy, Blog Post Creator is just a webpage that shows a form where the user can type in the text of his/her article, and then save it by submitting the form:

1. Open up your text editor. Put the following code in a new file:

```php
<?php
  $action = (!empty($_POST['btn_submit']) &&
    ($_POST['btn_submit'] === 'Save')) ? 'save_article'
      : 'show_form';
  switch($action){
    case 'save_article':
    try {
      $connection = new Mongo();
```

```php
        $database   = $connection->selectDB('myblogsite');
        $collection = $database->
        selectCollection('articles');
        $article = array{
          'title' => $_POST['title'],
          'content' => $_POST['content'],
          'saved_at' => new MongoDate()
        };
        $collection->insert($article);
    } catch(MongoConnectionException $e) {
        die("Failed to connect to database ".
          $e->getMessage());
    }
    catch(MongoException $e) {
        die('Failed to insert data '.$e->getMessage());
    }
    break;
    case 'show_form':
    default:
  }
?>
<!DOCTYPE html PUBLIC "-//W3C//DTD XHTML 1.0 Transitional//EN"
  "http://www.w3.org/TR/xhtml1/DTD/xhtml1-transitional.dtd">
<html xmlns="http://www.w3.org/1999/xhtml" xml:lang="en"
  lang="en">
  <head>
    <meta http-equiv="Content-Type" content="text/html;
      charset=utf-8"/>
    <link rel="stylesheet" href="style.css"/>
    <title>Blog Post Creator</title>
  </head>
  <body>
    <div id="contentarea">
      <div id="innercontentarea">
        <h1>Blog Post Creator</h1>
        <?php if ($action === 'show_form'): ?>
          <form action="<?php echo $_SERVER['PHP_SELF'];?>"
            method="post">
            <h3>Title</h3>
            <p>
              <input type="text" name="title" id="title/">
            </p>
            <h3>Content</h3>
            <textarea name="content" rows="20"></textarea>
            <p>
```

```
          <input type="submit" name="btn_submit"
            value="Save"/>
        </p>
      </form>
    <?php else: ?>
      <p>
        Article saved. _id:<?php echo $article['_id'];?>.
        <a href="blogpost.php">
          Write another one?</a>
      </p>
    <?php endif;?>
    </div>
  </div>
 </body>
</html>
```

2. Save the file as `blogpost.php`.

3. Open another new file in your text editor and put the following CSS rules in it:

```
body {
  background-color: #e1ddd9;
  font-size: 12px;
  font-family: Verdana, Arial, Helvetica, SunSans-Regular,
  Sans-Serif;
  color:#564b47;
  padding:20px;
  margin:0px;
  text-align: center;
}
div#contentarea {
  text-align: left;
  vertical-align: middle;
  margin: 0px auto;
  padding: 0px;
  width: 550px;
  background-color: #ffffff;
  border: 1px #564b47;
}
div#innercontentarea{ padding: 10px 50px; }
div#innercontentarea form input[type=text]{ width: 435px; }
div#innercontentarea form textarea[name=content] { width: 435px; }
```

4. Save the file as `style.css`.

5. Open `blogpost.php` in your browser. Type in some arbitrary text in the title and content field, and click on the **Save** button:

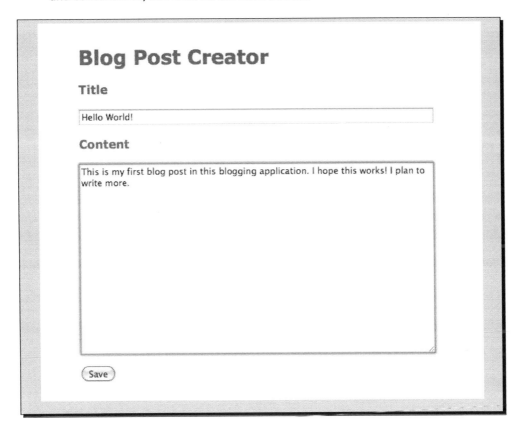

6. If the blog has been saved successfully, the page reloads with a message **Article saved**. The hyperlink on the page takes you back to the form so you can write more blog posts:

What just happened?

We just built the Blog Post Creator! We wrote a PHP script `blogpost.php` that conditionally either shows an HTML form where the user can write the title/content of a new blog post, or it saves the user-submitted data to MongoDB. By default the script displays the following HTML form:

```
<form action="blogpost.php" method="post">
   <h3>Title</h3>
   <p><input type="text" name="title" id="title/"></p>
   <h3>Content</h3>
   <textarea name="content" rows="20"></textarea>
   <p><input type="submit" name="btn_submit" value="Save"/></p>
</form>
```

We also created a CSS file named `styles.css` to apply styling rules to the HTML output.

When the user clicks the **Save** button after writing, the following portion of the code gets executed, which connects to MongoDB and selects a database and a collection where the data will be stored:

```
$connection = new Mongo();
$database   = $connection->selectDB('myblogsite');
$collection = $database->selectCollection('articles');
```

In the first line of the previous code, PHP connects to the MongoDB server by instantiating a `Mongo` object. Next, the `selectDB()` method is invoked on the `Mongo` object, with an argument `myblogsite`. This enables us to select a database named myblogsite on the MongoDB server. The `selectDB()` method returns a `MongoDB` object, which represents the database. Next we invoked the `selectCollection()` method on the `MongoDB` object, passing the name of the collection we want to select as the argument (articles), which in turn returns a `MongoCollection` object. This object represents the collection where we will store the data.

We construct an array with the user-submitted data, and pass this array as an argument to the `insert()` method of the `MongoCollection` object:

```
$article            = array();
$article['title']   = $_POST['title'];
$article['content'] = $_POST['content'];
..............................................................................
$collection->insert($article);
```

The `insert()` method stores the data in the collection. The `$article` array automatically receives a field named `_id`, which is the autogenerated unique `ObjectId` of the inserted BSON document.

Creating databases and collections implicitly

Did you notice that we selected a database and a collection that did not even exist in Mongo? This is one of the convenient features of MongoDB, we do not have to run any CREATE DATABASE or CREATE TABLE statement beforehand, as we would have to do in MySQL or any other relational database. The database and collection namespaces get created on the fly, and we can go ahead and start saving objects. So selectDB() either selects an existing database or creates it implicitly if it is not there. The same thing goes for selectCollection().

Shortcut approach for selecting database/collection

We can select a collection by doing this as well

```
$connection = new Mongo();
$collection = $connection->myblogsite->articles;
```

The second assignment of the previous code performs the same operation as calling selectDB('myblogsite') and selectCollection('articles') sequentially. This is a shortcut approach for selecting databases and collections.

Performing 'safe' inserts

An important thing that you must know about MongoDB is that when you invoke an insert() method, the program control does not wait for the response from the MongoDB database. That is, it just signals MongoDB to insert the document, and then immediately moves on to execute the next statement in the code. The actual insert and pooling of connection is taken care of by MongoDB itself. This is an asynchronous approach for inserting documents in MongoDB and it is the default behavior. If we want to change this—that is, we want to wait for the response of the database—we need to send an optional safe=true argument to the insert() method (by default this is set to false):

```
try {
  $status = $connection->insert(array('title' => 'Blog Title',
    'content' => 'Blog Content'),
    array('safe' => True));
    echo "Insert operation complete";
} catch (MongoCursorException $e) {
  die("Insert failed ".$e->getMessage());
}
```

In the previous code snippet, the program will wait for the MongoDB database to respond to the `insert` command, before executing the `echo` statement in the next line. In case the `insert` command does not succeed, a `MongoCursorException` will be thrown. Also the `insert()` method returns an array when in safe mode (as opposed to returning a Boolean value in regular mode) that contains information about the status of the insert.

Benefits of safe inserts

Using safe inserts comes in handy in any of the following situations:

- Using safe mode guards us against all kinds of user level errors during inserts. For example, if we try to insert a document with a non-unique `_id`, a safe insert will raise an exception.

- MongoDB may also run out of disk space when inserting documents. Safe inserts check against such potential pitfalls.

- In a multi-server setup, that is, when the data is being stored on multiple machines (a replica set), using safe inserts ensures that the data is written on at least one machine.

However, this does not mean we should use safe inserts in all scenarios in a real-world application. Safe inserts incur extra overhead, so they will not be as fast as the regular ones. We should identify the use cases where we are more concerned about the safety of the data rather than speed, and use safe inserts on those cases only.

Specifying a timeout on insert

When doing a `'safe'` insert, we can supply an optional timeout parameter, which specifies how long (in milliseconds) the program will wait for a database response when doing an insert:

```
try {
  $collection->insert($document, array('safe' => True,
    'timeout' => True));
} catch (MongoCursorTimeoutException $e) {
  die('Insert timeout expired '.$e->getMessage());
}
```

In case the database fails to insert the document within the specified timeout period, the PHP runtime throws a `MongoCursorTimeoutException`.

Setting the user generated _id

Although MongoDB assigns a unique _id to a document upon insertion, we can set the _id field of the document explicitly by ourselves. This is useful for situations when we want to give each document a unique identifier derived from our own rule. For example, the following code block creates a hash of the current Unix timestamp appended with the $username string and sets it as the _id of a document:

```
$username = 'Joe';
try{
  $document = array('_id' => hash('sha1', $username.time()),
    'user' => $username,
    'visited' => 'homepage.php');
  $collection->insert($document, array('safe' => True));
} catch(MongoCursorException $e) {
  die('Failed to insert '.$e->getMessage());
}
```

When setting the _id in this way, we should always do a 'safe' insert. This ensures when there is more than one document in the collection with the same _id, a MongoCursorException is thrown while doing the insert.

The MongoDate object

You may have noticed that we added an extra field named saved_at to the article when we inserted it. The value of saved_at is a MongoDate object, which represents the ISODate data type in BSON. When instantiated, a MongoDate gives the current Unix timestamp. We can use the built-in strtotime() function in PHP to instantiate MongoDate objects that represent any date/time information we want to store in MongoDB, and the date() function to print the timestamp in a human-readable format.

```
$timestamp = new MongoDate(strtotime('2011-05-21 12:00:00'));
print date('g:i a, F j', $timestamp->sec); //prints 12 pm, May 21
```

Have a go hero – allow storing tags for an article

Modify the HTML in the blogpost.php script to show a text field labeled tags, where the user will type in one or more tags for an article he creates. The tags will be comma separated. Modify the PHP code to store the user-submitted tags in an array field named tags of the article document being inserted.

Querying documents in a collection

We have learned how to store data in MongoDB. It is time that we learn about how to retrieve them. In *Chapter 1, Getting Started with MongoDB* we invoked the `find()` method on a collection to get all the documents in that collection. We did that using the mongo interactive shell, this time we will do that programmatically using PHP. Also, we are going to learn how we can specify query parameters in MongoDB.

Time for action – retrieving articles from a database

In this example, we are going to build the home page of our blog site, which will show the title and the content excerpt of every article stored in the database. Clicking on an article will take us to another page where we can see the full content of the article. Let's get to it:

1. Open up the text editor and create a new file named `blogs.php`. Put the following code in that file:

```php
<?php
  try {
    $connection = new Mongo();
    $database   = $connection->selectDB('myblogsite');
    $collection = $database->selectCollection('articles');
  } catch(MongoConnectionException $e) {
    die("Failed to connect to database ".$e->getMessage());
  }
  $cursor = $collection->find();
?>
<!DOCTYPE html PUBLIC "-//W3C//DTD XHTML 1.0 Transitional//EN"
  "http://www.w3.org/TR/xhtml1/DTD/xhtml1-transitional.dtd">
<html xmlns="http://www.w3.org/1999/xhtml" xml:lang="en"
  lang="en">
  <head>
    <meta http-equiv="Content-Type" content="text/html;
      charset=utf-8"/>
    <link rel="stylesheet" href="style.css" />
    <title>My Blog Site</title>
  </head>
  <body>
    <div id="contentarea">
      <div id="innercontentarea">
        <h1>My Blogs</h1>
        <?php while ($cursor->hasNext()):
          $article = $cursor->getNext(); ?>
        <h2><?php echo $article['title']; ?></h2>
```

```
      <p>
        <?php echo substr($article['content'], 0,
          200).'...'; ?>
      </p>
      <a href="blog.php?id=<?php echo $article['_id'];
        ?>">Read more</a>
      <?php endwhile; ?>
    </div>
  </div>
</body>
</html>
```

2. Create another file named `blog.php` with the following code:

```php
<?php
  $id = $_GET['id'];
  try {
    $connection = new Mongo();
    $database   = $connection->selectDB('myblogsite');
    $collection = $database->selectCollection('articles');
  } catch(MongoConnectionException $e) {
    die("Failed to connect to database ".$e->getMessage());
  }
  $article  = $collection->findOne(array('_id' =>
    new MongoId($id)));
?>
<!DOCTYPE html PUBLIC "-//W3C//DTD XHTML 1.0 Transitional//EN"
  "http://www.w3.org/TR/xhtml1/DTD/xhtml1-transitional.dtd">
<html xmlns="http://www.w3.org/1999/xhtml" xml:lang="en"
  lang="en">
  <head>
    <meta http-equiv="Content-Type" content="text/html;
      charset=utf-8"/>
    <link rel="stylesheet" href="style.css" />
    <title>My Blog Site</title>
  </head>
  <body>
    <div id="contentarea">
      <div id="innercontentarea">
        <h1>My Blogs</h1>
        <h2><?php echo $article['title']; ?></h2>
        <p><?php echo $article['content']; ?></p>
      </div>
    </div>
  </body>
</html>
```

3. Open your browser and navigate to the `blogs.php` file. It lists all the current articles in your blog:

My Blogs

Hello World!

Lorem ipsum dolor sit amet, consectetur adipisicing elit, sed do eiusmod tempor incididunt ut labore et dolore magna aliqua. Ut enim ad minim veniam, quis nostrud exercitation ullamco laboris nisi...

Read more

Learnt something important today

Lorem ipsum dolor sit amet, consectetur adipisicing elit, sed do eiusmod tempor incididunt ut labore et dolore magna aliqua. Ut enim ad minim veniam, quis nostrud exercitation ullamco laboris nisi...

Read more

Blogging is fun!

Lorem ipsum dolor sit amet, consectetur adipisicing elit, sed do eiusmod tempor incididunt ut labore et dolore magna aliqua. Ut enim ad minim veniam, quis nostrud exercitation ullamco laboris nisi...

Read more

4. Click on the **Read more** link of the first article on the list. It executes the `blog.php` script and displays the full content of the first blog post:

My Blogs

Hello World!

Lorem ipsum dolor sit amet, consectetur adipisicing elit, sed do eiusmod tempor incididunt ut labore et dolore magna aliqua. Ut enim ad minim veniam, quis nostrud exercitation ullamco laboris nisi ut aliquip ex ea commodo consequat. Duis aute irure dolor in reprehenderit in voluptate velit esse cillum dolore eu fugiat nulla pariatur. Excepteur sint occaecat cupidatat non proident, sunt in culpa qui officia deserunt mollit anim id est laborum. Sed ut perspiciatis unde omnis iste natus error sit voluptatem accusantium doloremque laudantium, totam rem aperiam, eaque ipsa quae ab illo inventore veritatis et quasi architecto beatae vitae dicta sunt explicabo. Nemo enim ipsam voluptatem quia voluptas sit aspernatur aut odit aut fugit, sed quia consequuntur magni dolores eos qui ratione voluptatem sequi nesciunt. Neque porro quisquam est, qui dolorem ipsum quia dolor sit amet, consectetur, adipisci velit, sed quia non numquam eius modi tempora incidunt ut labore et dolore magnam aliquam quaerat voluptatem. Ut enim ad minima veniam, quis nostrum exercitationem ullam corporis suscipit laboriosam, nisi ut aliquid ex ea commodi consequatur? Quis autem vel eum iure reprehenderit qui in ea voluptate velit esse quam nihil molestiae consequatur, vel illum qui dolorem eum fugiat quo voluptas nulla pariatur?

What just happened?

Let's go through the code we wrote in step 1. In the first block of code, we connect to the database and select the collection that we wish to query on. Nothing new there. Then we invoke the `find()` method on the collection to retrieve all documents currently in that collection:

```
$cursor = $collection->find();
```

The `find()` method returns a `MongoCursor` object, an object that we can use to iterate through the results of a database query. In the HTML portion of the code, we iterate the `MongoCursor` object to fetch each article one by one and display its title and first 200 characters of its content:

```
<?php while ($cursor->hasNext()):
    $article = $cursor->getNext(); ?>
    <h2><?php echo $article['title']; ?></h2>
    <p><?php echo substr($article['content'], 0, 200).'...'; ?></p>
    <a href="blog.php?id=<?php echo $article['_id']; ?>">Read more</a>
<?php endwhile; ?>
```

When we click on the **Read more** link, it takes us to the `blog.php` file which we wrote in step 2. This file receives the `_id` of the article as an HTTP GET parameter. We invoke the `findOne()` method on the articles collection, sending the `_id` value as a parameter to the method. The `findOne()` method is used to retrieve a single document, unlike `find()` which we use to retrieve a cursor of a set of documents that we can iterate over:

```
$id = $_GET['id'];
..........................................
$article = $collection->findOne(array('_id'=>
    new MongoId($id)));
```

This basically tells MongoDB to return the document that has the same `_id` as the specified value. This is similar to doing `SELECT * FROM articles WHERE id = <somevalue>` in SQL. The `find()` method returns a `MongoCursor` object. We call the `getNext()` method on it to get the first (in this case, the only) document in the query result. Finally, we display the title and content of the retrieved document using HTML markup.

The Mongo Query Language

Data is retrieved from MongoDB using the Mongo Query Language. Queries are expressed as JSON objects (or BSON objects to be more correct), which are passed as arguments to the find() method. For example, the next query applied in mongo shell, gets all documents from a collection named movies that have their genre fields set to 'sci-fi':

```
>db.movies.find({"genre":"sci-fi"})
{ "_id" : ObjectId("4db439153ec7b6fd1c9093ec"), "name" : "Source Code",
"genre" : "sci-fi", "year" : 2011 }
```

To do the same thing in PHP, we invoke find() on the MongoCollection object representing the movies collection. The query is expressed as an associative array:

```
//get all movies where genre == sci-fi
$moviesCollection->find(array("genre" : "sci-fi"));
```

We can also specify multiple query parameters:

```
//get all movies where genre is comedy and year is 2011
$moviesCollection->find(array('genre' => 'comedy', 'year' => 2011));
```

When we don't pass any query arguments to find(), it gets an empty array by default (an empty JSON object in MongoDB) and matches all documents in the collection:

```
//get ALL movies
$moviesCollection->find();
```

We could have also done $moviesCollection->find(array()), this also returns all documents (find() receives an empty array as a default parameter).

The MongoCursor object

A query in MongoDB, performed with find(), returns a cursor. We can iterate over this cursor to retrieve all the documents matched by the query. In PHP, the return value of the find() method is a MongoCursor object. In the following code snippet, we get all movies of the action genre and iterate over them in a while loop:

```
$cursor = $movieCollection->find(array('genre' => 'action'));
while ($cursor->hasNext()) {
  $movie = $cursor->getNext();
  //do something with $movie
  ...................................... .
}
```

The hasNext() checks whether or not there are any more objects in the cursor. getNext() returns the next object pointed by the cursor, and then advances the cursor. The documents do not get loaded into memory unless we invoke either getNext() or hasNext() on the cursor, this is good for keeping the memory usage low.

We can do this in a foreach loop as well:

```
$cursor = $movieCollection->find(array('genre' => 'action'));
if ($cursor->count() === 0) {
  foreach ($cursor as $movie) {
    //do something with $movie
  }
}
```

The count() method of the MongoCursor returns the number of objects in the cursor. We check if this number is zero (which means no matching results found), so that we can just skip the execution of the foreach section.

Returning documents in an array

We can use the built-in iterator_to_array() function in PHP to change the cursor returned by the query into an array. The array contains all the objects in the cursor, and we can access them or iterate over them the same way we do with a regular array in PHP. Programmers who find the cursor approach a little too difficult prefer this trick.

```
$cursor = $movieCollection->find({'genre': 'action'});
$array = iterator_to_array($cursor);
if (!empty($array)) {
  foreach($array as $item){

    //do something with $item

    .....................................  . .

  }

}
```

However, there is a downside of using iterator_to_array(). If the size of the data returned is very large, let's say 1 GB, using iterator_to_array() may lead to a major performance decrease, as PHP will try to load the entire data into memory. So you should avoid using this approach unless you are sure that the dataset is reasonably small.

Conditional Queries

In addition to doing queries based on equality, we can also do conditional queries in MongoDB using the conditional operators ($gt/$gte, $lt/$lte, $ne, and so on) of the Mongo query language. The next few lines of code demonstrate the uses of such operators:

```
//get all items with field 'x' greater than 100
$collection->find(array('x' => array('$gt' => 100)));

//get all items with field 'x' lower than 100
$collection->find(array('x' => array('$lt' => 100)));

//get all items with field 'x' greater than or equal to 100
$collection->find(array('x' => array('$gte' => 100)));

//get all items with field 'x' lower than or equal to 100
$collection->find(array('x' => array('$lte' => 100)));

//get all items with field 'x' between 100 and 200
$collection->find(array('x' => array('$gte' => 100, '$lte' => 200)));

//get all items with field 'x' not equal to 100
$collection->find(array('x' => array('$ne' => 100)));
```

Important! When using the MongoDB conditional query operators in PHP (or any special operator that has $ as a prefix), we must use the operator within single quotes (') and not double quotes ("). If we do use double quotes, we need to escape it since PHP treats $ prefixed strings within double quotes as variables:

```
//Using single quotes (') is ok.
$collection->find(array('x' => array('$gt' => 100)));
//$ is escaped within double quotes (")
$collection->find(array('x' => array("\$gt" => 100)));
//this will cause an error
$collection->find(array('x' => array("$gt" => 100)));
```

Visit http://www.mongodb.org/display/DOCS/
Advanced+Queries#AdvancedQueries-ConditionalOperators to learn some more of these conditional operators in Mongo.

Pop Quiz – what does this query do?

1. What does the following query do?

```
$movies->find(array('genre' => 'comedy',
  'year' => array('$gt' => 2009, '$lt' => 2011)));
```

   a. Gets all movies released after the year 2009

   b. Gets all movies released after the year 2009 and before the year 2011

   c. All of the above

   d. None of the above

Doing advanced queries in MongoDB

We have got the basics of querying MongoDB, so now we are going to move into a little more advanced stuff, such as sorting and limiting query results, returning a subset of fields, querying over a range of dates, and so on. We will use these concepts to build a page that will show a paginated list of blog posts in the database. The page will show the most recently saved articles first and we will be able to browse through all the articles using a pair of navigation links. We will call this page the "Blog Dashboard".

Time for action – building the Blog Dashboard

In this example, we are going to build the Blog Dashboard, a page that lists most recently saved articles first, showing five articles at a time. The user is able to browse through all articles using the navigation links at the bottom of the list. For now we will not implement any functionality in the dashboard other than viewing each article. Moving forward in this chapter, we will use this page as our codebase to build on top of as we learn more advanced MongoDB topics:

1. Create a new file named dashboard.php in your text editor, and add the following PHP, HTML/CSS code there:

```php
<?php
  try {
    $mongodb = new Mongo();
    $articleCollection = $mongodb->myblogsite->articles;
  } catch (MongoConnectionException $e) {
    die('Failed to connect to MongoDB '.$e->getMessage());
  }
  $currentPage = (isset($_GET['page'])) ? (int) $_GET['page']
    : 1;
```

```php
$articlesPerPage = 5;
$skip = ($currentPage - 1) * $articlesPerPage;
$cursor = $articleCollection->find(array(),array('title',
   'saved_at'));
$totalArticles = $cursor->count();
$totalPages = (int) ceil($totalArticles / $articlesPerPage);
$cursor->sort(array('saved_at'=>-1))->skip($skip)
   ->limit($articlesPerPage);
?>
<html>
  <head>
    <title>Dashboard</title>
    <link rel="stylesheet" href="style.css"/>
    <style type="text/css" media="screen">
      body { font-size: 13px; }
      div#contentarea { width : 650px; }
    </style>
  </head>
  <body>
    <div id="contentarea">
      <div id="innercontentarea">
        <h1>Dashboard</h1>
        <table class="articles" cellspacing="0"
          cellpadding="0">
          <thead>
            <tr>
              <th width="55%">Title</th>
              <th width="27%">Created at</th>
              <th width="*">Action</th>
            </tr>
          </thead>
          <tbody>
            <?php while($cursor->hasNext()):
              $article = $cursor->getNext();?>
              <tr>
                <td>
                  <?php echo substr($article['title'], 0, 35)
                    . '...'; ?>
                </td>
                <td>
                  <?php print date('g:i a, F j',
                    $article[saved_at]->sec);?>
                </td>
                <td class="url">
                  <a href="blog.php?id=<?php echo
```

```
                  $article['_id'];     ?>">View
                </a>
              </td>
            </tr>
          <?php endwhile;?>
        </tbody>
      </table>
    </div>
    <div id="navigation">
      <div class="prev">
        <?php if($currentPage !== 1): ?>
          <a href="<?php echo
            $_SERVER['PHP_SELF'].'?page='.($currentPage - 1);
            ?>">Previous </a>
        <?php endif; ?>
      </div>
      <div class="page-number">
        <?php echo $currentPage; ?>
      </div>
      <div class="next">
        <?php if($currentPage !== $totalPages): ?>
          <a href="<?php echo
            $_SERVER['PHP_SELF'].'?page='.($currentPage + 1);
            ?>">Next</a>
        <?php endif; ?>
      </div>
      <br class="clear"/>
    </div>
  </div>
</body>
</html>
```

2. Open `style.css` and add the following CSS rules to it:

```
table.articles {
  width: 100%;
  line-height: 1;
  text-align: left;
}
table.articles th{
  border-bottom: 1px solid #ccc;
  padding: 8px 0;
  font-weight: bold;
}
table.articles td {
```

```
    border-bottom: 1px solid #eee;
    padding: 6px 0;
}
div#navigation {
    margin: 0px 150px;
    padding: 5px 90px;
    text-align:center;
}
div#navigation div.prev  { display:block; float:left; width:40%; }
div#navigation div.page-number { float:left; width:20%; }
div#navigation div.next { float:right; width:40%; }
.clear { clear: both; }
```

3. Open your browser and go to the `dashboard.php` page. Use the **Previous/Next** links to browse through the articles in the database. Click on the **View** link next to an article to view its full content:

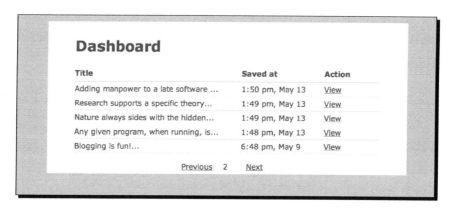

What just happened?

We wrote a new PHP program `dashboard.php` that implements the Blog Dashboard. We added some new styling rules in the `style.css` file for this new page. We executed `dashboard.php` in the browser and used the links at the bottom to navigate through all the blog posts in the database. In the next few sections, we are going to dig deeper into the code and learn advanced query features in Mongo.

Returning a subset of fields

In this example, we sent a second optional argument to `find()`, an array containing names of fields that we want to see in the retrieved documents:

```
$cursor = $articleCollection->find(array(),
    array('title' => 1, 'saved_at' => 1);
```

The first argument is an empty array, so the query matches all documents in the articles collection. The second argument tells MongoDB to only fetch the values for `title` and the `saved_at` fields of each document. This is useful in situations when we are only interested in some specific fields instead of all of them. For example, the next argument returns the username and e-mail for a user with a specific user ID:

```
//SELECT username, email FROM users WHERE user_id = 1;
$users->find(array('user_id' => 1), array('username', 'id'));
```

Sorting the query results

The `sort()` method invoked on the `MongoCursor` object sorts the query results based on the value of a specified field. Sorting order can be both ascending and descending. In our example, we sorted the articles on their create dates in descending order:

```
$cursor->sort(array('saved_at'  => -1)) //-1 means descending order
```

To reverse the sorting order, we would do the following:

```
$cursor->sort(array('saved_at'  => 1)) //1 means ascending order
```

We can also sort on multiple fields, even with different sort orders:

```
//sort on field 'x' in ascending order and on 'y' in descending order

$cursor->sort(array('x' = > 1, 'y' => -1));
```

Using count, skip, and limit

Calling `count()` on a `MongoCursor` object returns the number of items in the cursor:

```
$cursor = $articleCollection->find(); //gets all articles
$cursor->count(); //returns number of articles retrieved
```

`skip()` lets you skip a number of results in a cursor. It needs an integer as an argument, which is the number of results to skip:

```
//get all articles
$cursor = $articleCollection->find();
//skip the first five articles in the cursor
$cursor->skip(5);
//start iterating from the sixth article in the result set
while($cursor->hasNext()) {
  $cursor->getNext();
  .......................................................
}
```

Finally, `limit()` enables us to limit the number of results returned:

```
$cursor = $articlesCollection->find();
$cursor->limit(10); //get first 10 documents from the result set
```

We can chain all these methods together to achieve the combined effect. The next statement gets documents from the database sorted on `saved_at` in descending order, skips the first five documents in the result set and fetches the next five:

```
$cursor->sort(array('saved_at' => -1))->skip(5)->limit(5);
```

Performing range queries on dates

We know PHP stores date and time information in MongoDB as `MongoDate` objects. Let's take a look at how we can perform range queries on `MongoDate` fields using the conditional operators we have seen earlier in this chapter.

The next query returns all articles from the database that have been created within the last week:

```
$lastweek = new MongoDate(strtotime('-1 week'));
$cursor = $articleCollection->find(array('saved_at' =>
  array('$gt' => $lastweek)));
```

We can also specify two specific end points in date range queries:

```
$start = new MongoDate(strtotime('2011-05-01 00:00:00'));
$end  = new MongoDate(strtotime('2011-05-31 23:59:59'));
$articleCollection->find(array('saved_at'=>
  array('$gte' => $start,
  '$lte' => $end)));
```

Have a go hero – rewrite blogs.php

Rewrite the blog homepage script, `blogs.php`, to achieve the following changes:

- The page should show the most recently saved articles at the top
- Instead of showing all articles, only show the 10 most recent articles at the top
- Enable pagination on the homepage so that users can browse the older articles

Updating documents in MongoDB

We have covered creation and retrieval of documents in MongoDB. It is time that we learn how we can update a document.

Updates are performed by the `update()` method of the `MongoCollection` object. This is how the method signature looks:

```
public bool MongoCollection::update ( $criteria, $newobj, $options )
```

`$criteria` is an array that specifies the document that is going to be updated. The database is queried with `$criteria` to select the document intended to be updated.

`$newobj` is the document (represented as an array) that is going to replace the old document.

`$options` specifies optional arguments to `update()`. We will talk about what options are available later.

In this next section, we are going to see this method in action by building a module to edit existing blog posts in the database.

Time for action – building the Blog Editor

We are now going to build the Blog Editor, a page that loads an article, specified by the `_id`, from the database into an HTML form. The user changes the title and/or the content of the article, hits save, and the article gets updated with the modified content.

1. Create a new PHP file named `edit.php`. Add the following code to the file:

```php
<?php
$action = (!empty($_POST['btn_submit']) &&
    ($_POST['btn_submit'] === 'Save')) ? 'save_article'
    : 'show_form';
$id = $_REQUEST['id'];
```

```php
    try {
      $mongodb = new Mongo();
      $articleCollection = $mongodb->myblogsite->articles;
    } catch (MongoConnectionException $e) {
      die('Failed to connect to MongoDB '.$e->getMessage());
    }
    switch($action){
      case 'save_article':
        $article           = array();
        $article['title']   = $_POST['title'];
        $article['content'] = $_POST['content'];
        $article[saved_at]  = new MongoDate();
        $articleCollection->update(array('_id' => new
          MongoId($id)),
            $article);
        break;
      case 'show_form':
      default:
        $article = $articleCollection->findOne(array('_id' =>
          new MongoId($id)));
    }
?>
<!DOCTYPE html PUBLIC "-//W3C//DTD XHTML 1.0 Transitional//EN"
  "http://www.w3.org/TR/xhtml1/DTD/xhtml1-transitional.dtd">
<html xmlns="http://www.w3.org/1999/xhtml" xml:lang="en"
  lang="en">
  <head>
    <meta http-equiv="Content-Type" content="text/html;
      charset=utf-8"/>
      <link rel="stylesheet" href="style.css" />
      <title>Blog Post Editor</title>
  </head>
  <body>
    <div id="contentarea">
      <div id="innercontentarea">
        <h1>Blog Post Creator</h1>
        <?php if ($action === 'show_form'): ?>
          <form action="<?php echo $_SERVER['PHP_SELF'];?>"
            method="post">
            <h3>Title</h3>
            <p><input type="text" name="title" id="title"
              value="<?php echo $article['title']; ?>"/></p>
```

```
<h3>Content</h3>
<textarea name="content" rows="20">
  <?php echo $article['content']; ?>
</textarea>
<input type="hidden" name="id" value="<?php echo
  $article['_id'];?>" />
<p>
  <input type="submit" name="btn_submit"
    value="Save"/>
</p>
</form>
<?php else: ?>
  <p>
    Article saved. _id: <?php echo $id;?>.
    <a href="blog.php?id=<?php echo $id;?>">
      Read it.
    </a>
  </p>
<?php endif;?>
</div>
</div>
</body>
</html>
```

2. Open the `dashboard.php` file in your text editor, and change the following HTML markup:

```
<td>
  <a href="blog.php?id=<?php echo $article['_id'];?>">View</a>
</td>
```

To this:

```
<td>
  <a href="blog.php?id=<?php echo $article['_id'];?>">View</a>
  | <a href="edit.php?id=<?php echo $article['_id'];?>">Edit</a>
</td>
```

3. Open the `dashboard.php` file in the browser. Click on the `Edit` link on any one article.

4. Change **Title/Content** of the article loaded in the form on the `edit.php` page. Click on the **Save** button when done:

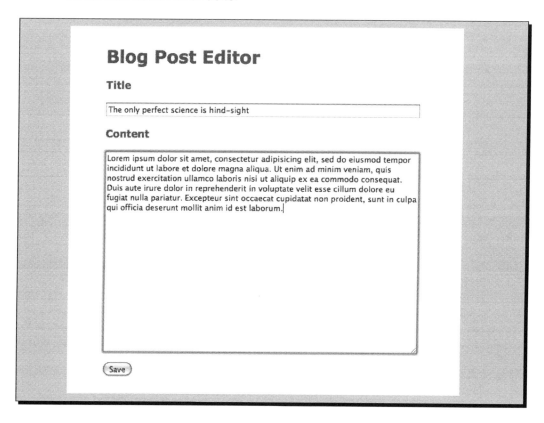

What just happened?

We created a new PHP file, `edit.php` that receives an article `_id` via the HTTP GET parameter and loads it into an HTML form. We modified the code in the `dashboard.php` file to add an **Edit** link for each article. Clicking on this link takes us to the `edit.php` page, where we can change the **Title/Content** of the article and click on **Save**. The article is saved to the database with the changed values and the `saved_at` field is set to the time of update.

Let's take a closer look at the code. We sent the article ID as the $criteria parameter for the update() method. We constructed an array from the user-submitted data (**Title/Content**) and passed it as the second argument to update(). The saved_at field is reset to the current time:

```
$article    = array();
$article['title']    = $_POST['title'];
$article['content']    = $_POST['content'];
$article['saved_at'] = new MongoDate();
$articleCollection->update(array('_id' => new MongoId($id)),
    $article);
```

Optional arguments to the update method

Let's take a look at some of the optional parameters we can send to the update() method:

- safe: This is the same as doing a 'safe' insert. When set to True, the PHP-MongoDB driver waits for the database response for the update operation. Default is false:

```
$collection->update($criteria, $newobj, array('safe' => True));
```

- multiple: Even if we get more than one document matched by the criteria, update() updates just one of them. Setting multiple to True switches this default behavior that is, all matched documents are updated:

```
$collection->update($criteria, $newobj, array('multiple' =>
    True));
```

- timeout: Specifies a timeout (in milliseconds) on the update operation. Must be used along with the safe parameter:

```
//100 milliseconds timeout on the update operation
$collection->update($criteria, $newobj, array('safe => True,
    'timeout' => 100));
```

Performing 'upsert'

MongoDB allows us to perform an interesting operation named Upsert. Upsert is short for "Update if exists, INSERT otherwise". That means if the document we are looking to update does not actually exist in the database, MongoDB is going to create the document with the given values instead. This is achieved by setting an optional upsert flag to True in the update() method.

Take the following code for example, it looks up the user with the e-mail ID `alice@wonderland.com` and sets her first name and last name. If the user does not exist in the database, it is going to create the user with the given values (both with the e-mail and the first and last names).

```
$users->update(array('email' => 'alice@wonderland.com'),
    array('firstname' => 'Alice', 'lastname'=> 'Liddell'),
    array('upsert' => True));
```

Using update versus using save

An alternate approach for updating documents in MongoDB is using the `save()` method on a `MongoCollection` object:

```
$collection->save($document);
```

The difference between `update()` and `save()` is that when using `save()`, if the document does not exist in the database it gets created. This is almost the same as doing `upsert=True` in `update()`. This way `save()` can be used instead of `insert()` as well:

```
$document = array('name' => 'Adam Smith', 'age' => 27);
$collection->save($document); //inserts the object
$document['age'] = 31;
$collection->save($document); //updates the object
```

Using modifier operations

Using modifiers enables us to update documents efficiently and conveniently. Instead of replacing the whole document, modifiers change only part of the document, leaving the other parts intact. Such atomic operations have the advantage of saving data with less latency in querying and returning the documents. To use these modifiers, we have to specify the operators marked by the `$` prefix. Let's take a look at some of the important modifiers.

Setting with $set

`$set` allows us to set the value of a particular field of a document. For example, if we just wanted to change the title of an article in our blog editor, we would do the following:

```
$articles->update(array('_id' => MongoId('4dcd2abe5981')),
    array('$set' => array('title' => 'New
    Title')));
```

The previous code sets the title of the article with the ID '4dcd2abe5981', to 'New Title'. The other fields are unchanged.

Incrementing with $inc

$inc lets us increment the value of a field by a specified number. For example, let's assume we are keeping track of how many times an article gets modified in our blog by a field named update_count, and we need to increase its value by 1 each time an article content gets modified:

```
$articles->update(array('_id' => MongoId('4dcd2abe5981')),
   array('$set' => array('content' => 'New Content'),
   '$inc' => array('update_count' => 1)));
```

The previous code snippet changes the content of the article with the ID '4dcd2abe5981', and increases its update_count value by 1. Incase the update_count field did not exist in the document, using $inc will add this field and set its value to 1.

Deleting fields with $unset

$unset is just the opposite of $set. We can use it to remove a field from a document:

```
$articles->update(array('_id' => MongoId('4dcd2abe5981')),
   array('$unset' => array('title' => True)));
```

The previous statement removes the title field from an article object.

Renaming fields with $rename

Another handy modifier operator is $rename, which can be used to change the name of a field in a document:

```
$articles->update(array(),
   array('$rename' => array('saved_at' =>
   'created_at')),
   array('multiple' => True));
```

The previous statement renames the saved_at field for all documents in an articles collection to created_at.

Have a go hero – merge Blog editor and creator into a single module

We created blogpost.php for inserting articles and edit.php for updating articles. Your homework is to develop a new module that does the job of both these modules. Here is how the new module will work:

1. By default, the page will show an HTML form where the user can type in the title and content of a blog post.

2. If the page receives the ID of an article as GET parameter, it will load the title and the content of the article in the HTML form.

3. When the user clicks on the **Save** button in the form, the article is saved in the database. In case of a new article, the article is inserted. Otherwise the article is updated. (Hint: use the `save()` method, or the `upsert` feature.)

4. When an article is updated, only the title and content of the article should be updated, rather than replacing the entire article object. Also, assign a new field called `modified_at` to record the last time the article was updated.

You get bonus points for handling errors gracefully!

Deleting documents in MongoDB

We are down to the last letter of CRUD, the DELETE operation. We will learn how to delete documents from a collection in MongoDB.

Time for action – deleting blog posts

We will modify the code of the Blog Dashboard once again to add a **Delete** link to each article displayed. Clicking on this link will display a JavaScript confirmation box, and clicking on **Yes** on that box will delete the article and reload the page:

1. Open up `dashboard.php` in your editor. Delete the old code in that file, and add the following code to it:

```php
<?php
  try{
    $mongodb = new Mongo();
    $articleCollection = $mongodb->myblogsite->articles;
  } catch (MongoConnectionException $e) {
    die('Failed to connect to MongoDB '.$e->getMessage());
  }
  $currentPage = (isset($_GET['page'])) ? (int) $_GET['page']
    : 1;
  $articlesPerPage = 5; //number of articles to show per page
  $skip = ($currentPage - 1) * $articlesPerPage;
  $cursor = $articleCollection->find(array(),
    $fields=array('title',
    'saved_at'));
  $totalArticles = $cursor->count();
  $totalPages = (int) ceil($totalArticles / $articlesPerPage);
  $cursor->sort(array('created_at' => -1))->skip($skip)
    ->limit($articlesPerPage);
?>
<!DOCTYPE html PUBLIC "-//W3C//DTD XHTML 1.1//EN"
  "http://www.w3.org/TR/xhtml11/DTD/xhtml11.dtd">
```

```
<html xmlns="http://www.w3.org/1999/xhtml" xml:lang="en">
  <head>
    <title>Dashboard</title>
    <link rel="stylesheet" href="style.css"/>
    <style type="text/css" media="screen">
      body { font-size: 13px; }
      div#contentarea { width : 650px; }
    </style>
    <script type="text/javascript" charset="utf-8">
      function confirmDelete(articleId) {
        var deleteArticle = confirm('Are you sure you want to
          delete this article?');
        if(deleteArticle){
          window.location.href = 'delete.php?id='+articleId;
        }
        return;
      }
    </script>
  </head>
  <body>
    <div id="contentarea">
      <div id="innercontentarea">
        <h1>Dashboard</h1>
        <table class="articles" cellspacing="0" cellpadding="0">
          <thead>
            <tr>
              <th width="50%">Title</th>
              <th width="24%">Saved at</th>
              <th width="*">Action</th>
            </tr>
          </thead>
          <tbody>
            <?php while($cursor->hasNext()):
            $article = $cursor->getNext();?>
            <tr>
              <td>
                <?php echo substr($article['title'], 0, 35) .
                  '...'; ?>
              </td>
              <td>
                <?php print date('g:i a, F j',
                  $article['saved_at']->sec);?>
              </td>
              <td>
                <a href="blog.php?id=<?php $article['_id'];?>">
```

```
                      View
                    </a>
                    | <a href="edit.php?id=<?php $article['_
                      id'];?>">
                      Edit
                    </a>
                    | <a href="#" onclick="confirmDelete('<?php echo
                    $article['_id']; ?>')">
                      Delete
                    </a>
                  </td>
                </tr>
              <?php endwhile;?>
            </tbody>
          </table>
        </div>
        <div id="navigation">
          <div class="prev">
            <?php if($currentPage !== 1): ?>
              <a href="<?php $_SERVER['PHP_SELF'].'?page='.
                ($currentPage - 1); ?>">
              Previous</a>
            <?php endif; ?>
          </div>
          <div class="page-number">
            <?php echo $currentPage; ?>
          </div>
          <div class="next">
            <?php if($currentPage !== $totalPages): ?>
              <a href="<?php echo
                $_SERVER['PHP_SELF'].'?page='.($currentPage + 1);
                ?>">
              Next
              </a>
            <?php endif; ?>
          </div>
          <br class="clear"/>
        </div>
      </div>
    </body>
</html>
```

2. Create another PHP script named `delete.php`. Put the following code in it:

```php
<?php
$id = $_GET['id'];
try{

    $mongodb = new Mongo();
    $articleCollection = $mongodb->myblogsite->articles;
} catch (MongoConnectionException $e) {
    die('Failed to connect to MongoDB '.$e->getMessage());
}
$articleCollection->remove(array('_id' => new MongoId($id)));
?>
<!DOCTYPE html PUBLIC "-//W3C//DTD XHTML 1.0 Transitional//EN"
    "http://www.w3.org/TR/xhtml1/DTD/xhtml1-transitional.dtd">
<html xmlns="http://www.w3.org/1999/xhtml" xml:lang="en"
    lang="en">
    <head>
        <meta http-equiv="Content-Type" content="text/html;
            charset=utf-8"/>
        <link rel="stylesheet" href="style.css"/>
        <title>Blog Post Creator</title>
    </head>
    <body>
        <div id="contentarea">
            <div id="innercontentarea">
                <h1>Blog Post Creator</h1>
                <p>Article deleted. _id: <?php echo $id;?>.
                    <a href="dashboard.php">Go back to dashboard?</a>
                </p>
            </div>
        </div>
    </body>
</html>
```

3. Run `dashboard.php` in the browser. Click on the **Delete** link on any one article. Click **OK** on the confirmation dialogue box to delete the article:

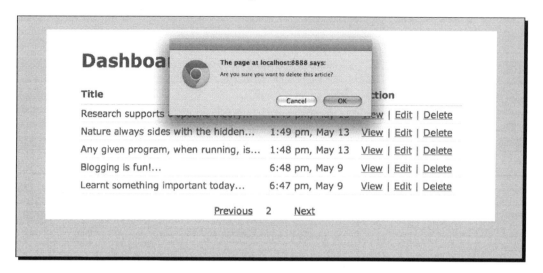

What just happened?

We edited the dashboard page HTML to display a **Delete** link in each row. We added some JavaScript code to the page so that when we click the delete link, a pop-up box asks for confirmation. Clicking **OK** takes us to the page `delete.php`, which deletes the article and shows us a confirmation message.

In the `delete.php` script, we used the `remove()` method to delete an article from the database. The `remove()` method takes an array as its parameter, which it uses to query the document it is going to delete. If multiple documents match the query, all of them are deleted.

```
//delete document(s) from the movies collection where genre is drama
$movies->remove(array('genre' => 'drama') );
```

 If no query argument is passed, `remove()` will delete all documents in the collection.

Optional arguments to remove

`remove()` has the following optional arguments:

- `safe`: Performs 'safe' delete that is, when set to `True`, the program control waits for the database response for the delete operation. Default is false:

```
$collection->remove(array('username' => 'joe'),
  array('safe' => True))
```

- `timeout`: Specify a timeout in milliseconds for the delete operation. It can only be used when doing safe delete:

```
$collection->remove(array('userid' => 267),
  array('safe' => True, 'timeout' => 200));
```

- `justOne`: When set to `True`, `remove()` will delete only one document matched by the query, instead of all of them:

```
//remove just one movie with genre = drama
$movies->remove(array('genre' =>'drama'),
  array('justOne' => True));
```

Managing relationships between documents

When building an application, we have to map the real-world objects into a data model that fits the use case scenarios of the application. These real-world objects are related to each other to some degree. A typical blog application, for example, will have articles written by authors, comments posted to articles, categories created by authors and assigned to articles, and so on. We know from our discussion in Chapter 1, *Getting Started with MongoDB* that MongoDB (and NoSQL databases in general) is non-relational by nature; there are no FOREIGN KEYs or JOINs. Then how do we simulate the relation between two documents in MongoDB?

There are two ways we can do that, embedding a document within the other document, or creating a reference from one document to the other.

Embedded documents

In this approach, the top-level document contains the related document in itself. For example, an author document may have an address document embedded in it:

```
{
    "_id"       : ObjectId("4dd491695072aefc456c9aca"),
    "username"  : "alphareplicant",
    "email"     : "roybatty@androids.org",
    "fullname"  : "Roy Batty",
    "joined_at" : ISODate("2011-05-19T03:41:29.703Z"),
    "address"   : {
        "street"  : "13 Tannhauser Gate",
        "city"    : "Caprica",
        "state"   : "CC",
        "zipcode" : 512
    },
}
```

Referenced documents

A document may also have a reference to another document. For example, an article document may refer to an author document by storing the ID of the author as a field:

```
{
    _id       : ObjectId("4dcd2abe5981aec801010000"),
    title     : "The only perfect site is hind-site",
    content   : "Loren ipsum dolor sit amet…",
    saved_at  : ISODate('2011-05-16T18:42:57.949Z'),
    author_id : ObjectId("4dd491695072aefc456c9aca")
}
```

Referential integrity of such documents is handled at the application level, rather than at the database level. That means you have to write code to handle the relationship between such objects.

Time for action – posting comments to blog posts

We are going to modify blog.php so that readers can post comments on an article. The reader will enter his name, e-mail address, and the comment in a form right below the article. We are also going to create a new PHP script, comment.php, that receives the user-submitted comment, saves it in the database, and redirects to the original blog post where the user can see his own submitted comment:

1. Open `blog.php` in your text editor and replace the existing code in it with the following:

```php
<?php
  $id = $_GET['id'];
  try {
    $connection = new Mongo();
    $database   = $connection->selectDB('myblogsite');
    $collection = $database->selectCollection('articles');
  } catch(MongoConnectionException $e) {
    die("Failed to connect to database ".$e->getMessage());
  }
  $article = $collection->findOne(array('_id' =>
    new MongoId($id)));
?>
<!DOCTYPE html PUBLIC "-//W3C//DTD XHTML 1.0 Transitional//EN"
  "http://www.w3.org/TR/xhtml1/DTD/xhtml1-transitional.dtd">
<html xmlns="http://www.w3.org/1999/xhtml" xml:lang="en"
  lang="en">
  <head>
    <meta http-equiv="Content-Type" content="text/html;
      charset=utf-8"/>
    <link rel="stylesheet" href="style.css" />
    <title>My Blog Site</title>
  </head>
  <body>
    <div id="contentarea">
      <div id="innercontentarea">
        <h1><?php echo $article['title']; ?></h1>
        <p><?php echo $article['content']; ?></p>
        <div id="comment-section">
          <h3>Comments</h3>
          <?php if (!empty($article['comments'])): ?>
          <h3>Comments</h3>
          <?php foreach($article['comments'] as $comment):
            echo $comment['name'].' says...';?>
          <p><?php echo $comment['comment']; ?></p>
          <span>
            <?php echo date('g:i a, F j', $comment['posted_at']->
              sec); ?>
          </span><br/><br/><br/>
          <?php endforeach;
          endif;?>
          <h3>Post your comment</h3>
          <form action="comment.php" method="post">
```

```
            <span class="input-label">Name</span>
            <input type="text" name="commenter_name"
              class="comment-input"/>
            <br/><br/>
            <span class="input-label">Email</span>
            <input type="text" name="commenter_email"
              class="comment-input"/>
            <br/><br/>
            <textarea name="comment"
              rows="5"></textarea><br/><br/>
            <input type="hidden" name="article_id"
              value="<?php echo $article['_id']; ?>"/>
            <input type="submit" name="btn_submit" value="Save"/>
          </form>
        </div>
      </div>
    </div>
  </body>
</html>
```

2. Add the following style rules to `style.css`:

```
div#comment-section { border-top: 1px solid #ccc; }
div#comment-section form input.comment-input{ width: 200px; }
div#comment-section form textarea[name=comment] { width: 255px; }
span.input-label { font-weight:bold; padding-right:10px; }
```

3. Create a new file named `comment.php`, add the following code in it:

```php
<?php
  $id = $_POST['article_id'];
  try {
    $mongodb = new Mongo();
    $collection = $mongodb->myblogsite->articles;
  } catch (MongoConnectionException $e) {
    die('Failed to connect to MongoDB '.$e->getMessage());
  }
  $article = $collection->findOne(array('_id' => MongoId($id)));
  $comment = array(
    'name' => $_POST['commenter_name'],
    'email' => $_POST['commenter_email'],
    'comment' => $_POST['comment'],
    'posted_at' => new MongoDate()
  );
  $collection->update(array('_id' => new MongoId($id)),
    array('$push' => array('comments' => $comments)));
  header('Location: blog.php?id='.$id);
```

4. Navigate to `blogs.php` in your browser, click on the **Read More** link of the top article to read its full content in the `blog.php` page.

5. Once the page loads, enter an arbitrary **Name** and **Email** in the input boxes under the comments section, put some text in the textarea box as well. Then click on the **Save** button and the page will reload with the comment you just posted:

What just happened?

We modified the code in the `blog.php` script to load the comments posted on an article, just underneath the content area, and show an HTML form where the reader can post comments:

```
<div id="comment-section">
  <?php if (!empty($article['comments'])):
    <h3>Comments</h3>
  foreach($article['comments'] as $comment):
    echo $comment['name'].' says...';?>
  <p><?php echo $comment['comment']; ?></p>
  <span>
    <?php echo date('g:i a, F j', $comment['posted_at']->sec); ?>
  </span><br/><br/><br/>
  <?php endforeach;
```

```
   endif;?>
   <h3>Post your comment</h3>
   <form action="comment.php" method="post">
     <span class="input-label">Name</span>
     <input type="text" name="commentor_name" class="comment-
       input"/>
     <br/><br/>
     <span class="input-label">Email</span>
     <input type="text" name="commentor_email" class="comment-
       input"/>
     <br/><br/>
     <textarea name="comment" rows="5"></textarea>
     <br/><br/>
     <input type="hidden" name="article_id" value="<?php echo
       $article['_id']; ?>"/>
     <input type="submit" name="btn_submit" value="Save"/>
   </form>
 </div>
```

The action of the form is `comment.php`, the script that stores the user-submitted comment to MongoDB. Comments for an article are stored in an array field of the document named `comments`. Each element of `comments` is an embedded document that contains several fields: name and e-mail of the commenter, the actual comment, and a timestamp. We construct an object with the user-submitted data and put a timestamp in it:

```
$comment = array(
  'name' => $_POST['commenter_name'],
  'email' => $_POST['commenter_email'],
  'comment' => $_POST['comment'],
  'posted_at' => new MongoDate()
);
```

We push this object to the `comments` field using the `$push` modifier:

```
$collection->update(array('_id' => new MongoId($id)),
  array('$push' => array('comments' =>
  $comments)));
```

Embedded versus referenced – Which one to use?

When designing the data model of your application in MongoDB, you will be faced with a choice of using either the embedded or referenced approach for creating relationship between two different objects. Here are some general rules that you can follow:

- Each top-level object in the data model should have a collection of its own. In a blog, the articles and the authors are two top-level objects and so each of them should be stored in a separate collection. They will be related to each other by reference.

- If the relation between two objects is such that one contains the other, the latter should be embedded in the former. For example, an article may contain one or more comments by embedding them in itself.

Embedding gets preference

In MongoDB, embedding documents is preferable to referencing. This is because embedded objects are more efficient in terms of performance. The documents share disk space. Also, embedded documents are loaded to memory when you load their container documents, whereas to get a referenced document you have to hit the database again. So embedded documents tend to be a little faster. But this does not mean you should always go for embedded objects! When designing the data model, embedding should be the first choice, but if you see a reason that it should not be embedded, you must reference it.

Querying embedded objects

MongoDB allows you to reach into an object and query the embedded documents. There are two ways to do that. Before we learn about them, let's assume that we have the following documents in a collection named users:

```
{
  name : "Gordon Freeman",
  address : {
    city  : "Springfield",
    state : "Florida"
  }
}
```

```
{
  name : "Lara Croft",
  address : {
    city : "Miami",
    state: "Florida"
  }
}
```

Now, if we need to get all users from Springfield, Florida; we will query the collection as follows:

```
$users->find(array('address' => array('city' => 'Springfield',
  'state' => 'Florida'))) ;
```

This will get us the user Gordon Freeman. This approach is called querying by subobjects. But this has a limitation, the subobjects have to match exactly with the embedded objects. For example, the following query will not return anything:

```
$users->find(array('address' => array('state' => 'Florida'))) ;
```

The previous query is looking for address documents with only one field (state), and therefore, will not match any of the documents in the collection. To get around these, we have to use the next query:

```
$users->find(array('address.state' => 'Florida'));
```

This will get us both Gordon Freeman and Lara Croft. This is called a **dot** notation query. It uses the dot (.) operator to conveniently look into embedded objects and query by their field values. We can rewrite the first query using dot notation as follows:

```
$users->find(array('address.city' => 'Springfield',
  'address.state' => 'Florida'));
```

Have a go hero – get comments by username

Write a MongoDB query to get all comments posted by a user named Bob.

Summary

It is time to wrap up this rather lengthy chapter. Let's take a look at what we covered. In this chapter, we built a very simple blogging application using MongoDB as the database. Through the practical example we learned how to:

- Insert documents into MongoDB
- Perform safe inserts with timeout
- Query documents with Mongo query language
- Retrieve and iterate over queried documents using cursors
- Update documents in MongoDB
- Performing `'upsert'` operation
- Performing atomic update with `$set`, `$unset`, `$inc`, and so on
- Delete documents in MongoDB
- Querying embedded documents

We also learned about referenced and embedded objects, their use cases, and relative advantages over each other. In the next chapter, we will use these concepts to build something more practical and reusable. Stay tuned!

3

Building a Session Manager

In the previous chapter, we learned how to use PHP to store and retrieve data to and from a MongoDB database and built a very basic web application while we were at it. This time we will use that knowledge to build something more practical. We are going to build a session manager in PHP, a module that will handle the HTTP session of a visitor in a website, using MongoDB for storing the session data. Why a session manager? Because it is one of those components that you are going to need when building a user facing web application; implementing basic but important functionalities such as signing in a user (authentication), tracking his/her activities, authorizing his/her actions, and logging him/her out. We will use object-oriented programming principles for building the module, so that it can be used in any web application with little or no change. We will also build a separate module for user authentication, which will be used by the session manager for logging a user in.

So to sum it up, in this chapter we will:

- Learn the basics of HTTP sessions
- Learn how PHP handles sessions
- Build the session manager, a module that handles sessions using MongoDB
- Build a user authentication module
- Learn how to log in and log out a user using the user authentication module
- Learn best practices for securing a user session

Understanding HTTP sessions

Before we start building the session manager, let's get the basics of HTTP sessions right. So what is a session? By design, HTTP is *stateless*. You make a request to a web server, it replies to you with a response, and then it forgets about the request. It has no memory of what requests it served you earlier. But this stateless nature of HTTP goes against the notion of interactive web applications. These applications need to keep track of users' activities on the website. They need to know who the user is, if the user is allowed to see a webpage, where the user has been before coming to this page. On an e-commerce site, for example, the user has to follow a step-by-step (or page-by-page to be more precise) process to log out of his/ her account. How does a web application running on top of a stateless protocol implement persistence of user state? The answer is a *session*. By definition, a session is a series of HTTP requests, performed consecutively by a user from a single client to a certain web application. The first request made by the user initiates the session, subsequent requests to the server are considered as part of the session. The underlying logic of session handling is simple. The application generates a session identifier, a value that is unique for each user. If there are 100 users making requests to the application at the same time, each of them is given a unique session ID. The application uses the session ID to identify a user and preserve his/her state in between requests.

Understanding PHP native session handling

Nowadays, most of us are doing web development using MVC web frameworks, built and open sourced by other developers. These frameworks have, among other things, their own modules for handling sessions. They take care of all the magic behind session handling and expose a simple API to the developers. This surely comes in handy; after all, the goal of such frameworks is to make us more productive by taking care of the low level plumbing. However, this makes some of us never really understand how session handling works under the hood. Since we are going to implement our own session handler, we should at least have an idea how PHP handles sessions.

Time for action – testing native PHP session handling

In the next example, we are going to see how we can use the built-in mechanisms in PHP for handling sessions.

1. Open up your text editor and put the following code in a new file:

```php
<?php
session_start();
  //Generate a random number
  $random_number = rand();
```

```
    //Put the number into session
    $_SESSION['random_number'] = $random_number;
?>
<!DOCTYPE html PUBLIC "-//W3C//DTD XHTML 1.0 Transitional//EN"
  "http://www.w3.org/TR/xhtml1/DTD/xhtml1-transitional.dtd">
<html xmlns="http://www.w3.org/1999/xhtml" xml:lang="en"
  lang="en">
  <head>
    <meta http-equiv="Content-Type" content="text/html;
      charset=utf-8"/>
    <link rel="stylesheet" href="style.css" />
    <title>Understanding PHP sessions...Page 1</title>
  </head>
  <body>
    <div id="contentarea">
      <div id="innercontentarea">
        <h2>Understanding PHP sessions...Page 1</h2>
        <p>Random number generated
          <span style="font-weight:bold;">
            <?php echo $_SESSION['random_number']; ?>
          </span>
        </p>
        <p>PHP session id
          <span style="text-decoration:underline;">
            <?php echo session_id(); ?>
          </span>
        </p>
        <a href="basic_session2.php">Go to next page</a>
      </div>
    </div>
  </body>
</html>
```

Save the file as `basic_session1.php`.

2. Create another file named `basic_session2.php`. Put the following code in it:

```
<?php
  session_start();
?>
<!DOCTYPE html PUBLIC "-//W3C//DTD XHTML 1.0 Transitional//EN"
  "http://www.w3.org/TR/xhtml1/DTD/xhtml1-transitional.dtd">
<html xmlns="http://www.w3.org/1999/xhtml" xml:lang="en"
  lang="en">
  <head>
    <meta http-equiv="Content-Type" content="text/html;
      charset=utf-8"/>
    <link rel="stylesheet" href="style.css" />
```

```
        <title>Understanding PHP sessions...Page 2</title>
    </head>
    <body>
      <div id="contentarea">
        <div id="innercontentarea">
          <h2>Understanding PHP sessions...Page 2</h2>
          <p>My Favorite movie is
            <span style="font-weight:bold;">
              <?php echo $_SESSION['random_number]; ?>
            </span>
          </p>
          <p>PHP session id
            <span style="text-decoration:underline;">
              <?php echo session_id(); ?>
            </span>
          </p>
        </div>
      </div>
    </body>
</html>
```

3. Open `basic_session1.php` in the browser. Note the random number displayed on the page:

Understanding PHP sessions...Page 1

Random number generated **1787867281**

PHP session id 3bb369863cb9733bca16ddc4cffa0255

Go to next page

4. Navigate to `basic_session2.php` by clicking on the **Go to next page** link. It should show the same number:

Understanding PHP sessions...Page 2

The random number generated in previous page is still **1787867281**

PHP session id 3bb369863cb9733bca16ddc4cffa0255

What just happened?

We just implemented session handling with built-in PHP functions. We created two pages. In the first page we put some data into the session. We navigated to the second page and read the same piece of data from the session to verify if it is the same.

In PHP, a session is initiated by calling the built-in `session_start()` method. Calling this method causes PHP to give the client a unique session ID (unless the client is already in session, in that case it retrieves the current session ID). The session ID is a 32-character string. You can get the value of this string by calling the `session_id()` function.

 `session_start()` must send session data to the web browser via HTTP headers. This is why calling `session_start()` in a PHP script must precede any HTML output, `echo` statements, calls to `var_dump()` or `print_r()` or even whitespaces. Otherwise you would get a "Header already sent" error.

PHP uses file-based session handling by default. When a new session is initiated, PHP creates a text file, typically under the `/tmp` directory on the server (or whatever filepath is set as the value of `session.save_path` in the `php.ini` configuration). The name of the file is prefixed with `sess_`, followed by the value of the session ID. For example, if the session in the previous example was `54305ebe20f19907658d2bd0991628c3`, the name of the file would be `sess_54305ebe20f19907658d2bd0991628c3`. Whatever data we put into the `$_SESSION` super global array, it is going to be serialized and stored in this file. If you open it up in a text editor after running the previous example, its content should look similar to the following:

```
random_number|i:23353609;
```

At the same time, PHP issues a cookie named `PHPSESSID` to the browser. The content of this cookie is the value of the session ID. In the subsequent HTTP requests, PHP checks the value of this cookie, then checks the stored session files for a match, and identifies the user's session. The data in the session file is de-serialized and put back into the global `$_SESSION` array. The `PHPSESSID` cookie obviously doesn't live forever. The lifetime of this cookie is defined by the `session.cookie_lifetime` setting in `php.ini`. When the cookie expires the (browser deletes the cookie if it is past expiration time), the session is terminated. Calling `session_start()` at this point will initiate a new session.

 A session can also be actively terminated by the server by calling `session_destroy()`.

Limitations of native PHP session handling

Although simple and effective, the native session handling in PHP is not suitable for large-scale web applications. Suppose you deploy your application to multiple web servers with a load balancer in front of them routing the traffic. The servers will have to share the session directory on a networked filesystemand the extra overhead will slow down your application. Also, file-based session handling has critical security concerns when the website is deployed on a shared hosting environment. A malicious user on that system can easily view the session files under the `/tmp` directory and may attempt to *hijack* the session.

Implementing session handling with MongoDB

In this section, we are going to learn how we can extend the session handling mechanism of PHP to use a MongoDB database for managing sessions instead of using the filesystem. Before we delve into implementation, we are going to briefly cover the basics, mainly the `session_set_save_handler()` function.

Extending session handling with session_set_save_handler

The `session_set_save_handler()` function allows us to define our own functions for storing and retrieving session data. The function takes six arguments, each one being the name of a callback function. This is what the method signature looks like:

```
bool session_set_save_handler(callback $open, callback $close,
                    callback $read, callback $write,
                    callback $destroy, callback $gc)
```

Let's see what each of these callback functions do:

- `open()`: This method is called whenever a session is initiated with `session_start()`. It takes two arguments, the path to where the session will be stored and the name of the session cookie. It returns TRUE to indicate successful initiation of a session.

- `close()`: This is called at the successful end of a PHP script using session handling. This also needs to return TRUE.

- `read()`: This method is called whenever we are trying to retrieve a variable from the `$_SESSION` super global array. It takes the session ID as an argument and returns a string value of the `$_SESSION` variable.

- `write()`: This function is executed whenever we are trying to add or change something in `$_SESSION`. This takes the session ID and the serialized representation of the data to be stored in `$_SESSION` as its two arguments.

- `destroy()`: This is called whenever we are trying to terminate a session by calling the built-in `session_destroy()` method. It takes the session ID as its only parameter and returns TRUE upon success.

- `gc()`: This function is executed by the PHP session garbage collector. It takes the maximum lifetime of session cookies as its argument, and removes any session older than the specified lifetime. It also returns TRUE on success. The `session.gc_probability` setting in `php.ini` specifies the probability of the session garbage collector running.

The SessionManager class

We are going to build the `SessionManager` class, a module that uses a collection in a MongoDB database for storing/retrieving/handling sessions. We will register the instance level methods of this class with `session_set_save_handler()` as callback functions for handling sessions. We will build the class with the following design goals in mind:

- The session created by this class will have a 1 hour lifespan (it can be changed by configuring the class level constants).

- The session will have a timeout of 10 minutes. That is, the session will expire before its expiration time if the user in that session is inactive for more than 10 minutes (also configurable).

- The session data will be serialized into a field of the document in the collection representing the session.

Time for action – building the SessionManager class

Now that we have covered enough of the basics, it is time that we finally get into coding the `SessionManager` class.

1. Create a new file named `dbconnection.php`. Add the following code to that file:

```php
<?php
  class DBConnection
  {
    const HOST   = 'localhost';
    const PORT   = 27017;
    const DBNAME = 'myblogsite';
    private static $instance;
    public $connection;
    public $database;
    private function __construct()
    {
```

```php
$connectionString = sprintf('mongodb://%s:%d',
  DBConnection::HOST,
  DBConnection::PORT);
try {
  $this->connection = new Mongo($connectionString);
  $this->database = $this->connection->
    selectDB(DBConnection::DBNAME);
} catch (MongoConnectionException $e) {
  throw $e;
}
}
static public function instantiate()
{
  if (!isset(self::$instance)) {
    $class = __CLASS__;
    self::$instance = new $class;
  }
  return self::$instance;
}
public function getCollection($name)
{
  return $this->database->selectCollection($name);
}
}
```

2. Create another PHP script named `session.php`. Put the following code in it:

```php
<?php
require_once('dbconnection.php');
class SessionManager{
  //name of collection where sessions will be stored
  const COLLECTION = 'sessions';
  //Expire session after 10 mins in inactivity
  const SESSION_TIMEOUT = 600;
  //Expire session after 1 hour
  const SESSION_LIFESPAN = 3600;
  //name of the session cookie
  const SESSION_NAME = 'mongosessid';
  const SESSION_COOKIE_PATH = '/';
  //Should be the domain name of you web app, for example
  //mywebapp.com. DO NOT use empty string unless you are
  //running on a local environment.
  const SESSION_COOKIE_DOMAIN = '';
  private $_mongo;
  private $_collection;
```

```php
//represents the current session
private $_currentSession;
public function __construct()
{
  $this->_mongo = DBConnection::instantiate();
  $this->_collection = $this->_mongo->
    getCollection(SessionManager::COLLECTION);
  session_set_save_handler(
    array(&$this, 'open'),
    array(&$this, 'close'),
    array(&$this, 'read'),
    array(&$this, 'write'),
    array(&$this, 'destroy'),
    array(&$this, 'gc')
  );
  //Set session garbage collection period
  ini_set('session.gc_maxlifetime',
    SessionManager::SESSION_LIFESPAN);
  //set session cookie configurations
  session_set_cookie_params(
    SessionManager::SESSION_LIFESPAN,
    SessionManager::SESSION_COOKIE_PATH,
    SessionManager::SESSION_COOKIE_DOMAIN
  );
  //Replace 'PHPSESSID' with 'mongosessid' as the
  //session name
  session_name(SessionManager::SESSION_NAME);
  session_cache_limiter('nocache');
  //start the session
  session_start();
}
public function open($path, $name)
{
  return true;
}
public function close()
{
  return true;
}
public function read($sessionId)
{
  $query = array(
    'session_id' => $sessionId,
    'timedout_at' => array('$gte' => time()),
```

```php
          'expired_at' => array('$gte' => time() -
            SessionManager::SESSION_LIFESPAN)
        );
        $result = $this->_collection->findOne($query);
        $this->_currentSession = $result;
        if (!isset($result['data'])) {
          return '';
        }
        return $result['data'];
      }
      public function write($sessionId, $data)
      {
        $expired_at = time() + self::SESSION_TIMEOUT;
        $new_obj = array(
          'data' => $data,
          'timedout_at' =>
            time() + self::SESSION_TIMEOUT,
          'expired_at' =>
            (empty($this->_currentSession)) ?
            time()+ SessionManager::SESSION_LIFESPAN
            : $this->_currentSession['expired_at']
        );
        $query = array('session_id' => $sessionId);
        $this->_collection->update(
          $query,
          array('$set' => $new_obj),
          array('upsert' => True)
        );
        return True;
      }
      public function destroy($sessionId)
      {
        $this->_collection->remove(array('session_id' =>
          $sessionId));
        return True;
      }
      public function gc()
      {
        $query = array( 'expired_at' => array('$lt' => time()));
        $this->_collection->remove($query);
        return True;
      }
      public function __destruct()
      {
```

```
        session_write_close();
    }
}
//initiate the session
$session = new SessionManager();
```

What just happened?

In step 1, we created a class DBConnection that handles the connection with the MongoDB database. In our earlier examples in the previous chapters, we repeated the same code block connecting to MongoDB and selecting a database/collection in multiple files. This time we decided to get a little organized, and put all connection handling logic inside the DBConnection class for the purpose of code reuse. Calling the initialize() static method on this class returns an instance of it, we can then select a collection by invoking the getCollection() method on this instance.

```
$mongo = DBConnection::instantiate();
$collection = $mongo->getCollection('sessions');
```

> The DBConnection class implements the **Singleton** design pattern. This design pattern ensures that there is only a single connection open to MongoDB, within the context of a single HTTP request. To learn more about Singleton and other such patterns, visit this page from the PHP online manual: http://php.net/manual/en/language.oop5.patterns.php.

In step 2, we built the SessionManager class. The class is contained in the session.php script. At the end of the script, we initiate a session by instantiating a SessionManager object. If we need to start a session in a PHP page, all we have to do is to require/include the session.php script in that page. We'll watch the SessionManager in action soon, for now let's look closer into the different methods of this class.

How the SessionManager works

Let's dig deeper into the SessionManger code to see how it implements session handling.

The constructor

The constructor for the class (the __construct() method) opens a connection to MongoDB as well as initializes important session configurations, such as session lifespan, name of the session cookie, path and domain for the cookie, and so on. Most importantly, it calls the session_set_save_handler() method to register its own public methods as callbacks for session handling. Finally, it initiates the session by calling the session_start() method.

The open and close methods

Since we don't need to do anything with these methods, we do nothing other than returning TRUE from them.

The read method

The read() method receives the session ID as its parameter. It queries the collection for a document with the session ID whose expiration timestamp is set to future, and which is going to time out in the future. If it finds such a document, it returns the value of the *data* field for this document.

```
$query = array(
                'session_id' => $sessionId,
                'timedout_at' => array('$gte' => time()),
                'expired_at' => array('$gte' => time())
            );
$result = $this->_collection->findOne($query);
return $result['data'];
```

Note that this method does not do any of the serialization/de-serialization of the data. This is handled by PHP itself.

The write method

The write() method receives the session ID and the session data as its arguments. It looks up the collection for a document with the session ID, overwrites the data if it finds one, and resets its timedout_at timestamp to 10 minutes into the future (the default session timeout is set to 10 minutes). In case it doesn't find such a document, it inserts one (remember upsert?).

```
$new_obj = array( 'data' => $data,
                  'timedout_at' => time() + self::SESSION_TIMEOUT,
                  'expired_at' => (empty($this->_currentSession))
                  ? time()+ SessionManager::SESSION_LIFESPAN
                        : $this->_currentSession['expired_at']
                );
$query = array('session_id' => $sessionId);
$this->_collection->update( $query,
                            array('$set' => $new_obj),
                            array('upsert' => True)
                );
```

The destroy method

The destroy() method receives the session ID as a parameter. When it is called, it removes the document from the collection with the specified session ID.

The gc method

Finally, the garbage collector method (gc()) removes any document in the collection that was created more than an hour ago.

Influencing the session garbage collector

The session garbage collection process in PHP executes the gc() method to clear out old sessions. You can influence the execution of this garbage collector by changing the runtime configurations in PHP. The session. gc_maxlifetime specifies the number of seconds after which a session is considered as garbage. The session.gc_probability and session.gc_divisor settings define the probability of an expired session being cleaned by the garbage collector. If the value of session. gc_probability is 1 and the value of session.gc_divisor is set to 100, then there is 1 percent chance (1/100 = 0.01) that the garbage collector will run on each session initialization. You can use the ini_ set() built-in function to change these values at runtime!

Pop quiz – what does session_destroy() do?

Which session handling callback method gets called when we call the session_destory() method in our code?

a. close()

b. destroy()

c. gc()

Putting the SessionManager in action

Now that we have the SessionManager class, it is time that we put it into action. We are going to implement the same use case we did with the native PHP session handling earlier in this chapter. This time we are going to use the SessionManager for storing and retrieving data to and from the session.

Time for action – putting SessionManager into action

We are going to repeat the example of testing native PHP session handling, with a twist. The `SessionManager` will be used for handling the session.

1. Create a new PHP script in your text editor with the following code:

```php
<?php
//Session started by requiring the script
require('session.php');
//Generate a random number
$random_number = rand();
//Put the number into session
$_SESSION['random_number'] = $random_number;
?>
<!DOCTYPE html PUBLIC "-//W3C//DTD XHTML 1.0 Transitional//EN"
  "http://www.w3.org/TR/xhtml1/DTD/xhtml1-transitional.dtd">
<html xmlns="http://www.w3.org/1999/xhtml" xml:lang="en"
  lang="en">
  <head>
    <meta http-equiv="Content-Type" content="text/html;
      charset=utf-8"/>
    <link rel="stylesheet" href="style.css" />
    <title>Using the SessionManager...Page 1</title>
  </head>
  <body>
    <div id="contentarea">
      <div id="innercontentarea">
        <h2>Using the SessionManager...Page 1</h2>
        <p>Random number generated
          <span style="font-weight:bold;">
            <?php echo $_SESSION['random_number']; ?>
          </span>
        </p>
        <p>PHP session id
          <span style="text-decoration:underline;">
            <?php echo session_id(); ?>
          </span>
        </p>
        <a href="mongo_session2.php">Go to next page</a>
      </div>
    </div>
  </body>
</html>
```

Save the file as `mongo_session1.php`.

2. Create another file named `mongo_session2.php` and put the following code in it:

```php
<?php
  //Session started by requiring the script
  require('session.php');
?>
<!DOCTYPE html PUBLIC "-//W3C//DTD XHTML 1.0 Transitional//EN"
  "http://www.w3.org/TR/xhtml1/DTD/xhtml1-transitional.dtd">
<html xmlns="http://www.w3.org/1999/xhtml" xml:lang="en"
  lang="en">
  <head>
    <meta http-equiv="Content-Type" content="text/html;
      charset=utf-8"/>
    <link rel="stylesheet" href="style.css" />
    <title>Using the SessionManager...Page 1</title>
  </head>
  <body>
    <div id="contentarea">
      <div id="innercontentarea">
        <h2>Using the SessionManager...Page 2</h2>
        <p>The random number generated in previous page is still
          <span style="font-weight:bold;">
            <?php echo $_SESSION['random_number']; ?>
          </span>
        </p>
        <p>PHP session id
          <span style="text-decoration:underline;">
            <?php echo session_id(); ?>
          </span>
        </p>
      </div>
    </div>
  </body>
</html>
```

3. Open `mongo_session1.php` in your browser. Note the random number shown in the page:

Using the SessionManager...Page 1

Random number generated **411554082**

PHP session id 57e1d857831e169a1db9cdea35db0db9

Go to next page

4. Click on the **Go to next page** link at the bottom to navigate to `mongo_session2.php`. Verify if it shows the same random number:

> ### Using the SessionManager...Page 2
>
> The random number generated in previous page is still **411554082**
>
> PHP session id 57e1d857831e169a1db9cdea35db0db9

What just happened?

We repeated the example of testing PHP sessions with the `SessionManager`. The first script we created, `mongo_session1.php` initiates a session by requiring the `session.php` script (a `SessionManager` object is instantiated in this script). It puts a random number in the session. When we navigate to `mongo_session2.php`, PHP treats it as the same session. We read the random number from the session and display it on the screen.

If at this point you query the collection used for storing the session (the collection is named *sessions*, you can change it by changing the `COLLECTION` constant of `SessionManager`) in `mongo` shell, you would see the document that represents this session.

```
>db.sessions.findOne({'session_id':'71ce0c6f71b358cb204cb518c9948b5d'})
{
  "_id" : ObjectId("4dea21fa170b7b0b58fd0bf7"),
  "created_at" : 1307189754,
  "data" : "random_number|i:392780258;",
  "expired_at" : 1307190759,
  "session_id" : "71ce0c6f71b358cb204cb518c9948b5d"
}
```

Notice the `data` field of the document. It has been serialized by PHP to store the random number value.

Building the user authentication module

It is time to put the `SessionManager` to some real use and implement user authentication and authorization logic to it. In this section, we are going to build a class that represents a user in the web application. This class can be used to log a user in (authentication), enable him/her to view pages that he/she is allowed to see (authorization), and log him/her out when he/she wishes.

Time for action – building the User class

In this example, we are going to build the `User` class. An instance of this class will represent a user in the system. Before we do that, we are going to generate some dummy user accounts in the system by running a PHP script to insert some data into a collection named *users*.

1. Open your text editor and put the following code in a new file:

```php
<?php
require('dbconnection.php');
$mongo = DBConnection::instantiate();
$collection = $mongo->getCollection('users');
$users = array(
        array(
            'name' => 'Luke Skywalker',
            'username' => 'jedimaster23',
            'password' => md5('usetheforce'),
            'birthday'  => new MongoDate(
              strtotime('1971-09-29 00:00:00')),
            'address' => array(
              'town' => 'Mos Eisley',
              'planet' => 'Tatooine'
            )
        ),
        array(
            'name' => 'Leia Organa',
            'username' => 'princessleia',
            'password' => md5('eviltween'),
            'birthday'  => new MongoDate
              (strtotime('1976-10-21 00:00:00')),
            'address' => array(
              'town' => 'Aldera',
              'planet' => 'Alderaan'
            )
        ),
        array(
            'name' => 'Chewbacca',
            'username' => 'chewiethegreat',
            'password' => md5('loudgrowl'),
            'birthday'  => new MongoDate
              (strtotime('1974-05-19 00:00:00')),
            'address' => array(
              'town' => 'Kachiro',
```

```
                              'planet' => 'Kashyyk'
                    )
                )
            );

    foreach($users as $user)
    {
      try{
        $collection->insert($user);
      } catch (MongoCursorException $e) {
        die($e->getMessage());
      }
    }

    echo 'Users created successfully';
```

Save the file as `create_users.php`.

2. Run the `create_users.php` script to generate the dummy user data.

3. Create a new file named `user.php`. Put the following code in the file and save it:

```php
<?php
  require_once('dbconnection.php');
  require_once('session.php');
  class User
  {
    const COLLECTION = 'users';
    private $_mongo;
    private $_collection;
    private $_user;
    public function __construct()
    {
      $this->_mongo = DBConnection::instantiate();
      $this->_collection = $this->_mongo->
        getCollection(User::COLLECTION);
      if ($this->isLoggedIn()) $this->_loadData();
    }
    public function isLoggedIn()
    {
      return isset($_SESSION['user_id']);
    }
    public function authenticate($username, $password)
```

```php
{
  $query = array(
    'username' => $username,
    'password' => md5($password)
  );
  $this->_user = $this->_collection->findOne($query);
  if (empty($this->_user)) return False;
  $_SESSION['user_id'] = (string) $this->_user['_id'];
  return True;
}
public function logout()
{
  unset($_SESSION['user_id']);
}
public function __get($attr)
{
  if (empty($this->_user))
    return Null;
  switch($attr) {
    case 'address':
      $address = $this->_user['address'];
      return sprintf('Town: %s, Planet: %s', $address['town'],
        $address['planet']);
    case 'town':
      return $this->_user['address']['town'];
    case 'planet':
      return $this->_user['address']['planet'];
    case 'password':
      return NULL;
    default:
      return (isset($this->_user[$attr])) ?
        $this->_user[$attr] : NULL;
  }
}
private function _loadData()
{
  $id = new MongoId($_SESSION['user_id']);
  $this->_user = $this->_collection->findOne(array('_id'
    => $id));
}
}
```

What just happened?

In steps 1 and 2, we created and executed a script called `create_users.php` for generating some dummy users in the database. This will come in handy when we test the `User` class later on. Next we created the `user.php` script that contains the `User` class.

Let's walk through the code of `User`. In the constructor of this class, we obtain a database connection and select the appropriate collection. These objects are stored in private member variables of the class. The `authenticate()` method of the class is used to authenticate a valid user. The method receives the username and password as its arguments. It queries the database with the username and MD5 hash of the password. If a matching document is found, the `ObjectId` of the document is casted to string and stored in `$_SESSION` as `user_id`. The method returns `TRUE` to indicate that the user is successfully authenticated. Otherwise the method returns `FALSE`.

```
$query = array(
        'username' => $username,
        'password' => md5($password)
      );
$this->_user = $this->_collection->findOne($query);
$_SESSION['user_id'] = (string) $this->_user['_id'];
```

The `isLoggedIn()` method checks whether the user is already logged in by simply checking the existence of `user_id` in `$_SESSION`. The `logout()` method terminates the authenticated session by unsetting the `user_id` field.

If the user is logged in; the `_loadData()` private method is called within the constructor to query the database with the ID and populate the values of user attributes. Finally, the `__get()` magic method is used to read the attributes (name, address, birth date, and so on.) of a `User` object.

Creating the login, logout, and user profile page

In this section, we are going to put the `User` class into use and develop the pages for logging the user in, viewing his/her profile, and logging him/her out. These pages implement some of the essential use cases of a web application. Implementing these use cases allows us to achieve state persistence on the application, something we have been talking about since the beginning of this chapter.

Time for action – creating the login, logout, and profile page

The login page will show a form where the user can type in the username and password. If he/she is authenticated, he/she will be redirected to his/her profile page. The profile page will show his/her basic information and can only be accessed when he/she is logged in. The user can log out by clicking on the link on the profile page.

1. Create a new file named `login.php` with the following code:

```php
<?php
  $action = (!empty($_POST['login']) &&
         ($_POST['login'] === 'Log in')) ? 'login'
                                   : 'show_form';
  switch($action)
  {
      case 'login':
          require('session.php');
          require('user.php');
          $user = new User();
          $username = $_POST['username'];
          $password = $_POST['password'];
          if ($user->authenticate($username, $password)) {
              header('location: profile.php');
              exit;
          } else {
            $errorMessage = "Username/password did not match.";
              break;
          }
      case 'show_form':
      default:
          $errorMessage = NULL;
  }
?>
<!DOCTYPE html PUBLIC "-//W3C//DTD XHTML 1.0 Transitional//EN"
   "http://www.w3.org/TR/xhtml1/DTD/xhtml1-transitional.dtd">
<html xmlns="http://www.w3.org/1999/xhtml" xml:lang="en"
   lang="en">
   <head>
     <meta http-equiv="Content-Type" content="text/html;
       charset=utf-8"/>
       <link rel="stylesheet" href="style.css" />
       <title>User Login</title>
   </head>
   <body>
```

```
            <div id="contentarea">
              <div id="innercontentarea">
                <h1>Log in here</h1>
                <div id="login-box">
                  <div class="inner">
                    <form id="login" action="login.php" method="post"
                      accept-charset="utf-8">
                    <ul>
                      <?php if(isset($errorMessage)): ?>
                        <li><?php echo $errorMessage; ?></li>
                      <?php endif ?>
                      <li>
                      <label>Username </label>
                      <input class="textbox" tabindex="1"
                        type="text" name="username"
                        autocomplete="off"/>
                      </li>
                      <li>
                        <label>Password </label>
                        <input class="textbox" tabindex="2"
                          type="password" name="password"/>
                      </li>
                      <li>
                        <input id="login-submit" name="login"
                          tabindex="3" type="submit"
                          value="Log in" />
                      </li>
                      <li class="clear"></li>
                    </ul>
                  </form>
                </div>
              </div>
            </div>
          </div>
        </body>
      </html>
```

2. Create a PHP script named `profile.php` and put the following code in it:

```php
<?php
  require('session.php');
  require('user.php');
  $user = new User();
  if (!$user->isLoggedIn()){
      header('location: login.php');
      exit;
```

```
      }
?>
<!DOCTYPE html PUBLIC "-//W3C//DTD XHTML 1.0 Transitional//EN"
  "http://www.w3.org/TR/xhtml1/DTD/xhtml1-transitional.dtd">
<html xmlns="http://www.w3.org/1999/xhtml" xml:lang="en"
  lang="en">
  <head>
    <meta http-equiv="Content-Type" content="text/html;
      charset=utf-8"/>
    <link rel="stylesheet" href="style.css" />
    <title>Welcome <?php echo $user->username; ?></title>
  </head>
  <body>
    <div id="contentarea">
      <div id="innercontentarea">
        <a style="float:right;" href="logout.php">Log out</a>
        <h1>Hello <?php echo $user->username; ?></h1>
        <ul class="profile-list">
          <li>
            <span class="field">Username</span>
            <span class="value">
              <?php echo $user->username; ?>
            </span>
            <div class="clear"> </div>
          </li>
          <li>
            <span class="field">Name</span>
            <span class="value">
              <?php echo $user->name; ?>
            </span>
            <div class="clear"> </div>
          </li>
          <li>
            <span class="field">Birthday</span>
            <span class="value">
              <?php echo date('j F, Y',$user->birthday->sec); ?>
            </span>
            <div class="clear"> </div>
          </li>
          <li>
            <span class="field">Address</span>
            <span class="value">
              <?php echo $user->address; ?>
            </span>
```

```
            <div class="clear"> </div>
          </li>
        </ul>
      </div>
    </div>
  </body>
</html>
```

3. Create another PHP script named `logout.php` and add the following code to it:

```php
<?php
require_once('session.php');
require_once('user.php');
$user = new User();
$user->logout();
header('location: login.php');
exit;
```

4. Open the `style.css` file and add the following CSS rules to it:

```css
div#login-box{
  margin: 50px auto 250px auto;
  border: 1px solid #ddd;
  width: 305px;
}
div#login-box div.inner{ padding: 10px; }
form#login ul { list-style: none; }
form#login ul li { margin: 10px 0; }
form#login ul li label {
  float: left;
  padding: 6px 0 0 0;
  width: 70px;
  display: block;
  font-size:12px;
  line-height: 1;
}
form#login ul li input.textbox {
  font-size:13px;
  font-weight: normal;
  width: 147px;
}
form#login ul li input#login-submit {
  margin: 0px 0 0 70px;
  float:right;
}
```

```
ul.profile-list {
  margin:15px 0 0 0;
  list-style: none;
  font-family: Arial, sans-serif;
  font-size: 13px;
}
ul.profile-list li {
  padding:0 0 12px 0;
}
ul.profile-list span.field{
  display: block;
  float:left;
  margin: 3px 10px 0 0;
  width: 110px;
}
ul.profile-list span.value{
  float:left;
  padding: 3px 7px;
  width: 210px;
  background:#f7f5ed;
  color:#666;
}
```

5. Open `login.php` in the browser, type in the username `jedimaster23` and the password `usetheforce` in the appropriate input boxes. Hit the **Log in** button:

6. Once successfully logged in, you will be redirected to the profile page:

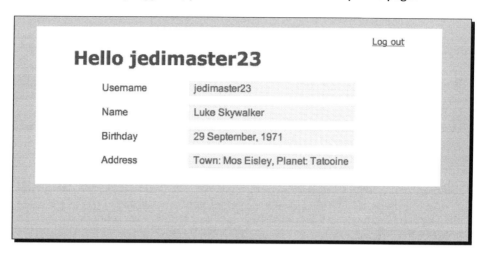

7. Click on the **Log out** link at the top right corner to log out. You will be redirected to the login.php page again.

What just happened?

We created a page login.php that shows a login form by default. When a user enters the correct username and password into the form, it authenticates him/her by using the authenticate() method of the User object and redirects to the profile page.

```
$user = new User();
$username = $_POST['username'];
$password = $_POST['password'];
if ($user->authenticate($username, $password)) {
  header('location: profile.php');
  exit;
}
```

The profile page checks whether the user is indeed logged in, if not it redirects him/her to the login page. Otherwise it displays the user profile information.

```
$user = new User();
if (!$user->isLoggedIn()){
  header('location: login.php');
  exit;
}
```

When the user clicks **Log out** in the top right corner of the profile page, the user is logged out and redirected to the login page again.

```
$user = new User();
$user->logout();
header('location: login.php');
exit;
```

Have a go hero – implement user authentication in the blogging web app

Now that we have the modules for handling sessions and user authentication, your task is to plug them into the blogging application we built in the previous chapter to implement authentication and authorization. Here are the specifications:

- Each document in the article collection must have a field `author_id` that references the `_id` of a user document. This will let us know who is the author of an article.

- Only logged in users are allowed to write articles.

- When the logged in user navigates to the dashboard, he/she should only see the articles written by him/her.

- A user can edit or delete an article only if he/she is the writer of that article.

Using good session practices

We will end this chapter by discussing some techniques to make user sessions in a web application more secure. Web application security is a broad and complicated topic, and beyond the scope of this book. There are numerous books and articles written on web security, which you should read. We will look at some practices that we can adopt at the application level to minimize the risk of user sessions being compromised.

Setting low expiry times of session cookies

Each session cookie issued by the application should have a low expiry time. Keeping the expiry time too long increases the risk of the session being compromised. However, when setting this value, you should be mindful about the activity of users on your website. If you make the expiry time too short, your users will be irritated, as they will be logged out while they are doing something important on your application. You can set the expiry time by either using the `session_set_cookie_params()` function or by changing the `session.cookie_lifetime` configuration through `ini_set()`. Note that this doesn't guarantee preventing session hijacking through cookies (nothing actually guarantees, it only reduces the chance!). You might want to consider encrypting your session cookies when sending them over HTTP.

Using session timeouts

Session timeouts should not be confused with session expiry time. This is the maximum amount of time a user is allowed to stay inactive on the website, after which the application will revoke the user's session and he/she will be asked to log in again. This is an effective way to reduce the window of opportunity for a malicious user to hijack his/her session (it also prevents the user's session from being physically stolen when he/she is away from his/her computer for too long, while logged into the website). Session timeouts are implemented as application logic. In the `SessionManager` class, we set a 10 minutes timeout value for the user.

Setting proper domains for session cookies

Each cookie set by the application has a domain attribute that specifies which website or websites are allowed to read that cookie. If the domain is set to example.com only, then only the application running on http://example.com will be able to read it. The domain can be set to example.com to allow all subdomains of example.com to use that cookie (both x.example.com and y.example.com will be able to read it). When setting the session cookie, make sure to set the domain name of the cookie to the domain name of your website (either using `session_set_cookie_params()` or setting `session.cookie_domain` through `ini_set()`).

 We deliberately set the cookie domain to an empty string in the `SessionManager` (which allows any site to read from that cookie!) to make it work on a local machine. When you use this in a real world setting, make sure you change this to the domain name of your application.

Checking for browser consistency

When a web browser makes a request to the server, it sends out a **User Agent** string in the HTTP header, which identifies the name, manufacturer, and version of that browser and operating system it is running on. The session handling code of a web application can log the User Agent string at the initiation of the session, and verify against it at subsequent session requests. This is not a bulletproof idea to prevent session hijacking, since the User Agent is not unique to a computer. Nonetheless, this reduces the risk as we are making things harder for the hijacker.

Have a go hero – store and verify User Agent in SessionManager

Modify the `SessionManager` to store the User Agent of an HTTP request when a user logs in. When the user makes subsequent requests to the application, check the User Agent of each request against the stored value to verify if it is the same user. Deny access to authorized pages (and log him/her out) when a mismatch is found.

Summary

Let's take a look at what we covered in this chapter. We learned:

- How web applications achieve state persistence by sessions
- How native session handling in PHP works
- How to use MongoDB for storing sessions
- How to implement user authentication/authorization using MongoDB as the session storage
- How we can improve session security

In the next chapter, we will learn how to aggregate queries on a MongoDB database.

4

Aggregation Queries

In this chapter, we will focus on learning how to perform aggregation queries in MongoDB. In Chapter 2, Building your First MongoDB Powered Web App, we learned how to query a collection using the `find()` *method. Aggregation queries are different from the queries we have done so far. These queries perform certain computations/calculations on the documents and the result of the computation is sent back to the user. For instance, grouping the documents on the value of a certain field and counting their values is a kind of aggregation operation. If you have experience with SQL, aggregation queries are the ones that use* COUNT/SUM/AVG/GROUP BY *statements. MongoDB uses MapReduce, a functional programming paradigm to perform aggregation and batch processing of data. In this chapter, we are going to familiarize ourselves with the concepts of MapReduce. We will learn how to perform MapReduce queries both in the mongo shell and in PHP. We will also learn to use utility functions (*`group()`, `distinct()`, `count()`, *and so on) in MongoDB that are used for aggregation.*

So, in this chapter we will:

- Learn about MapReduce
- Learn how to do MapReduce in mongo shell
- Learn how to perform MapReduce in PHP
- Learn about the `group()` function
- Learn to use the `distinct()` function
- Learn about the `count()` function

Generating sample data

Before we start learning about aggregation in MongoDB, we are going to need some sample data in the first place to perform aggregation on. We will populate a collection with some dummy data. Each document in the collection will have the following fields:

- `title`: A string, represents the title of the article

- `description`: Content of the article, also a string

- `author`: A string representing the name of the author

- `category`: Category of the article

- `rating`: An integer between 1 and 10

- `tags`: An array, contains between 1 to 5 distinct tags of the article

- `published_at`: A timestamp

A sample document from the collection will look similar to the following:

```
{
    "_id"    : ObjectId("4dfb49545981ae0a02680700"),
    "title"     : "Programmers will act rational when all other
        possibilities have been exhausted.",
    "author"     : "Spock",
    "category"    : "Programming",
    "rating"  : 6,
    "tags"      : ["security", "code","howto"],
    "published_at" : ISODate("2011-06-13T12:32:20Z")
}
```

Time for action – generating sample data

We are going to write a PHP script that will generate the sample data in a collection named `sample_articles`. We will execute the script in the command line and query the collection in `mongo` shell to verify the generated data:

1. Fire up your text editor and create a PHP script named `generate_data.php` with the following code in it:

```php
<?php
  require('dbconnection.php');
  $titles  = array(
    'Nature always sides with the hidden flaw',
    'Adding manpower to a late software project makes it later.',
    'Research supports a specific theory depending on the amount
      of funds dedicated to it.',
```

```
  'Always draw your curves, then plot your reading.',
  'Software bugs are hard to detect by anybody except may be
    the end user.',);
$authors = array('Luke Skywalker', 'Leia Organa', 'Han Solo',
  'Darth Vader', 'Spock', 'James Kirk',
  'Hikaru Sulu', 'Nyota Uhura');
$description = "Lorem ipsum dolor sit amet, consectetur
  adipisicing elit, sed do eiusmod tempor incididunt ut labore
  et dolore magna aliqua. ".
  "Ut enim ad minim veniam, quis nostrud exercitation ullamco
  laboris nisi ut aliquip ex ea commodo consequat. ";
$categories = array('Electronics', 'Mathematics', 'Programming',
  'Data Structures', 'Algorithms',
  'Computer Networking');
$tags = array('programming', 'testing', 'webdesign', 'tutorial',
  'howto', 'version-control', 'nosql', 'algorithms',
  'engineering', 'software', 'hardware', 'security');
function getRandomArrayItem($array)
{
  $length = count($array);
  $randomIndex = mt_rand (0, $length - 1);
  return $array[$randomIndex];
}
function getRandomTimestamp()
{
  $randomDigit = mt_rand (0, 6) * -1;
  return strtotime($randomDigit . ' day');
}
function createDoc()
{
  global $titles, $authors, $categories, $tags;
  $title    = getRandomArrayItem($titles);
  $author   = getRandomArrayItem($authors);
  $category = getRandomArrayItem($categories);
  $articleTags = array();
  $numOfTags   = rand(1,5);
  for ($j = 0; $j < $numOfTags; $j++){
    $tag = getRandomArrayItem($tags);
    if(!in_array($tag, $articleTags)){
      array_push($articleTags, $tag);
    }
  }
  $rating = mt_rand(1, 10);
  $publishedAt = new MongoDate(getRandomTimestamp());
  return array('title' => $title,
```

```
            'author' => $author,
            'category' => $category,
            'tags' => $articleTags,
            'rating' => $rating,
            'published_at' => $publishedAt);
    }
    $mongo = DBConnection::instantiate();
    $collection = $mongo->getCollection('sample_articles');
    echo "Generating sample data...<br/>";
    for ($i = 0; $i < 1000; $i++)
    {
        $document = createDoc();
        $collection->insert($document);
    }
    echo "Finished!";
```

2. Execute the `generate_data.php` script in your browser (you may also run it from the command line).

3. Start up the mongo shell. Enter the following commands to view the data generated by the PHP script:

```
> use myblogsite
switched to db myblogsite
> db.sample_articles.find()
```

What just happened?

We just created and executed a PHP script that inserts 1000 dummy articles in a collection named `sample_articles`. The script uses the `DBConnection` class that we created in the previous chapter to connect to MongoDB and select the myblogsite database. The script contains some arrays that hold the dummy data for the article objects (titles, author names, categories, tags, and so on). The script loops 1000 times and within each loop it randomly picks an item from each of those arrays, constructs a document with those items, and inserts the document in the `sample_articles` collection.

 If you want to generate this data in a separate database, just change the DBNAME constant in the `DBConnection` class in the `dbconnnection.php` file.

Understanding MapReduce

MapReduce is a design pattern for data processing. The idea behind MapReduce is simple. A large task is broken down into smaller subtasks. Each subtask is performed independently. The results of all these subtasks are then combined to produce the final result. It should be obvious that MapReduce has two principal phases:

- **The map phase**: Breakdown the task into smaller subtasks and execute them to produce intermediate results
- **The reduce phase**: Combine the intermediate results and produce the final output

If you have done functional programming in the past, the idea should not be new to you. In the paradigm of functional programming, `map()` takes an array as an input and performs an operation on each element on the array. `reduce()` takes the result array of `map()` as its input and combines all the elements in that array into a single element by performing some operation. To elaborate the idea, consider the array of integers [1, 2, 3, 4, 5]. We have to find the sum of the squares of all these numbers. `map()` takes this array and applies the function $f(x) = x2$ on each integer in the array and produces the output [1, 4, 9, 16, 25]. Now, `reduce()` takes this output array, sums all the numbers in it, and outputs the number 55 (1+4+9+16+25 = 55).

The Internet search giant Google, took this simple idea and applied it into distributed computing systems. In the year 2004, Google published a paper that demonstrated how the MapReduce model could be used to process large datasets concurrently in a large cluster of machines. One machine in the cluster assumes the role of a master node; it partitions the input into smaller subtasks and distributes them among multiple worker nodes. The workers run in parallel to process the subtasks and return the results back to the master. The master combines the results and produces the final output. By dividing the tasks between multiple workers, we gain speed and scalability (add more workers when the problem gets bigger). Google's proposed programming model was soon adopted by other companies and developers, and they rolled out their own frameworks that implement MapReduce. (**Apache Hadoop** is perhaps the most prominent of them). NoSQL databases started using this model for running batch processing tasks and aggregation queries at scale.

Visualizing MapReduce

The next figure illustrates how MapReduce solves a hypothetical problem of counting occurrences of each word in a stream of text inputs:

The **MAP** steps take each line of text as input and output the word count for each line. The **REDUCE** steps iteratively combines the word count and eventually produces the final word count for all lines in the text.

Further reading on MapReduce

Kristina Chodorow, core developer of the MongoDB project, wrote an interesting blog post explaining MapReduce, which is available at `http://www.snailinaturtleneck.com/blog/2010/03/15/mapreduce-the-fanfiction/`

Oren Eini's blog has a nice visual explanation of MapReduce available at `http://ayende.com/blog/4435/map-reduce-a-visual-explanation`

The original publication on MapReduce by Google is avaliable at `http://labs.google.com/papers/mapreduce.html`

Pop Quiz – MapReduce basics

1. The concept MapReduce has been derived from which programming paradigm?

   a. Object-oriented programming

   b. Functional Programming

   c. Aspect-oriented programming

   d. Procedural programming

2. When running a MapReduce job in a distributed environment that is on a cluster of machines, which of the following task a master node is supposed to do?

   a. Distribute the tasks among worker nodes

   b. Monitor progress of the job

   c. Combine the results of all worker nodes

   d. both a. and c.

Performing MapReduce in MongoDB

In this section, we are going to learn how we can use MapReduce over MongoDB to perform aggregation queries. We are going to define the map and reduce functions in JavaScript in the mongo interactive shell. Then we will apply these functions over the sample data we generated earlier in the chapter.

Time for action – counting the number of articles for each author

In this example, we are going to use MapReduce to find out how many articles there are in the database per author. The output of this operation will be a collection of documents, where each document will contain an author name and the number of articles written by the author.

1. Fire up the mongo shell and switch to the myblogsite database:

```
$./mongodb/bin/mongo
MongoDB shell version: 1.8.1
connecting to: test
>use myblogsite
switched to db myblogsite
>
```

2. Define the map function using the following command in the shell:

```
>var map = function() { emit(this.author, 1); }
```

3. Now, define the reduce function:

```
> var reduce = function(key, values) {
...var count = 0;
...for (var i = 0; i < values.length; i++){
... count += values[i];
... }
... return count;
... };
>
```

4. Apply the MapReduce operation on the sample_articles collection using the next command:

```
> db.runCommand({
... mapreduce: 'sample_articles',
... map: map,
... reduce: reduce,
... out: 'articles_per_author'
... })
{
    "result" : "articles_per_author",
```

```
   "timeMillis" : 70,
   "counts" : {
      "input" : 1000,
      "emit" : 1000,
      "output" : 8
   },
   "ok" : 1
}
```

5. Enter the next command to view the result of the MapReduce operation:

```
> db.articles_per_author.find()
   { "_id" : "Darth Vader", "value" : 126 }
   { "_id" : "Han Solo", "value" : 130 }
   { "_id" : "Hikaru Sulu", "value" : 119 }
   { "_id" : "James Kirk", "value" : 115 }
   { "_id" : "Leia Organa", "value" : 134 }
   { "_id" : "Luke Skywalker", "value" : 132 }
   { "_id" : "Nyota Uhura", "value" : 127 }
   { "_id" : "Spock", "value" : 117 }
>
```

What just happened?

We just used MapReduce to perform an aggregation operation. We defined the map and the reduce functions within the mongo shell, and produced a new collection named articles_ per_author that holds the result of the aggregation, that is, the number of articles written by each author. This is similar to executing the query SELECT COUNT(id) IN sample_ articles GROUP BY author in SQL. In the following sections, we will see how MapReduce works in MongoDB.

Defining the Map function

The map function takes the documents in the collection and produces a new set of key/ value pairs. In this example, the map function that we defined processes each document in the collection, and produces a key/value pair where the key is the author name for the document and value is an array containing the integer 1. We assigned the function to a variable named map:

```
var map = function() { emit(this.author, 1); }
```

Each time map encounters a document with the same key (author name), it simply adds a 1 in the values array. This is being handled by calling `emit()` inside the map function. The output of map looks like this:

```
{
    "Luke Skywalker"  :  [1],
    "Spock"           :  [1],
    "Han Solo"        :  [1, 1, 1],
    "James Kirk"      :  [1, 1],

    ...................

}
```

Defining the Reduce function

The key/value pairs emitted by the `map` function are fed into the `reduce` function. Reduce takes each author and sums up the 1s in the values array to produce the total count:

```
//receives arguments like this reduce('Han Solo', [1, 1, 1,…])
var reduce = function(key, values) {
  var count = 0;
  for (var i = 0; i < values.length; i++){
    count += values[i];
  }
  return count;
}
```

In the previous code snippet, the `reduce` function is defined and assigned to a JavaScript variable named `reduce`.

Applying the Map and Reduce

When we are done defining the `map` and `reduce` functions, we have to apply them on the collection to produce the output. This is done by invoking the `runCommand()` method in `mongo` shell:

```
> db.runCommand({
... mapreduce: 'sample_articles',
... map: map,
... reduce: reduce,
... out: 'articles_per_author'
... })
```

The `runCommand()` method takes the following arguments:

- `mapreduce`: The name of the collection on which the MapReduce is going to be performed.

- `map`: The reference to the user-defined map function.

- `reduce`: Reference to the user-defined reduce function.

- `out`: Name of the collection where the result of the operation is going to be stored. If the collection does not exist, it gets created. If it does exist, the contents of this collection will be replaced with the documents produced by the operation (default behavior).

After we apply this command in the shell, we can see the following output on the screen that gives us some of the statistics of the MapReduce operation:

```
{
    "result"          :  "articles_per_author",
    "timeMillis"      :  43,
    "counts"          :  {
        "input"   :  1000,
        "emit"    :  1000,
        "output"  :  8
    },
    "ok"  :  1
}
```

The `result` field shows the name of the collection where the aggregation results are stored. `timeMillis` shows the number of milliseconds it took to compute the results. The `input`, `emit`, and `output` fields of count respectively, show how many documents have been fed into the `map` function, how many have been emitted, and how many have been produced as output. `ok` simply signals that the operation was completed successfully.

Viewing the results

Finally, we can view the results of the aggregation by invoking the `find()` command on the newly created collection:

```
> db.articles_per_author.find()
{ "_id" : "Darth Vader", "value" : 126 }
{ "_id" : "Han Solo", "value" : 130 }
{ "_id" : "Hikaru Sulu", "value" : 119 }
```

The collection contains documents that have author names as their `_id`s and the `value` fields contain the number of articles for the particular author.

Performing MapReduce on a subset of the collection

It is also possible to specify a query parameter in the `runCommand()` so that MapReduce will be applied only on the documents in the collection that match the query. For example, if we wanted the article count per author only for the article in the `'Programming'` category, we could do the following:

```
> db.runCommand({
... mapreduce: 'sample_articles',
... query: {category: 'Programming'},
... map: map,
... reduce: reduce,
... out: 'articles_per_author'
... })
```

 Visit `http://www.mongodb.org/display/DOCS/MapReduce` on the MongoDB documentation website to see more optional arguments for MapReduce.

Concurrency

Although the idea behind MapReduce is to achieve concurrency by distributing jobs among multiple machines/processes, as of this writing the MapReduce jobs running on a MongoDB server are single threaded. This is because of the limitations imposed by current JavaScript engines. The developers at 10gen are looking for alternative ways to achieve parallelism of MapReduce jobs.

 Concurrency can be achieved by **sharding** the database. Sharding is the process of partitioning the data into multiple nodes, and is performed when the volume of data becomes too large to be handled in a single machine. This is an advanced topic and not covered in this book. If you are interested you can visit the page for sharding in the MongoDB online documentation available at `http://www.mongodb.org/display/DOCS/Sharding+Introduction`.

Performing MongoDB MapReduce within PHP

Now that we are familiar with the concept of MapReduce and have learned how to do it in the MongoDB shell, we are going to see how to perform a MapReduce operation from a PHP program, using the API exposed by the PHP-MongoDB driver.

Time for action – creating a tag cloud

In this example, we will run a MapReduce job that counts the frequency of tags in our sample collection. We will perform the operation within a PHP script and use the result to build a tag cloud using CSS and HTML:

1. Create a new script named `tagcloud.php` using your text editor and put the following code in it:

```php
<?php
  require('dbconnection.php');
  $mongo = DBConnection::instantiate();
  //get an instance of MongoDB object
  $db = $mongo->database;
  //define the map function
  $map = new MongoCode("function() {".
    "for (i = 0; i < this.tags.length; i++) {".
      "emit(this.tags[i], 1);".
    "}".
  "}");
  //define the reduce function
  $reduce = new MongoCode("function(key, values) {".
    "var count = 0;".
    "for (var i = 0; i < values.length; i++){".
      "count += values[i];".
    "}".
    "return count;".
  "}");
  //Run the map and reduce functions, store results in a
    collection
  //named tagcount
  $command = array(
    'mapreduce' => 'sample_articles',
    'map' => $map,
    'reduce' => $reduce,
    'out' => 'tagcount'
  );
  $db->command($command);
  //load all the tags in an array, sorted by frequenct
  $tags = iterator_to_array($db->selectCollection('tagcount')
    ->find()
    ->sort(array('value' => -1)));
  //custom function for finding the tag with the highest frequency
  function getBiggestTag($tags)
```

```php
  {
    //reset the array to the first element
    reset($tags);
    //get the first key of the associative array
    $firstKey = key($tags);

    //return the value of the first tag document
    return (int)$tags[$firstKey]['value'];
  }
  $biggestTag = getBiggestTag($tags);
  //compare each tag with the biggest one and assign a weight
  foreach($tags as &$tag) {
    $weight = floor(($tag['value'] / $biggestTag) * 100);
    switch($weight){
      case ($weight < 10):
        $tag['class'] = 'class1';
        break;
      case (10 <= $weight && $weight < 20):
        $tag['class'] = 'class2';
        break;
      case (20 <= $weight && $weight < 30):
        $tag['class'] = 'class3';
        break;
      case (30 <= $weight && $weight < 40):
        $tag['class'] = 'class4';
        break;
      case (40 <= $weight && $weight < 50):
        $tag['class'] = 'class5';
        break;
      case (50 <= $weight && $weight < 60):
        $tag['class'] = 'class6';
        break;
      case (70 <= $weight && $weight < 80):
        $tag['class'] = 'class7';
        break;
      case (80 <= $weight && $weight < 90):
        $tag['class'] = 'class8';
        break;
      case ($weight >= 90):
        $tag['class'] = 'class9';
        break;
    }
  }
?>
```

```html
<html xmlns="http://www.w3.org/1999/xhtml" xml:lang="en"
  lang="en">
  <head>
    <meta http-equiv="Content-Type" content="text/html;
      charset=utf-8"/>
    <link rel="stylesheet" href="style.css" />
    <title>Tag Cloud</title>
  </head>
  <body>
    <div id="contentarea">
      <div id="innercontentarea">
        <h1>Tag Cloud</h1>
        <ul id="tagcloud">
          <?php foreach($tags as $tag):  ?>
            <li>
              <a href="#" class="<?php echo $tag['class'];?>">
                <?php echo $tag['_id']; ?></a>
            </li>
          <?php endforeach;?>
        </ul>
      </div>
    </div>
  </body>
</html>
```

2. Create a CSS file named `style.css` and put the following styling rules in it:

```css
body {
  background-color: #e1ddd9;
  font-size: 12px;
  font-family: Verdana, Arial, Helvetica, SunSans-Regular,
    Sans-Serif;
  color:#564b47;
  padding:20px;
  margin:0px;
  text-align: center;
}
div#contentarea {
  text-align: left;
  vertical-align: middle;
  margin: 0px auto;
  padding: 0px;
  width: 550px;
  background-color: #ffffff;
  border: 1px #564b47;
```

```
}
div#innercontentarea{ padding: 10px 50px; }
ul#tagcloud { padding: 2px; line-height: 3em;
  text-align: center; margin: 0;}
ul#tagcloud li { display: inline; }
ul#tagcloud a { padding: 0px; }
//css classes for tags in increasing order of font-weight
ul#tagcloud a.class1 { font-size: 0.7em; font-weight: 100; }
ul#tagcloud a.class2 { font-size: 0.8em; font-weight: 200; }
ul#tagcloud a.class3 { font-size: 0.9em; font-weight: 300; }
ul#tagcloud a.class4 { font-size: 1.0em; font-weight: 400; }
ul#tagcloud a.class5 { font-size: 1.2em; font-weight: 500; }
ul#tagcloud a.class6 { font-size: 1.4em; font-weight: 600; }
ul#tagcloud a.class7 { font-size: 1.6em; font-weight: 700; }
ul#tagcloud a.class8 { font-size: 1.8em; font-weight: 800; }
ul#tagcloud a.class9 { font-size: 2.2em; font-weight: 900; }
ul#tagcloud a.class10 { font-size: 2.5em; font-weight: 900; }
```

3. Run `tagcloud.php` in the browser to generate the **Tag Cloud**:

What just happened?

We just performed a MapReduce operation using the PHP driver for MongoDB and produced a tag cloud using the result. First, we initiated a connection to the MongoDB server using the DBConnection class and got the reference to a MongoDB object that represents the myblogsite database in the server. Next, we defined the map and the reduce functions using MongoCode objects. A MongoCode object represents JavaScript code that can be executed on the server. It takes valid JavaScript code as a string parameter to the a constructor. So we wrote the JavaScript map and reduce functions as strings and passed them as constructor to a couple of MongoCode objects. For each tag in the tags array of each document, map() emits the tag and an array of 1s (a 1 is appended each time the tag is encountered). reduce() sums up the 1s and outputs the total count for the tag.

Next, we invoked the command() method on the MongoDB object. This method is similar to the db.runCommand() method in mongo shell. The result of the aggregation is written to a collection named tagcount (as specified by the out option). The next statement fetches all the documents in the newly created collection and loads them into an array:

```
$tags = iterator_to_array($db->selectCollection('tagcount')->find());
```

Next, we constructed the logic for building the tag cloud. We defined CSS classes with increasing font sizes and weights:

```
ul#tagcloud a.class1 { font-size: 0.7em; font-weight: 100; }
ul#tagcloud a.class10 { font-size: 2.5em; font-weight: 900; }
```

We found the tag with the highest frequency, and got its value. Based on this value, we assigned a relative weight to each tag in the result set. Next, we assigned a CSS class to each tag depending on its relative weight:

```
function getBiggestTag($tags)
{
  reset($tags);
  $firstKey = key($tags);
  return (int)$tags[$firstKey]['value'];
}
$biggestTag = getBiggestTag($tags);
foreach($tags as &$tag) {
  $weight = floor(($tag['value'] / $biggestTag) * 100);
  switch($weight){
    case ($weight < 10):
      $tag['class'] = 'class1';
```

```
            break;
..................................................................................................
        case ($weight >= 90):
            $tag['class'] = 'class9';
            break;
    }
}
```

Finally, we rendered the tag cloud using HTML and CSS.

Have a go hero – repeat the earlier example with PHP

Repeat the example of grouping the articles by author name. But this time, perform the MapReduce within a PHP program. Display an HTML table that shows the article count for each author.

Performing aggregation using group()

Besides MapReduce, aggregation in MongoDB can also be performed using the group() method on a collection. group() can be viewed as a short-circuit approach for doing MapReduce. It is easier to learn and use (easier because it is a lot similar to using GROUP BY in SQL). The group() method takes the following parameters:

- key: Specifies the key or set of keys by which the documents will be grouped.

- initial: The base aggregator counter, specifies initial values before aggregation.

- reduce: A reduce that aggregates the documents. It takes two arguments, the current document being iterated over, and the aggregation counter.

In addition to these, group() can also receive the following optional arguments:

- cond: A query object. Only the documents matching this query will be used in grouping.

- finalize: A function that runs on each item in the result set (before returning the item). It can either modify or replace the returning item.

In the next section, we are going to learn how we can use the group() method to aggregate objects in a collection.

Time for action – calculating the average rating per author

In this example, we are going to calculate the average rating each author received for his or her articles—published within the last 24 hours—using the `group()` method. We are going to execute this method within a PHP program. The program will output a HTML table, displaying the total number of articles and average rating for each author:

1. Open up your text editor and create a new PHP script named `avg_rating.php`. Put the following code in it:

```php
<?php
require('dbconnection.php');
$mongo = DBConnection::instantiate();
$collection = $mongo->getCollection('sample_articles');
$key = array('author' => 1);
//set both the aggregation counter and total rating to zero
$initial = array('count' => 0, 'total_rating' => 0);
//reduce function, increases counter by 1 and adds up the
  ratings
$reduce = "function(obj, counter) { counter.count++;".
  "counter.total_rating += obj.rating;}";
//finalize function, finds the average rating
$finalize = "function(counter) { counter.avg_rating ="
  .."Math.round(counter.total_rating /counter.count);}";
//query condition, selects the documents created over last 24
//hours for running the group()
$condition = array('published_at' => array('$gte' =>
  new MongoDate(strtotime('-1 day'))));
$result = $collection->group($key,
  $initial,
  new MongoCode($reduce),
  array(
    'finalize' =>
    new MongoCode($finalize),
    'condition' => $condition
  )
);
?>
<html xmlns="http://www.w3.org/1999/xhtml" xml:lang="en">
  <head>
    <title>Author Rating</title>
    <link rel="stylesheet" href="style.css"/>
  </head>
  <body>
    <div id="contentarea">
      <div id="innercontentarea">
        <h1>Authors' Ratings</h1>
```

```html
<table class="table-list" cellspacing="0"
  cellpadding="0">
  <thead>
    <tr>
      <th width="50%">Author</th>
      <th width="24%">Articles</th>
      <th width="*">Average Rating</th>
    </tr>
  </thead>
  <tbody>
    <?php foreach($result['retval'] as $obj): ?>
      <tr>
        <td><?php echo $obj['author']; ?></td>
        <td><?php echo $obj['count']; ?></td>
        <td>
          <?php echo $obj['avg_rating']; ?>
        </td>
      <tr>
    <?php endforeach; ?>
  </tbody>
</table>
      </div>
    </div>
  </body>
</html>
```

2. Open the `style.css` file and add the following CSS rules to it:

```css
table.table-list {
  width: 100%;
  line-height: 1;
  text-align: left;
}
table.table-list th{
  border-bottom: 1px solid #ccc;
  padding: 8px 0;
  font-weight: bold;
}
table.table-list td {
  border-bottom: 1px solid #eee;
  padding: 6px 0;
}
```

3. Open the `avg_rating.php` file in the browser to view the average rating per author:

Authors' Ratings

Author	Articles	Average Rating
Han Solo	25	6
Hikaru Sulu	21	6
Leia Organa	23	6
Luke Skywalker	23	6
James Kirk	10	6
Spock	14	7
Nyota Uhura	23	6
Darth Vader	22	5

What just happened?

We wrote and executed a PHP program that performs aggregation using `group()`. The script invoked the `group()` method on the `MongoCollection` object that represents the `sample_articles` collection. Let's examine the parameters sent to this method.

We supplied `array('author' => 1)` as the key parameter to group articles by author names.

We initialized an aggregation counter that has two fields, `count` and `total_rating`, both set to `zero`. `$reduce` iterates through the document, increments the `count` field of the aggregation counter by 1, and adds the rating of the current document to the `total_rating` field of the counter. `$finalize` calculates the average rating by dividing the total rating with the counter and rounding off the quotient. The `$condition` argument selects the articles that have been published within the last 24 hours to run the group operation on.

We passed all these parameters to the `group()` method on the `MongoCollection` object, which returns the result in an array:

```
$result = $collection->group($key, $initial, new MongoCode($reduce),
  array(
    'finalize' =>
    new MongoCode($finalize),
    'condition' => $condition
  )
);
```

The result of aggregation is contained in the `retval` field of `$result`. We iterated through this field to display the result in an HTML table.

Grouping by custom keys

We can also group documents based on a user-defined key by passing a JavaScript function as the key parameter to `group()`. The function needs to return an object based on some predefined rule. For example, suppose we want to group the articles based on the length of their title. Any article having less than 6 words in the title will be considered small, articles having between 6 to 10 words will be considered medium, all the other articles will be considered large. The following would be the key parameter to `group()`:

```
$key = new MongoCode("function(article) {".
  "len = article.title.split(' ').length;".
  "if( len < 6) {".
    "return {short:true};".
  "} else if(6 <= len && len < 10) {".
    "return {medium:true};".
  "}".
  "else return {large:true};}"
);
```

MapReduce versus group()

The obvious question that arises at this point is whether we should use `group()` or MapReduce for aggregation purposes. `group()` has its obvious perks; for programmers new to MongoDB and the concept of MapReduce, it is easier to understand and use. However, it is not without its limitations. `group()` returns the result in a single BSON object, and therefore has to be very small (less than 16 MB). It cannot be applied on a key having more than 10,000 distinct values. Also, using the `group()` method blocks the entire database (you cannot read/write anything while `group()` is running). For these reasons, when aggregating over a large dataset, MapReduce is the preferred option. Use `group()` when you are certain of no performance deficits.

> Jamund Ferguson has an interesting blog post comparing the performance of `group()` and MapReduce in MongoDB. It is worth reading and is available at `http://j-query.blogspot.com/2011/06/mongodb-performance-group-vs-find-vs.html`.

Have a go hero – find the maximum and minimum rating for each author

Use the `group()` method to find the maximum and minimum rating each author received for the articles.

Pop quiz – limitation of group()

1. Which of the following is a limitation of the `group()` command for running aggregation queries in MongoDB

   a. If the key used for grouping has more than 10,000 distinct values, `group()` cannot be applied.

   b. Result of group has to be less than 16 MB in size.

   c. `group()` is a blocking operation.

   d. All of the above.

Listing distinct values for a field

In this section, we will learn to use the `distinct()` method of MongoDB, which lists the distinct values for a specified field of the documents in a collection.

Time for action – listing distinct categories of articles

In this example, we will list the distinct categories of the article objects in the `sample_articles` collection by invoking the `distinct()` method from a PHP program:

1. Create a new PHP script named `distinct.php` and put the following code in it:

```php
<?php
  require('dbconnection.php');
  $mongo = DBConnection::instantiate();
  //get an instance of MongoDB object
  $db = $mongo->database;
  $result = $db->command(array('distinct' => 'sample_articles',
    'key' => 'category'));
?>
<html xmlns="http://www.w3.org/1999/xhtml" xml:lang="en">
  <head>
    <title>Categories</title>
    <link rel="stylesheet" href="style.css"/>
  </head>
  <body>
    <div id="contentarea">
      <div id="innercontentarea">
        <h1>Distinct Categories</h1>
        <ul>
```

```php
        <?php foreach($result['values'] as $value): ?>
          <li><?php echo $value; ?></li>
        <?php endforeach; ?>
      </ul>
    </div>
  </div>
</body>
</html>
```

2. Execute the `distinct.php` script in your browser:

Distinct Categories

- Programming
- Data Structures
- Mathematics
- Operating System
- Electronics
- Computer Networking
- Database Management
- Artificial Intelligence
- Algorithms

What just happened?

We wrote a PHP script that lists all the distinct values for the category field of each article document. We invoke the `command()` method, passing in the appropriate collection and field names:

```php
$result = $db->command(array(
  'distinct' => 'sample_articles',
  'key' => 'category'));
```

The distinct values for category are contained in the `values` field of the returned array `$result`. Next, we simply rendered an HTML unordered list to display all the distinct categories.

Using distinct() in mongo shell

If we want to run distinct() from the mongo shell, we can invoke the method on a collection, passing the key as an argument. The following command gives us all the distinct values of the category field in the sample_article collection:

```
> db.sample_articles.distinct('category')
[

    "Programming",

    "Data Structures",

    "Mathematics",

    "Operating System",

    ............................... . .

]

>
```

Counting documents with count()

We will end this chapter by examining the method count(), which is used to count the number of objects in a collection. count() takes a document selector as parameter and returns the number of documents matching the selector:

```php
<?php
  require('dbconnection.php');
  $mongo = DBConnection::instantiate();
  $collection = $mongo->getCollection('sample_articles');
  //get the number of articles written by Spock
  $collection->count(array('author' => 'Spock'));
```

If no argument is passed, count() returns the total number of documents in the collection:

```php
//returns total number of articles in collection
$collection->count();
```

Summary

Let's take a look at what we covered in this chapter:

- We learned about MapReduce
- We learned how to do aggregation queries in MongoDB using MapReduce
- We learned how we can perform MapReduce queries in PHP
- We covered how we can do aggregation using `group()`.
- We discussed advantages and disadvantages of using `group()` versus using MapReduce.
- We learned about the `discount()` and `count()` methods.

In the next chapter, we will put our newly learned skills into work and use them to solve real-world data processing problems. Keep reading!

5
Web Analytics using MongoDB

In this chapter, we are going to explore and experiment with an interesting use case of MongoDB: storing website analytics. There are certain features of MongoDB (which we will discuss in this chapter) that make it an excellent choice as a backend for storing web traffic data. We can use MapReduce to process and analyze the data, measure key metrics, and generate reports. We are going to learn how to do all that by adding analytics features into the blog application that we built in Chapter 2, Building your First MongoDB Powered Web App. We will build a logger in PHP that stores HTTP request data. Then we will use MapReduce to process the data and expose certain statistics in a web dashboard. Finally, we will learn how we can leverage the upsert and $inc feature of MongoDB to store page visit counts in real time.

So to sum it up, in this chapter we will:

- Discuss why MongoDB is a good choice for storing web analytics
- Learn how to implement logging using PHP and MongoDB
- Use MapReduce to analyze the logged data
- Implement real-time analytics using `'upsert'` and `'$inc'`

Why MongoDB is a good choice as a web analytics backend

MongoDB is good for storing and processing large datasets in general. Web analytics is one example of such a large data problem. Let's take a look at some of its features that make it a good choice for this purpose:

- MongoDB is well suited to handle large volumes of data. In situations where traditional relational database systems are too expensive in terms of system resources (because of the large volume of the data), MongoDB might prove to be a better alternative. The scalability features of MongoDB (replication, sharding, replica sets, and so on) aid in performing optimally as the size of data and number of operations on it continue to grow. A high traffic website can use it to store all the user activity on the site, so they can be processed and analyzed in the background.

- MongoDB supports asynchronous inserts. This means that your application code, whether it is PHP, C, or the JavaScript interface of the mongo shell, asks MongoDB to insert a document and moves on to the next instruction without waiting for the server to respond. This makes it an excellent tool for logging. For example, your web application can process an HTTP request, save various aspects of the request (such as time of request, user agent string, and so on) in the database, and then generate the output. Since the insertion is asynchronous, the output generation is not delayed.

- MapReduce may be considered as another useful feature from this perspective. You may find it confusing at first (I did!), but once you wrap your head around the concept, you will realize this is a powerful and flexible tool for data processing. You can run MapReduce on your analytics data and generate reports that may give clues on how to better optimize the website or how to improve its usability.

The Flexible schema feature of MongoDB makes it an excellent choice for web analytics storage. It is difficult to define a data structure for analytics data beforehand, because often we do not know what are the most important pieces of information we would have to store. Also, if we decide to store any additional information (or decide not to store any existing information going forward) the flexibility of the schema makes it very easy to introduce the required changes to the data structure.

Logging with MongoDB

Perhaps the most basic requirement of web analytics is to log visits to different pages in a web application. In this section, we are going to learn how we can implement a logger module that will log user requests to a web app in a MongoDB collection. Primarily, we are interested in the following aspects of an HTTP request:

- The page being visited
- The time of visit
- The IP address of the user
- The user agent string of the browser
- The query parameters (if any)
- The time taken to generate a response, in milliseconds

Time for action – logging page visits with MongoDB

We are going to implement user request logging in the blog web app that we created in Chapter 2, *Building your First MongoDB Powered Web App*. We will build a Logger class that will handle logging. We will modify the `blog.php` file, the script used for viewing individual blog posts, to log page views through the logger module:

1. Open up your text editor and create a new file named `log.php`. Add the following code to it:

```php
<?php
require_once('dbconnection.php');
define('LOGNAME', 'access_log');
class Logger
{
  private $_dbconnection;
  private $_db;
  public function __construct()
  {
    $this->_dbconnection = DBConnection::instantiate();
    //obtain a reference to the collection where the data
    //will be logged
    $this->_collection = $this->_dbconnection
      ->getCollection(LOGNAME);
  }
  public function logRequest($data = array())
  {
    $request = array();
    //obtain HTTP request information by accessing $_SERVER
```

```
$request['page']        = $_SERVER['SCRIPT_NAME'];
$request[viewed_at]    =
  new MongoDate($_SERVER['REQUEST_TIME']);
$request['ip_address']   = $_SERVER['REMOTE_ADDR'];
$request['user_agent']  = $_SERVER['HTTP_USER_AGENT'];
//split the query string and store HTTP
//parameters/values in an array
if (!empty($_SERVER['QUERY_STRING'])){
  $params = array();
  foreach(explode('&', $_SERVER['QUERY_STRING']) as
    $parameter) {
    list($key, $value) = explode('=', $parameter);
    $params[$key] = $value;
  }
  $request['query_params'] = $params;
}
//add addtional log data, if any
if (!empty($data)) {
  $request = array_merge($request, $data);
}
$this->_collection->insert($request);
    }
  }
}
```

2. Open the `blog.php` file and add the following lines at the beginning:

```
require('log.php');
$start = microtime();
```

Add the following code at the end of the blog.php file

```
$end = microtime();
$data = array('response_time_ms' => ($end - $start) * 1000);
$logger = new Logger();
$logger->logRequest($data);
```

3. Start the `mongo` interactive shell. Switch to the `myblogsite` database and create a collection named `access_log` by entering the following commands:

```
./mongodb/bin/mongo
MongoDB shell version: 1.8.1
connecting to: test
> use myblogsite
switched to db myblogsite
> db.createCollection('access_log',{capped:true, size:100000})
{ "ok" : 1 }
```

4. Open the `blogs.php` page in a browser. Click on **Read more** a few times to view blog posts:

5. Open the `mongo` shell again. View the documents in the `access_log` collection by entering the following commands:

```
$ ./mongodb/bin/mongo
MongoDB shell version: 1.8.1
connecting to: test
> use myblogsite
switched to db myblogsite
> db.access_log.find()
```

The following screenshot shows the output:

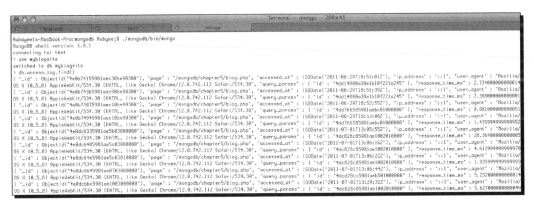

What just happened?

We implemented user request logging by creating a collection in MongoDB and inserting the HTTP request data into this collection. First we started the `mongo` shell and created a capped collection named `access_log` in the `mongo` interactive shell. A capped collection is a collection for which we can specify the maximum size (or the maximum number of objects it can store) and it will always maintain this size:

```
>db.createCollection('access_log', {capped: true, size:100000})
{ "ok" : 1 }
```

We will cover capped collection in detail shortly. Now, let's dig deeper into the code of `log.php`. This file contains a class named `Logger` that handles the request logging logic. In the constructor of the class, we created a connection to the MongoDB server and obtained a reference to the `access_log` collection. The `logRequest()` method obtains the HTTP request information we are interested in by accessing the `$_SERVER` super global array. It also splits the query string and stores the parameters and their values in an array. Finally, it merges the data with any additional data received as arguments and inserts it in the capped collection.

Next, we edited the `blog.php` script so that it loads `log.php` at runtime. We added timers at the start and end of this script so we can measure the time taken to render the page. At the end of the script, we instantiated `Logger` and called `logRequest()` on it, passing the response time taken as an optional argument:

```
$data   = array('response_time_ms' => ($end - $start) * 1000);
$logger = new Logger();
$logger->logRequest($data);
```

We visited some of the blog posts on the site in the browser and switched to the `mongo` shell once again. We invoked `find()` on `access_log` to see the data logged by the `Logger` class.

Capped collections

A capped collection is just like any other collection in MongoDB, except that if we specify the size of the collection in bytes, it will maintain this size by itself. That means when this collection grows larger than the specified size, it replaces the oldest documents (the documents that were inserted first) automatically with new ones.

A capped collection is created explicitly by calling `createCollection()`, unlike regular collections which are created implicitly. A second parameter has to be passed to this method specifying that this is a capped collection and the size of the collection in bytes.

```
//create a capped collection of 1000000 bytes named access_log
>db.createCollection('access_log', {capped:true, size: 100000})
```

This command will create the collection and pre-allocate the specified size on the disk. We can also specify the maximum number of objects to be stored in a capped collection (this must be accompanied by the size parameter):

```
//cap the number of documents to 1000
>db.createCollection('capped_coll',{capped:true, size:10000, max: 1000})
```

Sorting in natural order

Another notable feature of a capped collection is that it implements natural ordering. Natural ordering is the database's native approach of ordering documents in a collection. When we query a collection, without specifying to sort on a certain field, we will get the documents in the order they were inserted. In a regular collection, this is not guaranteed to happen because as we update the documents, their sizes change and they are moved around to fit into the collection. A capped collection on the other hand guarantees that the documents are returned in the order of their insertion:

```
//this will return the oldest documents first
db.access_log.find()
```

You can also reverse the order by sending in the {$natural : -1} parameter to sort():

```
//this will return the newest documents first
db.access_log.find().sort({$natural : -1})
```

This natural ordering behavior, coupled with the fixed size property makes capped collection an ideal logging backend (the order of items is preserved and the log is not allowed to grow beyond a specific size).

Updating and deleting documents in a capped collection

We can update documents in a capped collection the same way we update documents for a regular collection. But there is a catch; the document being updated is not allowed to grow in size (otherwise capped collection could not guarantee natural ordering). Also, we cannot delete documents from a capped collection. We can however use drop() to delete the collection entirely.

Specifying the size of a regular collection

It is possible to pre-allocate disk space for a collection that is not capped. We have to use the createCollection() method for it:

```
>db.createCollection('noncapped_coll', {size : 100000})
{ "ok" : 1 }
```

Convert a regular collection to a capped one

We can also turn a regular collection into a capped collection by using the following command:

```
>db.runCommand({'convertToCapped': 'regular_coll', size : 1000000})
{ "ok" : 1 }
```

This converts a non-capped collection named `regular_coll` into a capped collection.

Pop quiz – capped collection

1. Which of the following is a false statement?

    a. A capped collection cannot grow beyond the specified size

    b. Documents in a capped collection cannot be modified

    c. Documents in a capped collection are stored in order of insertion

2. What happens when a capped collection exceeds its pre-allocated size when we are inserting new documents into it?

    a. We get an error saying the collection has reached its limit

    b. MongoDB shuffles the allocated disk space to make room for the new documents

    c. The newly inserted objects automatically replace the oldest ones in the collection

3. Sorting by natural order means:

    a. The documents that were created last will be returned first (Last in First Out)

    b. The documents that were inserted first will be returned first (First in First Out)

    c. None of the above

Extracting analytics data with MapReduce

The log contains raw data about page visits, but we need to extract some meaningful information out of it. For example, it might be useful to know how many times a page has been viewed over a certain time period, or what is the average response time for a page. It is possible to do so by applying MapReduce on the log. In the next example, we are going to do just that.

Time for action – finding total views and average response time per blog post

In this example, we will write a PHP program where we will define the map and reduce functions to determine the number of visits per blog post over the last seven days and the average response time for rendering it. We will display the result in an HTML table:

1. Create a new PHP script named `page_views.php`. Add the following code to it:

```php
<?php
  require 'dbconnection.php';
  $dbConnection = DBConnection::instantiate();
  $db = $dbConnection->database;
  /* The map function, emits a counter and response_time_ms of
    each document */
  $map = "function() { emit(this.query_params.id, {count: 1,".
    "resp_time: this.response_time_ms}) }";
  // the reduce function, sums up the counters and response times
  $reduce = "function(key, values) { ".
    "var total_count = 0;".
    "var total_resp_time = 0;".
    "values.forEach(function(doc) {".
      "total_count += doc.count;".
      "total_resp_time += doc.resp_time;".
    "});".
    "return {count: total_count, resp_time:".
      "total_resp_time};".
  "}";
  /*finalize - finds average response time by dividing total
    response time by total sum of counters */
  $finalize = "function(key, doc) {".
    "doc.avg_resp_time = doc.resp_time / doc.count;".
    "return doc;".
  "}";
  $db->command(array(
    'mapreduce' => 'access_log',
    'map' => new MongoCode($map),
    'reduce' => new MongoCode($reduce),
    'query' => array('page' => '/blog.php',
      'viewed_at' => array('$gt' =>
        new MongoDate(strtotime('-7 days')))),
    'finalize' => new MongoCode($finalize),
```

```
        'out'    => 'page_views_last_week'
        )
    );
    $results = $dbConnection->getCollection('page_views_last_week')
        ->find();
    function getArticleTitle($id)
    {
        global $dbConnection;
        $article = $dbConnection->getCollection('articles')
            ->findOne(array('_id' => new MongoId($id)));
        return $article['title'];
    }
?>
<html xmlns="http://www.w3.org/1999/xhtml" xml:lang="en">
    <head>
        <title>Most viewed articles (Last 7 days)</title>
        <link rel="stylesheet" href="style.css"/>
        <style type="text/css" media="screen">
            body { font-size: 13px; }
            div#contentarea { width : 680px; }
        </style>
    </head>
    <body>
        <div id="contentarea">
            <div id="innercontentarea">
                <h1>Most viewed articles (Last 7 days)</h1>
                <table class="articles" cellspacing="0"
                    cellpadding="0">
                    <thead>
                        <tr>
                            <th width="50%">Article</th>
                            <th width="25%">Page views</th>
                            <th width="*">Avg response time</th>
                        </tr>
                    </thead>
                    <tbody>
                        <?php foreach($results->sort(array('value.count'
                        => -1))
                        as $result): ?>
                        <tr>
                            <td><?php echo getArticleTitle($result['_id']);
                            ?></td>
```

```
        <td><?php echo $result['value']['count']; ?></td>
        <td>
          <?php echo sprintf('%f ms',
            $result['value']['avg_resp_time']); ?>
        </td>
      </tr>
    <?php endforeach; ?>
    </tbody>
  </table>
</div>
    </div>
  </body>
</html>
```

2. Execute the newly created `page_views.php` script in the browser to see the analytics data:

Most viewed articles (Last 7 days)

Article	Page views	Avg response time
Always draw your curves, then plot your reading.	24	2.937500 ms
Learnt something important today	21	2.880952 ms
Nature always sides with the hidden flaw	19	2.842105 ms
Software bugs are hard to detect by anybody except may be the end user.	18	2.727778 ms
Patchers gonna patch!	17	2.505882 ms
Research supports a specific theory depending on the amount of funds dedicated to it.	16	3.225000 ms
Adding manpower to a late software project makes it later.	16	2.700000 ms
Blogging is fun!	15	2.893333 ms
Hello World!	14	2.721429 ms
There is never time to do it right, but always time to do it over.	14	2.900000 ms
Hello World Again!	14	2.992857 ms
Any given program, when running, is obsolete.	12	2.458333 ms

What just happened?

We just ran a MapReduce operation on the access_log collection and displayed the extracted information in an HTML table. We wrote the map, reduce, and finalize functions in JavaScript and supplied them as arguments to the command() method of the MongoDB object that represents the myblogsite database. We also supplied query arguments to limit the operation to the blog.php pages, viewed over the last seven days.

The map, reduce, and finalize functions

Let's look closely at the map, reduce, and finalize functions we used. The map function emits the id field in the query_param embedded document of each document in access_log. It also emits an object containing a counter and the value of the response_time_ms field of the document. The reduce function sums up the counter and response time values. The finalize function determines average response time by dividing the sum of response times by the sum of counters.

Displaying the result

The result of the MapReduce operation is stored in a collection named page_views_last_week. Each document of this collection has the blog ID in its _id field, and the counter and average response time in its values field:

```
> db.page_views_last_week.find()
{ "_id" : "4dc828a75981ae0e02000000", "value" : { "count" : 14, "resp_
time" : 38.1, "avg_resp_time" : 2.7214285714285715 } }
{ "_id" : "4dc828c85981ae1002010000", "value" : { "count" : 21, "resp_
time" : 60.5, "avg_resp_time" : 2.880952380952381 } }
{ "_id" : "4dc828e95981ae0f02000000", "value" : { "count" : 15, "resp_
time" : 43.4, "avg_resp_time" : 2.893333333333333 } }
................. . .
```

In the page_views.php script, we wrote a custom function to fetch the blog title by _id from the articles collection. Then we sorted the articles by their page views (sorting on the values.count field) in descending order, and render an HTML table with their values.

Running MapReduce in real time versus running it in the background

It is not generally a good idea to calculate analytics using such MapReduce in real time, especially if you are running a website that enjoys heavy user traffic. The log will be very large and, constantly growing, so running MapReduce on it would take time (MapReduce jobs are known to be consistent and continuous, but their speed depends on several factors). If we ran the page view calculation job like we did in our example, it will take a long time to load the page. Rather, you should run processes in the background (running a cron job, maybe every night) that execute the MapReduce jobs, stores the results in a collection, and have the analytics page simply read from that collection. This way we can keep the performance at an optimum level, although we will sacrifice real-time page view counts. But there is another way we can obtain page view stats in real time. We are going to learn about that in the next section.

Have a go hero – find out usage share of browsers for the site

Using MapReduce, find out the usage share of different browsers used by the visitors of your blog. Group the log data by different values of user agent strings and express the proportion of each browser as a percentage. There are bonus points available if you can display the result in a graphical manner (using a pie chart or a bar chart!).

Real-time analytics using MongoDB

In this section, we are going to build another analytics tool with MongoDB that keeps count of how many times a page has been viewed and displays in an HTML dashboard, in real time. Although it is possible to do that using the logger we built earlier in this chapter and MapReduce, this is not a very scalable solution as we discussed earlier. So we are going to take an alternative approach, by making use of upsert and the $inc modifier.

Time for action – building a real-time page visit counter

We will modify the logger to add a new method that keeps track of how many times a blog post has been viewed daily. The method will store this information in a new collection, whose schema is designed to fit this new use case. We will modify the blog.php file to call that method after rendering the page. We will display this information in an HTML table on a different page.

1. Open the log.php file and add the following method in the Logger class:

```
public function updateVisitCounter($articleId)
{
  $articleVistiCounterDaily = $this->_dbconnection
    ->getCollection('article_visit_counter_daily');
  $criteria = array(
```

```php
        'article_id' => new MongoId($articleId),
        'request_date' =>
          new MongoDate(strtotime('today'))
    );
    $newobj = array('$inc' => array('count' => 1));
    $articleVistiCounterDaily->update($criteria,
      $newobj,
      array('upsert' => True));
}
```

2. Open the `blog.php` file and add the following code at the end of the file:

```php
$logger->updateVisitCounter($id);
```

3. Create a new PHP script named `blogreader_bot.php` and add the following code to it:

```php
<?php
  require 'dbconnection.php';
  $mongo = DBConnection::instantiate();
  $articles = $mongo->getCollection('articles');
  $articleIds = array();
  foreach($articles->find(array(), array('_id' => TRUE)) as
    $article){
    array_push($articleIds, (string)$article['_id']);
  }
  function getRandomArrayItem($array)
  {
    $length = count($array);
    $randomIndex = mt_rand(0, $length - 1);
    return $array[$randomIndex];
  }
  echo 'Simulating blog post reading...';
  while(1) {
    $id = getRandomArrayItem($articleIds);
    //change the value of $url accordingly on your machine
    $url =
      sprintf('http://localhost:8888/
      mongodb/chapter5/blog.php?id=%s'   , $id);
    $curlHandle = curl_init();
    curl_setopt($curlHandle, CURLOPT_URL, $url);
    curl_setopt($curlHandle, CURLOPT_HEADER, false);
    curl_setopt($curlHandle, CURLOPT_RETURNTRANSFER, true);
    curl_exec($curlHandle);
    curl_close($curlHandle);
  }
```

4. Create another PHP script named `realtime_pageviews.php` and add the following code to it:

```php
<?php
  require 'dbconnection.php';
  $dbConnection = DBConnection::instantiate();
  $collection = $dbConnection
    ->getCollection('article_visit_counter_daily');
  function getArticleTitle($id)
  {
    global $dbConnection;
    $article = $dbConnection->getCollection('articles')
      ->findOne(array('_id' => new MongoId($id)));
    return $article['title'];
  }
  $objects = $collection->find(array('request_date' =>
    new MongoDate(strtotime('today'))));
?>
<html xmlns="http://www.w3.org/1999/xhtml" xml:lang="en">
  <head>
    <title>Daily Page views (in realtime)</title>
    <link rel="stylesheet" href="style.css"/>
    <style type="text/css" media="screen">
      body { font-size: 13px; }
      div#contentarea { width : 680px; }
    </style>
  </head>
  <body>
    <div id="contentarea">
      <div id="innercontentarea">
        <h1>Daily Page views (in realtime)</h1>
        <table class="articles" cellspacing="0"
          cellpadding="0">
          <thead>
            <tr>
              <th>Article</th>
              <th>Viewed</th>
            </tr>
          </thead>
          <tbody>
            <?php foreach($objects->sort(array('count' => -1))
              as $obj): ?>
            <tr>
              <td>
                <?php
                  echo getArticleTitle((string)
                  $obj['article_id']); ?>
              </td>
              <td><?php echo $obj['count']; ?></td>
            </tr>
```

```
      <?php endforeach; ?>
    </tbody>
  </table>
 </div>
 </div>
</body>
<script type="text/javascript">
  var REFRESH_PERIOD = 5000; //refresh every 5 seconds.
  var t = setInterval("location.reload(true);",
    REFRESH_PERIOD);
</script>
</html>
```

5. Open the terminal (the command prompt if you are running on Windows) and execute the `blogreader_bot.php` file in the command line:

```
$ php blogreader_bot.php
Simulating blog post reading...
```

6. While the `blogreader_bot.php` script is running, open the `realtime_pageviews.php` page in the browser. Notice the numbers under the **Viewed** column change as the page periodically refreshes itself every five seconds:

Daily Page views (in realtime)

Article	Viewed
Adding manpower to a late software project makes it later.	521
Learnt something important today	490
Always draw your curves, then plot your reading.	487
Software bugs are hard to detect by anybody except may be the end user.	486
There is never time to do it right, but always time to do it over.	479
Blogging is fun!	476
Any given program, when running, is obsolete.	472
Research supports a specific theory depending on the amount of funds dedicated to it.	467
Hello World Again!	461
Hello World!	454
Patchers gonna patch!	454
Nature always sides with the hidden flaw	449

What just happened?

That was quite a big example! Let's go through the steps to see what we did. First we added a method `updateVisitCounter()` to the existing `Logger` class. As the name suggests, this method keeps count of how many times a blog has been viewed today. It queries the `article_visit_counter_daily` collection with an `article_id` (received as its argument) and the date of request (today's date by default). If it finds a document, it increases the `count` field by 1; otherwise it inserts such a document with the `count` field set to 1 (we use the `upsert` and `$inc` features of MongoDB to achieve this).

Next, we modified `blog.php` again to call `updateVisitCounter()` at the end of the script.

Then we wrote a command-line PHP script `blogreader_bot.php` that simulates blog post visits. It runs in an indefinite loop, randomly picks an article from the articles collection, and 'views' the article using the PHP cURL library. You can also run this script in your browser if you don't have PHP CLI installed on your machine.

 If you have not worked with PHP and cURL before, check out this page in the PHP online documentation `http://bd.php.net/manual/en/book.curl.php`.

Next, we wrote another PHP program named `realtime_pageviews.php` that loads the data from the `article_visit_counter_daily` and displays page views per article in an HTML table. The page has a JavaScript code that automatically refreshes itself every five seconds.

```
<script type="text/javascript">
 var REFRESH_PERIOD = 5000; //refresh every 5 seconds.
 var t = setInterval("location.reload(true);", REFRESH_PERIOD);
</script>
```

We executed the `blogreader_bot.php` script in the command line to simulate page visits. We ran the `realtime_pageviews.php` file in the browser and watched the numbers changing when the page refreshed every five seconds.

 Create indexes on the look up fields

One way the solution mentioned earlier can be improved is by creating indexes on the fields that are being queried (the `article_id` and the `request_date` fields). This will make document look up much faster. We will cover the benefits of indexing and how to create them later in this book.

Have a go hero – get unique page visits in real time

Your task is to modify the previous code to count unique visits to a blog post in real time. The general idea is that when a user views a blog post for the first time, the counter for that article will increase by one. His subsequent visits to the same blog post will not affect the counter (at least for that day). Avoid using MapReduce as we have learned that they are not great in real-time scenarios. There are several ways you can detect a unique visitor to a page. You can check the user's browser (the user agent string) and IP address, although this is not a viable solution in all situations (two users using the same browser and platform on a proxy server will have the same IP address, and therefore will be mistakenly identified as one visitor). You can put a cookie in the user's browser when he visits the site, and read the cookie value to identify whether the user's visit is unique or not.

Summary

Let's take a look what we covered in this chapter:

- We learned what makes MongoDB a good analytics tool
- We learned how we can use MongoDB for logging page visits
- We learned how to use MapReduce to extract analytics information from raw data
- We learned how to implement real-time analytics using `upsert` and `$inc`

We also covered asynchronous inserts and capped collections in MongoDB.

In the next chapter, we will learn how MongoDB and a relational database system can be used together to build a robust and elegant data backend.

6

Using MongoDB with Relational Databases

We have covered different aspects of MongoDB in the previous chapters, hopefully enough to make you feel confident of building your own web applications on top of it. In this chapter, we are going to discuss an interesting concept: using MongoDB and a relational database system together. We are going to examine a fictional project that is built around a relational database, and identify use cases for which MongoDB is a better fit. The practical examples in this chapter will demonstrate how we can use MongoDB along with a relational database for data archiving, storing aggregation results, caching JOIN queries, and so on. Lastly, we will discuss some of the challenges of working with such a hybrid data model. We will be using MySQL as the RDBMS in the examples, but the concepts should apply to any other relational database.

In this chapter, we shall:

- Learn about the use cases where we can use MongoDB with a relational database system
- Learn how we can archive data in an RDBMS to MongoDB
- Learn to use MongoDB as a storage for expensive aggregation queries
- Learn how we can use MongoDB for storing entity metadata
- Discuss the challenges for using an RDBMS and MongoDB together

The motivation behind using MongoDB and an RDBMS together

Relational databases have been around for decades. Programmers have built countless applications, web-based or otherwise, on top of such databases. If the domain of the problem is relational, then using an RDBMS is an obvious choice. The real-world entities are mapped into tables, and the relationships among the entities are maintained using more tables (or foreign key constraints). But there could be some parts of the problem domain where using a relational data model will not be the best approach, and perhaps we may need a data store that supports a flexible schema. In such scenarios, we could use a document-oriented data storage solution such as MongoDB. The application code will have separate modules for accessing and manipulating the data of the RDBMS and that of MongoDB.

Potential use cases

Let's look at some potential use cases where we can employ MongoDB alongside a relational database system:

- **Storing results of aggregation queries**: The results of expensive aggregation queries (COUNT, GROUP BY, and so on) can be stored in a MongoDB database. This allows the application to quickly get the result from MongoDB without having to perform the same query again, until the result becomes stale (at which point the query will be performed and the result will be stored again). Since the schema of a MongoDB collection is flexible, we don't need to know anything about the structure of the result data beforehand. The rows returned by the aggregation query could be stored as BSON documents.

- **Data archiving**: As the volume of data grows, queries and other operations on a relational table increasingly take more time. One solution to this problem is to partition the data into two tables: an **Online table**, which contains the working dataset, and an **Archival table** that holds the old data. The size of the online table will remain more or less the same, but the archival table will grow larger. The drawback of this approach is that when the schema of the online table changes, we will have to apply the same changes to the archive table. This will be a very slow operation because of the volume of the data. Also, if we drop one or more columns in the online table, we will have to drop those columns in the archive tables too, thus losing the old data that might have been valuable. To get around this problem, we could use a MongoDB collection as the archive. Because of its flexible schema, we won't have to do anything if the structures of the old and the new tables differ.

- **Logging:** We can apply MongoDB for logging events in an application. We can use a relational database for the same purpose, but the INSERT operations on the log table will incur an extra overhead that will make the application response slower. We can also try simple file-based logging, but in that case, we would have to write our own, regular-expression-powered log parsing code to analyze the log data and extract information out of it. The asynchronous insert feature and the Mongo query language (and MapReduce) makes MongoDB a better choice for logging. We have learned how to log HTTP requests in MongoDB in Chapter 5, *Web Analytics using MongoDB*, so we won't go into much detail about it here.

- **Storing entity metadata:** The application that you built maps the entities of the domain into tables. The entities could be physical, real-world objects (users, products, and so on), or they could be something virtual (blog posts, categories, and tags). You determine what pieces of information you need to store for each of these entities, and then you design the database schema and define the table structures. But let's assume that we need to store some additional of information for some of these entities. We don't know what kind of information we need to store, and they vary from one entity to another (even though both entities are of the same type). To illustrate this, consider a table called **Player**, where we store specific data for all kinds of sportsmen such as tennis players, golfers, and race-car drivers. At some point, we realize that we need to store the key achievements of these players as well. We need to store how many PGA championships Tiger Woods has won, and how many times Roger Federar has lifted the Wimbledon cup. You can imagine how difficult it is to map all this data to a relational structure. We could instead put the metadata for the player in a MongoBD document, along with the primary key of the player. When we need to access it, we could just query the collection with the primary key and have the document loaded. (We could store the metadata in a serialized form in a table, but in that case, we would not be able to run any queries on the metadata.)

In the next sections, we will learn how to implement these use cases.

Defining the relational model

To demonstrate how MongoDB and RDBMS can work together, we are going to design the schema of the database for a fictional company named Acme Corp (the fans of the Looney Tunes cartoon series might be familiar with their products!). For the sake of simplicity, we will limit the tables of the database to three:

- **products:** This table lists all the products manufactured by Acme Corp.

- **customers:** This table contains a list of all the individuals who purchased Acme Corp products.

- **sales:** This table contains a record of each sales transaction of Acme Corp products.

The following diagram shows the schema diagram of the database:

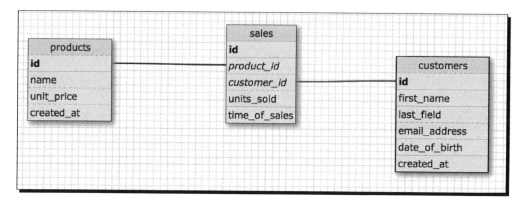

As shown in the diagram, the **product_id** field of **sales** is a foreign key referencing the primary key of **products**, and the **customer_id** references the primary key of **customers**.

Time for action – creating the database in MySQL

We are going to implement the database schema that we defined in the previous section. I have chosen MySQL as the RDBMS to use in this chapter. I am assuming you have some experience working with MySQL and have both the server and client installed and running on your machine.

1. Open your text editor and put the following SQL code in a new text file:

```
CREATE DATABASE `acmeproducts`;
USE acmeproducts;
CREATE TABLE `customers` (
    `id` int(11) NOT NULL auto_increment,
    `first_name` varchar(256) NOT NULL,
    `last_name` varchar(256) NOT NULL,
    `email_address` varchar(256) NOT NULL,
    `date_of_birth` datetime default NULL,
    `created_at` timestamp NOT NULL default CURRENT_TIMESTAMP,
    PRIMARY KEY  (`id`),
```

```
    UNIQUE KEY `email_address` (`email_address`)
) ENGINE=InnoDB;
CREATE TABLE `products` (
  `id` int(11) NOT NULL auto_increment,
  `name` varchar(256) NOT NULL,
  `unit_price` double NOT NULL,
  `created_at` timestamp NOT NULL default CURRENT_TIMESTAMP,
  PRIMARY KEY (`id`),
  UNIQUE KEY `name` (`name`)
) ENGINE=InnoDB;
CREATE TABLE `sales` (
  `id` int(11) NOT NULL auto_increment,
  `product_id` int(11) NOT NULL,
  `customer_id` int(11) NOT NULL,
  `units_sold` int(11) NOT NULL,
  `time_of_sales` timestamp NOT NULL default
    CURRENT_TIMESTAMP,
  PRIMARY KEY (`id`),
  KEY `sales_ibfk_1` (`product_id`),
  KEY `sales_ibfk_2` (`customer_id`)
) ENGINE=InnoDB;
ALTER TABLE `sales`
  ADD CONSTRAINT `sales_ibfk_1` FOREIGN KEY (`product_id`)
    REFERENCES `products` (`id`),
  ADD CONSTRAINT `sales_ibfk_2` FOREIGN KEY (`customer_id`)
    REFERENCES `customers` (`id`);
```

Save the file as `acmeproducts.sql`.

2. Launch the Terminal (command prompt in Windows) and run the following command to execute the SQL in `acmeproducts.sql` file, and create the database and tables. Enter your MySQL user password when prompted.

```
mysql -uXYZ -p -v < /path/to/acmeproducts.sql
```

(Replace `XYZ` with your MySQL username and `/path/to` with the actual file path to `acmeproducts.sql`). The output is as shown in the following screenshot:

```
Terminal — bash — 239×41
  mongod          mongo              bash            bash
Rubayeets-MacBook-Pro:~ Rubyeej$ mysql -uroot -p -v < acmeproducts.sql
Enter password:
--------------
CREATE DATABASE `acmeproducts`
--------------


--------------
CREATE TABLE `customers` (
  `id` int(11) NOT NULL auto_increment,
  `first_name` varchar(256) NOT NULL,
  `last_name` varchar(256) NOT NULL,
  `email_address` varchar(256) NOT NULL,
  `date_of_birth` datetime default NULL,
  `created_at` timestamp NOT NULL default CURRENT_TIMESTAMP,
  PRIMARY KEY (`id`),
  UNIQUE KEY `email_address` (`email_address`)
) ENGINE=InnoDB
--------------


--------------
CREATE TABLE `products` (
  `id` int(11) NOT NULL auto_increment,
  `name` varchar(256) NOT NULL,
  `unit_price` double NOT NULL,
  `created_at` timestamp NOT NULL default CURRENT_TIMESTAMP,
  PRIMARY KEY (`id`),
  UNIQUE KEY `name` (`name`)
) ENGINE=InnoDB
--------------


--------------
CREATE TABLE `sales` (
  `id` int(11) NOT NULL auto_increment,
  `product_id` int(11) NOT NULL,
  `customer_id` int(11) NOT NULL,
  `units_sold` int(11) NOT NULL,
  `time_of_sales` int(11) NOT NULL,
  PRIMARY KEY (`id`),
  KEY `product_id` (`product_id`),
  KEY `customer_id` (`customer_id`)
) ENGINE=InnoDB
```

What just happened?

The steps are pretty much self-explanatory in the previous example. We wrote the SQL command for creating a database named `acmeproducts`, defined the `products`, `customers`, and `sales` tables for this database, and added the foreign key constraints. Then we ran the command line MySQL client to execute the SQL code in the file, and created the database and tables.

Generate sample data

You should insert some sample data into these tables before continuing as we will need them for future examples. You can use a GUI interface with MySQL, such as phpMyAdmin for convenience, or write a PHP script to perform a batch insert of some randomly generated data.

Caching aggregation results in MongoDB

We are going to see how we can use MongoDB as a cache for aggregation queries. We are going to run aggregation operations on the database, which we defined in the previous section, store the result in MongoDB, and serve them to the user when he queries it.

Time for action – storing the daily sales history of products in MongoDB

In this example, we will run a SUM...GROUP BY query in the `sales` table to find out how many units are sold for each product, per day. We will store the result in a MongoDB collection. Then we will build a page where the user can enter the date and view the sales data by querying the collection.

1. Create a PHP script name `mysql.php` and put the following code in it:

```php
<?php
define('MYSQL_HOST', 'localhost');
define('MYSQL_PORT', 3306);
define('MYSQL_USER', 'XYZ');
define('MYSQL_PASSWD', '123123');
define('MYSQL_DBNAME', 'acmeproducts');
//function for connecting to MySQL
function getMySQLConnection(){
  $mysqli = new mysqli(MYSQL_HOST, MYSQL_USER, MYSQL_PASSWD,
    MYSQL_DBNAME, MYSQL_PORT);
  if (mysqli_connect_error()) {
    die(sprintf('Error connecting to MySQL. Error No: %d,'.
      'Error: %s', mysqli_connect_errno(),
      mysqli_connect_error()));
  }
  return $mysqli;
}
```

2. Open the `dbconnection.php` file and change the value of the DBNAME constant of the DBConnection class to acmeproducts_mongo.

```
const DBNAME = 'acmeproducts_mongo'.
```

3. Create a PHP file named `aggregates.php`, and put the following code in it:

```php
<?php
require 'mysql.php';
require 'dbconnection.php';
//query MySQL database to get daily sales data
```

```php
$query = 'SELECT name, DATE(time_of_sales) as date_of_sales,'.
  'SUM(units_sold) as total_units_sold '.
  'FROM sales s INNER JOIN products p ON'.
  '(p.id = s.product_id) '.
  'GROUP BY product_id, DATE(time_of_sales)';
$mysql = getMySQLConnection();
$result = $mysql->query($query);
if($result === False){
  die(sprintf("Error executing query %s" % $mysql->error));
}
$salesByDate = array();
//create documents with the query result
while($row = $result->fetch_assoc()) {
  $date = $row['date_of_sales'];
  $product = $row['name'];
    $totalSold = $row['total_units_sold'];
  $salesPerProduct = (isset($salesByDate[$date])) ?
   $salesByDate[$date] : array();
  $salesPerProduct[$product] = $totalSold;
  $salesByDate[$date] = $salesPerProduct;
}
$result->free();
$mysql->close();
//store the query result into a MongoDB collection
$mongodb =  DBConnection::instantiate();
$collection = $mongodb->getCollection('daily_sales');
foreach($salesByDate as $date => $sales) {
  $document = array(
    'sales_date' => new MongoDate(strtotime($date)),
    'items' => array()
  );
  foreach($sales as $product => $unitsSold) {
    $document['items'][$product] = $unitsSold;
  }
  $collection->insert($document);
}
```

4. Execute the `aggregates.php` script in the command-line (or in the browser) to run the aggregation, and store the result in MongoDB.

5. Create another PHP script named `daily_sales.php`, and add the following code to it:

```php
<?php
require 'dbconnection.php';
$action = (isset($_POST['action'])) ? $_POST['action']
  : 'default';
//function for validating the input date
function validateInput() {
  if (empty($_POST['year']) || empty($_POST['month']) ||
    empty($_POST['day'])) {
    return False;
  }
  $timestamp = strtotime($_POST['year'].'-'.$_POST['month'].
    '-'.$_POST['day']);
  if (!is_numeric($timestamp)) {
    return False;
  }
  return checkdate(date('m', $timestamp),
    date('d', $timestamp),
    date('Y', $timestamp)
  );
}
switch($action) {
  case 'Show':
    if(validateInput() === True) {
      $inputValidated = True;
      //query MongoDB collection to get sales data for
      //user-supplied date
      $date = sprintf('%d-%d-%d', $_POST['year'],
        $_POST['month'],
        $_POST['day']);
      $mongodate  = new MongoDate(strtotime($date));
      $mongodb    = DBConnection::instantiate();
      $collection = $mongodb->getCollection('daily_sales');
      $doc = $collection->findOne(array('sales_date' =>
        $mongodate));
    }
    else {
      $inputValidated = False;
    }
  break;
  default:
}
?>
```

```
<html xmlns="http://www.w3.org/1999/xhtml" xml:lang="en">
  <head>
    <title>Acme Corp | Daily Sales</title>
    <link rel="stylesheet" href="style.css"/>
  </head>
  <body>
    <div id="contentarea">
      <div id="innercontentarea">
        <h1>Daily Sales of Acme Products</h1>
        <form action="<? echo $_SERVER['PHP_SELF']; ?>"
          method="post">
          Enter Date (YYYY-MM-DD)
          <input type="text" name="year" size=4/> -
          <input type="text" name="month" size=2/> -
          <input type="text" name="day" size=2/>
          <input type="submit" name="action"
          value="Show"/>
        </form>
        <?php if($action === 'Show'):
          if ($inputValidated === True):?>
        <h3>
          <?php echo date('F j, Y', $mongodate->sec) ?>
        </h3>
        <?php if (!empty($doc)):?>
        <table class="table-list" cellspacing="0"
          cellpadding="0">
            <thead>
            <tr>
              <th width="50%">Item</th>
              <th width="25%"> </th>
              <th width="*">Units Sold</th>
            </tr>
          </thead>
          <tbody>
              <?php foreach($doc['items'] as $item =>
                $unitsSold): ?>
              <tr>
                <td><?php echo $item; ?></td>
                <td> </td>
                <td><?php echo $unitsSold; ?></td>
              </tr>
              <?php endforeach;?>
            </tbody>
          </table>
          <?php else:
```

```
        echo "<p> No sales record found.</p>";
    endif;
    else:
        echo "<h3>Invalid input. Try again.</h3>";
    endif;
  endif; ?>
  </div>
 </div>
</body>
</html>
```

6. Load the `daily_sales.php` page in the browser.

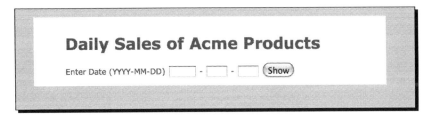

7. Enter a valid date in the input fields and click on the **Show** button. The page will reload with the data.

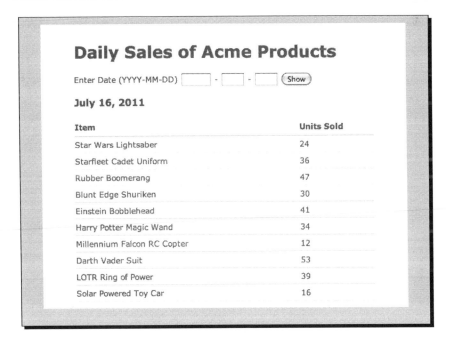

What just happened

Let's go through the steps of the last example and see what we did. First, we created a PHP script named `mysql.php` that houses a function we can use (and reuse) for connecting to the MySQL `acmeproducts` database on the machine. Next, we edited the `dbconnection.php` file to change the `DBNAME` constant of the `DBConnection` class. We will use this class to connect to a new Mongo database named `acmeproducts_mongo`. We created a PHP script named `aggregates.php` that runs the following aggregation query on the MySQL database. The result of the script is organized into a data structure similar to the following:

```
Array
(
   [2011-07-09] => Array
   (
      [Star Wars Lightsaber] => 23
      [Starfleet Cadet Uniform] => 39
      [Rubber Boomerang] => 9
      [Blunt Edge Shuriken] => 3
      [Einstein Bobblehead] => 26
      [Harry Potter Magic Wand] => 9
      [Millennium Falcon RC Copter] => 5
      [Darth Vader Suit] => 15
      [LOTR Ring of Power] => 37
      [Solar Powered Toy Car] => 53
   )
   [2011-07-10] => Array
   (
      [Star Wars Lightsaber] => 65
      [Starfleet Cadet Uniform] => 134
      [Rubber Boomerang] => 95
      [Blunt Edge Shuriken] => 114
      [Einstein Bobblehead] => 65
      [Harry Potter Magic Wand] => 84
      [Millennium Falcon RC Copter] => 64
      [Darth Vader Suit] => 97
      [LOTR Ring of Power] => 71
      [Solar Powered Toy Car] => 73
   )
)
```

The next few lines of code in the file save this data structure into a MongoDB collection named `daily_sales`. If we query the collection in mongo shell at this point, we will see something similar to the following:

```
> use acmeproducts_mongo
switched to db acmeproducts_mongo
> db.daily_sales.findOne()
{
  "_id" : ObjectId("4e20429a5981aec215000000"),
  "sales_date" : ISODate("2011-07-08T00:00:00Z"),
  "items" : {
    "Star Wars Lightsaber" : "18",
    "Starfleet Cadet Uniform" : "29",
    "Rubber Boomerang" : "34",
    "Blunt Edge Shuriken" : "68",
    "Einstein Bobblehead" : "41",
    "Harry Potter Magic Wand" : "42",
    "Millennium Falcon RC Copter" : "40",
    "Darth Vader Suit" : "43",
    "LOTR Ring of Power" : "18",
    "Solar Powered Toy Car" : "59"
  }
}
```

As you can see, each document of the collection stores a date in the `sales_date` field, and the `items` field stores the name of the product and the number of units of that product sold on that date.

Finally, we created a PHP page where the user can supply the date in the input field. The PHP code runs a query on the `sales_date` field of the `daily_sales` collection with it. The contents of the `items` field of the retrieved document are displayed in an HTML table.

Benefits of caching queries in MongoDB

The real benefit of using this technique becomes apparent when we try this on a table with a large number of rows. If we had to perform queries on it in real-time, triggered by a user who wants to see the result in a webpage, he would have to wait for a long time for the page to load, because such queries will obviously take a long time to complete on a massive table. Also, the database server will experience a heavy load when more than one user is running such queries multiple times. Rather, we should have a background process (cron job in UNIX terms) that kicks off automatically at the end of the day (or when the web traffic is at its least), runs the query, and stores the result in MongoDB so that it can be served to the user promptly.

Storing results of expensive JOINs

We can also use MongoDB to store results of JOIN queries among very large tables. Obviously, if the data in the tables participating in the JOIN changes, the result cache becomes stale. We can have an automated background process that frequently updates the cache. The frequency of the cache update would depend on the pattern of read-write operations on the joined tables.

Have a go hero – replacing Views with MongoDB

I am going to put forward an idea as food for thought. Is it feasible to use MongoDB instead of Views? **Views** are like virtual tables, they are stored queries that produce results when invoked. What do we gain if we use a MongoDB collection for storing such results instead of views? What are the disadvantages? Can you draw them out from both database and application points of view?

Using MongoDB for data archiving

We discussed the benefits of using MongoDB for archiving data from a relational table. Now we are going to see it in action. We will use a MongoDB collection to archive the old sales records of the fictional Acme Corp database. We will consider all sales records that are older than one month as eligible for archiving.

Time for action – archiving old sales records in MongoDB

In this example, we will write and execute a PHP script that queries all the sales records that are older than one month, migrate them to a MongoDB collection, and have them removed from the sales table.

1. Open up the text editor, create a new file and put the following code in it:

```php
<?php
  require 'mysql.php';
  require 'dbconnection.php';
  $cutoffDate = date('Y-m-d', strtotime('-30 day'));
  $mysql  = getMySQLConnection();
  //get all the sales records older than one month
  $query  = sprintf("SELECT * FROM sales WHERE".
    "DATE(time_of_sales) < '%s'", $cutoffDate);
  printf("Fetching old data from MySQL...\n");
  $result = $mysql->query($query);
  if($result === False) {
    die(sprintf("Error executing query %s" % $mysql->error));
  }
  printf("Migrating to MongoDB...\n");
  $mongo = DBConnection::instantiate();
  $collection = $mongo->getCollection('sales_archive');
  while($record = $result->fetch_assoc()) {
    try{
      $collection->insert($record);
    } catch(MongoCursorException $e) {
      die("Migration Failed ".$e->getMessage());
    }
  }
  printf("\tDone. %d records migrated.\n", $result->num_rows);
  $result->free();
  printf("Deleting old data from MySQL...\n");
  $query = sprintf("DELETE FROM sales WHERE
    DATE(time_of_sales)". "< '%s'", $cutoffDate);
  $status = $mysql->query($query);
  if($status === False) {
    die(sprintf("Error executing query %s" % $mysql->error));
  }
  $mysql->close();
  printf("Archiving complete.\n");
```

Save the file as `archive_sales_data.php`.

2. Run the `archive_sales_data.php` script in the command-line (or in the browser, in case you don't have PHP CLI installed).

```
$ php archive_sales_data.php
Fetching old data from MySQL...
Migrating to MongoDB...
Done. 12547 records migrated.
Deleting old data from MySQL...
Archiving complete.
```

3. Launch the mongo shell and query the `sales_archive` collection of the `acmeproducts_mongo` database to view all the archived data.

```
>use acmeproducts_mongo
switched to db acmeproducts_mongo

>db.sales_archive.find()
```

What just happened?

We created a script that archives all sales records older than one month to a MongoDB collection named `sales_archive`. First we query the sales table in the `acmeproducts` database to retrieve all records with `time_of_sales` older than one month. Next, we migrate all the retrieved records to MongoDB.

```
$mongo       = DBConnection::instantiate();
$collection = $mongo->getCollection('sales_archive');
while($record = $result->fetch_assoc()) {
  try{
```

```
        $collection->insert($record, array('safe' => True));
    } catch(MongoCursorException $e) {
        die("Migration Failed ".$e->getMessage());
    }
}
```

Notice how we turned on safe insert flag to ensure the insertion operation completes successfully (and terminate the script if it doesn't). Finally, when the migration is complete we delete the old data from the MySQL table.

>
> Having indexes on the fields used for searching old records speeds up the process. You can learn about MySQL indexing from this page `http://dev.mysql.com/doc/refman/5.0/en/mysql-indexes.html`.

Challenges in archiving and migration

Our migration example was pretty simple. We fetched a row from a MySQL table, formed a document with the data and inserted it in a MongoDB collection. But in real-world use cases, RDBMS to MongoDB migration will not always be this simple. Let's see what challenges we might face when we try to migrate and archive relational data in MonogDB.

Dealing with foreign key constraints

There might be situations where we would have to migrate data from multiple tables related to each other by foreign keys. In such cases, we can either have a separate collection for archiving each of the tables, and use application code to maintain relationships among the documents (referenced objects), or we could archive the records of the principle table in a single collection and store the related records as embedded documents in the documents of that collection. The best course of action should be chosen after considering the data model and application needs (such as the referenced versus embedded objects argument in Chapter 2, *Building your First MongoDB Powered WebApp*). In either case, we should be careful while deleting old data from the tables, so that data integrity is preserved. We may have to migrate and drop data from the RDBMS in a particular order. Having ON DELETE CASCADE turned on also helps.

Preserving data types

Also, in some cases you may need to preserve the data type when you migrate from MySQL to MongoDB. In our example, all data is stored as strings in the MongoDB database. In your code, you will have to define a map between the MySQL and BSON data types. During migration, check the MySQL data type of individual items (use `mysqli_result::fetch_field()` for this purpose) and typecast them appropriately before insertion.

Storing metadata in MongoDB

Earlier in this chapter, we discussed how MongoDB could be used as flexible storage for storing information about different entities that are difficult to map into relational tables. We are going to try it out in this section. The marketing department of the fictional Acme Corp wishes to collect some personal details of their customers (the ones the customer would willingly give to them of course! Acme Corp is not evil!). The details vary from one customer to another, and they are of different data types, such as strings, numbers, dates, arrays, objects and so on. These details will be stored in MongoDB. We will also need to store something in the documents that relates the row in the MySQL table to the metadata document.

Time for action – using MongoDB to store customer metadata

In this example, we will create a class named `Customer`. An instance of this class will represent a single row in the `customers` table of the database. The class will also have methods that store and retrieve the metadata of the customer.

1. Open a new file in your text editor and put the following code in it:

```php
<?php
require 'mysql.php';
require 'dbconnection.php';
class Customer{
  private $_mysql;
  private $_mongodb;
  private $_collection;
  private $_table;
  private $_id;
  private $_email;
  private $_dateOfBirth;
  private $_createdAt;
  public function __construct($id = null){
    $this->_mysql   = getMySQLConnection();
    $this->_mongodb = DBConnection::instantiate();
    $this->_collection = $this->_mongodb
      ->getCollection('customer_metadata');
    $this->_table = 'customers';
    if(isset($id)) {
      $this->_id = $id;
      $this->_load();
    }
  }
  private function _load(){
```

```php
    $query = sprintf("SELECT * FROM %s WHERE id = %d",
      $this->_table, $this->_id);
    $result = $this->_mysql->query($query);
    if($result === False) {
      throw new Exception('Error loading data: '
        .$this->_mysql->error);
    }
    elseif($result->num_rows === 0) {
      throw new Exception('No customer found with id '.
        $this->id);
      $this->__destruct();
    }
    else{
      $obj = $result->fetch_object();
      $this->_email       = $obj->email_address;
      $this->_dateOfBirth = $obj->date_of_birth;
      $this->_createdAt   = $obj->created_at;
      $result->free();
    }
    return;
  }
  public function __get($name){
    switch($name) {
      case 'id':
        return $this->_id;
      case 'email';
        return $this->_email;
      case 'dateOfBirth':
        return $this->_dateOfBirth;
      case 'createdAt':
        return $this->_createdAt;
      default:
        throw new Exception('Trying to access undefined'.
          'property '.$name);
    }
  }
  public function __set($name, $value){
    switch($name) {
      case 'email':
        if(filter_var($value, FILTER_VALIDATE_EMAIL) === False){
          throw new Exception('Trying to set invalid' .'email');
          return;
        }
        $this->_email = $value;
```

```
      break;
    case 'dateOfBirth':
      $timestamp = strtotime($value);
      if(is_numeric($timestamp) === False){
        throw new Exception('Trying to set invalid' .'date of
          birth. '. 'Expected format Y-m-d');
        return;
      }
      elseif($timestamp > time()){
        throw new Exception('Trying to set future'. 'date as
          birth date.');
        return;
      }
      elseif (checkdate(date('m', $timestamp),
        date('d', $timestamp),
        date('Y', $timestamp)) === False) {
        throw new Exception('Trying to set invalid' .'date of
          birth.');
        return;
      }
      $this->_dateOfBirth = date('Y-m-d H:i:s', $timestamp);
    break;
    default:
      throw new Exception('Trying to set'.
        'undefined/restricted property '.$name);
  }
}
public function save(){
  if(isset($this->_id)) {
    $query = sprintf("UPDATE %s SET ". "email_address='%s',".
      " date_of_birth='%s' WHERE id = %d", $this->_table,
    $this->_email,
    $this->_dateOfBirth,
    $this->_id);
  }
  else {
    $query = sprintf("INSERT INTO %s (". " email_address,".
      " date_of_birth) VALUES(" ."'%s', '%s')",
      $this->_table,
      $this->_email,
      $this->_dateOfBirth
    );
  }
  $status = $this->_mysql->query($query);
```

```php
    if ($status === False) {
      throw new Exception('Failed to save customer to'. 'MySQL
        database '.$this->_mysql->error);
    }
    elseif(!isset($this->_id)) {
      $this->_id = $this->_mysql->insert_id;
    }
    return $status;
  }
  public function delete() {
    if(!isset($this->_id)){
      return;
    }
    $query = sprintf("DELETE FROM %s WHERE id = %d",
      $this->_table, $this->_id);
    $status = $this->_mysql->query($query);
    if ($status === False) {
      throw new Exception('Failed to delete customer from'.
        'MySQL database '.$this->_mysql->error);
    }
    else{
      unset($this->_id);
    }
    return $status;
  }
  public function getMetaData(){
    if(!isset($this->_id)) {
      return;
    }
    $metadata = $this->_collection->findOne(array
      ('customer_id' => $this->_id));
    if ($metadata === NULL) {
      return array();
    }
    //remove _id and customer_id to avoid conflict during
      //future updates.
    unset($metadata['_id']);
    unset($metadata['customer_id']);
    return $metadata;
  }
  public function setMetaData($metadata){
    if(!isset($this->_id)) {
      throw new Exception('Cannot store metadata before'.'saving
        the object in MySQL');
    }
```

```php
        $metadata['customer_id'] = $this->_id;
        foreach($metadata as $key => $value) {
          if ($key === '_id') {
            unset($metadata[$key]);
          }
          elseif ((strpos($key, '$') !== FALSE) ||
            (strpos($key, '.') !== FALSE)) {
            unset($metadata[$key]);
          }
        }
        $currentMetaData = $this->getMetaData();
        $metadata = array_merge($currentMetaData, $metadata);
        $this->_collection->update(array('customer_id' =>
          $this->_id), $metadata, array('upsert' => True));
      }
      public function __destruct(){
        $this->_mysql->close();
        $this->_mongodb->connection->close();
      }
  }
```

Save the file as `customer.php`.

2. Create another file called `save_metadata.php`, and put the following code in it:

```php
<?php
  require 'customer.php';
  printf("Saving new customer object...\n");
  $customer              = new Customer();
  $customer->email       = 'joegunchy42@example.com';
  $customer->dateOfBirth = '1982-04-07';
  $status = $customer->save();
  printf("\tDone. ID %d\n", $customer->id);
  printf("Saving Metadata....\n");
  $metadata = array(
    'Middle Name' => 'The Gun',
    'Social Networking' => array(
      'Twitter Handle' => '@joegunchytw',
      'Facebook Username' => 'joegunchyfb'
    ),
    'Has a Blog?' => True
  );
  $customer->setMetaData($metadata);
  printf("\tDone\n");
  printf("Loading metadata...\n");
```

```
print_r($customer->getMetaData());
printf("Updating metadata...\n");
$metadata = array(
   'Marriage Anniversary' => new MongoDate(strtotime
      ('10 September 2005')),
   'Number of Kids' => 3,
   'Favorite TV Shows' => array(
      'The Big Bang Theory',
      'Star Trek Next Generation'
   )
);
print_r($customer->setMetaData($metadata));
printf("\tDone.\n");
printf("Reloading metadata...\n");
print_r($customer->getMetaData());
```

3. Run the save_metadata.php file from the command line:

```
$ php save_metadata.php
Saving new customer object...
Done. ID 13
Saving Metadata....
Done
Loading metadata...
Array
(
   [Middle Name] => The Gun
   [Social Networking] => Array
   (
      [Twitter Handle] => @joegunchytw
      [Facebook Username] => joegunchyfb
   )
   [Has a Blog?] => 1
)
Updating metadata...
Done.
Reloading metadata...
Array
(
   [Middle Name] => The Gun
   [Social Networking] => Array
```

```
        (
            [Twitter Handle] => @joegunchytw
            [Facebook Username] => joegunchyfb
        )
        [Has a Blog?] => 1
        [Marriage Anniversary] => MongoDate Object
        (
            [sec] => 1126306800
            [usec] => 0
        )
        [Number of Kids] => 3
        [Favorite TV Shows] => Array
        (
            [0] => The Big Bang Theory
            [1] => Star Trek Next Generation
        )
    )
```

What just happened?

In this example, we created a PHP class named `Customer` that represents a customer in the application. The class implements an object oriented design pattern named `ActiveRecord` (http://en.wikipedia.org/wiki/Active_record_pattern). In this pattern, each instance of the class represents a row in a certain database table. The class provides an interface to perform `select`/`insert`/`update`/`delete` operations on the row (collectively knows as **CRUD** operations), and also applies the business logic (data validation and the like).

If the constructor of the class is supplied with an ID, it loads the corresponding row from the database and populates the instance variables.

The magic method `_get()` offers an interface to read the values of some of the instance variables. The `_set()` method, on the other hand, allows to set the instance variables. It also performs validation of certain fields before setting them (e-mail, date of birth, and so on).

The `save()` method saves the object in the database. It either performs an `insert` or an `update` on the table (depending on whether the ID is supplied to the constructor), with the values of the instance variables. `delete()` simply deletes the record from the database.

Now, let's turn our attention to the really important methods of the class. The first is `getMetadata()`, which retrieves the document containing metadata of the Customer object from the `customer_metadata` collection. Each document contains a field named `customer_id` that holds the value of the ID field from the customers table in MySQL. The method queries the collection with this field and returns the metadata document, if it finds any.

```
public function getMetaData(){
  if(!isset($this->_id)) {
  return;
}
$metadata = $this->_collection->findOne(
  array('customer_id' => $this->_id));
  if ($metadata === NULL) {
    return array();
  }
  unset($metadata['_id']);
  unset($metadata['customer_id']
);
return $metadata;
}
```

Before returning the document, _id and customer_id fields are removed to avoid conflict during future updates of the metadata.

The setMetadata() method, as its name implies, stores the metadata for a customer. It ignores any field named _id to avoid conflict with the existing _id of the document. It also ignores any field that contains the characters "$" and ".", because these characters are used as query operators in MongoDB. It merges the metadata with the existing ones and performs an 'upsert' in the collection.

```
public function setMetaData($metadata){
  if(!isset($this->_id)) {
  throw new Exception('Cannot store metadata before saving the'.
    'object in MySQL');
  }
  $metadata['customer_id'] = $this->_id;
  foreach($metadata as $key => $value) {
    if ($key === '_id') {
      unset($metadata[$key]);
    }
    elseif ((strpos($key, '$') !== FALSE) ||
      (strpos($key, '.') !== FALSE)) {
      unset($metadata[$key]);
    }
  }
  $currentMetaData = $this->getMetaData();
  $metadata = array_merge($currentMetaData, $metadata);
  $this->_collection->update(array('customer_id' => $this->_id),
    $metadata, array('upsert' => True));
}
```

To test out the class, we wrote a simple script where we created a `Customer` object and saved it in the database. After that we used `setMetadata()` to store some personal details of the customer, and `getMetadata()` to read them back.

```
$metadata = array(
    'Middle Name' => 'The Gun',
    'Social Networking' => array(
        'Twitter Handle' => '@joegunchytw',
        'Facebook Username' => 'joegunchyfb'
    ),
    'Has a Blog?' => True
);
$customer->setMetaData($metadata);
print_r($customer->getMetaData());
```

At this point, you can query the collection in mongo shell with the `customer_id` to see the actual document.

```
> db.customer_metadata.findOne({customer_id:13})
{
    "_id" : ObjectId("4e21cc5e98d9701b770f2722"),
    "Middle Name" : "The Gun",
    "Social Networking" : {
        "Twitter Handle" : "@joegunchytw",
        "Facebook Username" : "joegunchyfb"
    },
    "Has a Blog?" : true,
    "Marriage Anniversary" : ISODate("2005-09-10T00:00:00Z"),
    "Number of Kids" : 3,
    "Favorite TV Shows" : [
        "The Big Bang Theory",
        "Star Trek Next Generation"
    ],
    "customer_id" : 13
}
```

Problems with using MongoDB and RDBMS together

Before you start building your next web application, powered by a hybrid data backend of MongoDB and MySQL (or any other relational database), you should consider some of the problems you might face.

- **Data consistency**: If you use MongoDB as a cache-tier on top of a relational database, you will need to keep it consistent with the changes in the underlying data. You can run background processes that are fired at a certain time, and update the stale data in MongoDB. A more elegant solution would be to define callback methods in the data access layer, which will automatically update the MongoDB data every time you insert/update/delete something in the tables.

- **Complexity of the software architecture**: From the application developer's point of view, having both MongoDB and an RDBMS as the data backends increases the complexity of the code. This is because he now has to provide and support two separate data access layers, one for the MongoDB database and the other for the relational one.

- **Cost of supporting an additional component**: If you add MongoDB to your existing technology stack, you now have a new component to support. The DBA has an additional task of keeping an eye on it, monitoring its performance. The system administrator needs to monitor how much system resources (CPU, memory, and disk space) it is taking up, and whether he would have to allocate new resources for it.

If you think you can handle all these challenges effectively, you should go ahead. Otherwise, try to solve the problem using your existing software stack. Alternatively, if the cost is reasonable (in terms of developer time), consider migrating the whole application to MongoDB.

Summary

Let's take a look at what we covered in this chapter:

- We discussed the possible use cases where we can use MongoDB and an RDBMS together as data backend in an application

- We learned how to use MongoDB as a query cache for storing and serving results of expensive SQL queries

- We learned how we can migrate data from an RDBMS to MongoDB, so the latter can be used as a data archive

- We saw how MongoDB can be used for storing metadata of different entities in the application

We also discussed some potential problems that a developer might face if he decides to adopt such a hybrid data backend solution. In the next chapter, we are going to focus on an interesting feature of MongoDB, which is **GridFS**. Keep reading!

7

Handling Large Files with GridFS

So far in this book we have dealt with data that is mostly textual. But Web 2.0 hardly contains itself within text data. Now we are using web applications to do things that we probably did not think of doing while the World Wide Web was being conceived. For example, watching blockbuster movies, listening to top charted music, uploading and sharing high-resolution pictures snapped with our digital cameras, and all using our web browsers! Where does MongoDB fit in all of this? Is it capable of handling large amounts of binary data? The answer in short, is yes. And in this chapter, we are going to learn how. Mainly we are going to tinker with GridFS, which enables MongoDB to store large files.

So we are going to learn:

- What GridFS is
- Advantages of using GridFS
- How to use PHP to upload files to GridFS
- How to serve files from GridFS
- When not to use GridFS and why

What is GridFS?

GridFS is MongoDB's solution for storing binary data in the database. It is a specification for handling large files in MongoDB. When I say specification, I mean it is not a feature of MongoDB itself; there is no code in MongoDB that implements it. GridFS just specifies how large files are to be handled in the database, and the language drivers (PHP, Python, Ruby, and so on) implement this specification and expose an API to the user of that driver (that's you) so you can use it to store/retrieve large files in MongoDB.

The rationale of GridFS

By design, a MongoDB document (a BSON object) cannot be larger than 16 megabytes. This is to keep performance at an optimum level. If there are documents larger than 16 MB, they are going to take up a lot of memory when you query them. GridFS specifies a mechanism for dividing a large file among multiple documents. The language driver that implements it, for example, the PHP driver, takes care of the splitting of the stored files (or merging the split chunks when files are to be retrieved) under the hood. The developer using the driver does not need to know of such internal details. This way GridFS allows the developer to store and manipulate files in a transparent and efficient way.

The specification

Let's learn about the GridFS specification briefly. GridFS stores a file in two separate collections: **files** and **chunks**. The basic idea is for every file to be stored in GridFS, `files` will have exactly one document that will contain the filename, size, time of upload, and any other metadata set by the user. The contents of the file will be stored in one or more documents in `chunks` (in the PHP implementation, each chunk stores up to 256 kilobytes of data). The next diagram illustrates the specification:

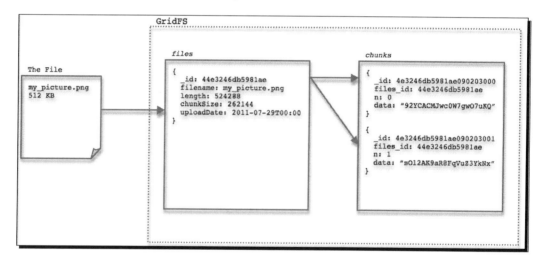

The previous diagram shows how an image file of 512 KB is stored in GridFS. The document in files contains the filename, size, time when the file was uploaded, and so on. The file is split into two 256 KB chunks, each chunk referring to the document in files with its `files_id` field.

To learn more about the specification visit the page in MongoDB online documentation available at `http://www.mongodb.org/display/DOCS/GridFS+Specification`.

Advantages over the filesystem

The obvious question that pops into mind is "What do I gain from using GridFS instead of the trusted old filesystem?". Here are some reasons that might convince you:

- With GridFS we could store millions of files under one (logical) directory. Traditional filesystems will not allow us to do so (even if they do, it will be at the cost of a serious performance decrease).

- In a distributed environment, where multiple machines have to access the files, GridFS is a much better choice than having a networked/distributed filesystem. The built-in replication schemes of MongoDB can be used to replicate and sync the files on multiple machines.

- If you have taken measures for backing up your MongoDB data, it will work for backing up the files stored in GridFS as well. You do not have to design a separate system for backing up your filesystem.

- You can store whatever metadata you consider important along with the file itself. For example, if your site allows users to upload photos/videos, you can also store any comments, likes, or ratings along with the file.

- Since files are stored in chunks, you can access random parts of a large file. Traditional tools that implement this feature on the filesystems are not very good.

 Relational database systems facilitate file storing as well. MySQL has a data type named BLOB (Very Large Objects) for storing large files in database. But it is known to perform poorly, in terms of speed, disk space, and memory consumption.

Pop quiz – what is the maximum size of BSON objects?

1. What is the maximum allowed size of BSON objects (MongoDB documents)?

    a. 4 MB

    b. 16 MB

    c. 32 MB

2. If a 20 MB file is stored in GridFS, how many chunks will it be split into?

    a. 40

    b. 60

    c. 80

Storing files in GridFS

Now that we have learned about GridFS, it is time to see it in action. For our first practical example of using GridFS, we will learn how we can store files to it using PHP. We will also look under the hood and see how the file is actually being stored.

Time for action – uploading images to GridFS

We are going to build a simple image uploader with PHP that will store images uploaded by the user to GridFS. Let's start:

1. Open your text editor and put the following code in a new file:

```php
<?php
require 'dbconnection.php';
$action = (isset($_POST['upload']) &&
  $_POST['upload'] === 'Upload') ? 'upload' : 'view';
switch($action) {
  case 'upload':
    //check file upload success
    if($_FILES['image']['error'] !== 0) {
      die('Error uploading file. Error code '.
        $_FILES['image']['error']);
    }
    //connect to MongoDB sevrer
    $mongo = DBConnection::instantiate();
    //get a MongoGridFS instance
    $gridFS = $mongo->database->getGridFS();
    $filename = $_FILES['image']['name'];
    $filetype = $_FILES['image']['type'];
    $tmpfilepath = $_FILES['image']['tmp_name'];
    $caption    = $_POST['caption'];
    //storing the uploaded file
    $id = $gridFS->storeFile($tmpfilepath,
    array('filename' => $filename,
      'filetype' => $filetype,
      'caption' => $caption));
    break;
    default:
  }
?>
<html xmlns="http://www.w3.org/1999/xhtml" xml:lang="en"
  lang="en">
  <head>
    <meta http-equiv="Content-Type" content="text/html;
```

```
            charset=utf-8"/>
        <link rel="stylesheet" type="text/css"
          href="styles.css"/>
        <title>Upload Files</title>
    </head>
    <body>
      <div id="contentarea">
        <div id="innercontentarea">
          <h1>Upload Image</h1>
          <?php if($action === 'upload'): ?>
            <h3>File Uploaded. Id <?php echo $id; ?>
              <a href="<?php echo $_SERVER['PHP_SELF']; ?>">
                Upload another?
              </a>
            </h3>
          <?php else: ?>
            <form
              action="<?php echo $_SERVER['PHP_SELF']; ?>"
              method="post"
              accept-charset="utf-8"
              enctype="multipart/form-data">
              <h3>Enter Caption 
                <input type="text" name="caption"/>
              <h3/>
              <p>
                <input type="file" name="image" />
              </p>
              <p>
                <input type="submit" value="Upload"
                  name="upload"/>
              </p>
            </form>
          <?php endif; ?>
        </div>
      </div>
    </body>
</html>
```

2. Save the file as `upload.php`.

3. Open the `dbconnection.php` file again and change the `DBNAME` constant to `'myfiles'`:

```
const DBNAME = 'myfiles';
```

4. Open the `upload.php` file in your browser. Choose any image from your computer for uploading, type in a caption in the **Enter Caption** box:

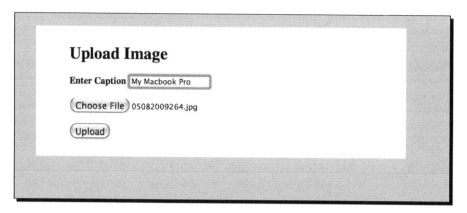

5. Click the **Upload** button. The file will be uploaded and the page will reload with the `_id` of the stored file. Click on the **Upload another?** link if you like to upload more images:

What just happened?

In the example we just tried out, we built a simple image uploader—a PHP page showing an HTML form with a file input field (and a text input field for the image caption). If the upload is successful and the file is stored in the database, the page reloads showing the `_id` for the stored file. Also, we modified the DBNAME constant in DBConnection class (in dbconnection.php script) to store uploaded files in a new database `myfiles`.

Let's walk through the code in `upload.php`. When a file is uploaded, the script opens a connection to the Mongo server and gets an instance of a `MongoGridFS` class by calling the `getGridFS()` method on the `MongoDB` object. Next, we invoked the `storeFile()` method on the `MongoGridFS` object to store the uploaded file in the database. The method takes the path of the file to be stored as its first argument. Any optional metadata that needs to be stored along with the file can be supplied as the second argument to `storeFile()`.

```
//storing the uploaded file
$id = $gridFS->storeFile($tmpfilepath,
  array('filename' => $filename,
  'filetype' => $filetype,
  'caption' => $caption));
```

The return value of the method is the `_id` of the document created in the files collection.

Alternatives to storeFile() method

You could also use the `storeUpload()` method to store the uploaded file directly. It is a bit more convenient, however, it does not allow specifying optional metadata at the time of creation. Also, you could use `storeBytes()` to store string data whereas `storeFile()` stores file data.

Looking under the hood

Let's take a look under the hood to see what is actually getting stored in `files` and `chunks`. Launch the mongo interactive shell, switch to the `myfiles` database, and query the files collection with the `_id` of the uploaded file (displayed on the `image.php` page when the upload is successful).

```
$./mongodb/bin/mongo
MongoDB shell version: 1.8.1
connecting to: test
> use myfiles
switched to db myfiles
>db.fs.files.findOne({_id:ObjectId("4e3267e95981ae1602010000")})
{
  "_id" : ObjectId("4e3267e95981ae1602010000"),
  "filename" : "05082009264.jpg",
```

```
    "filetype" : "image/jpeg",
    "caption" : "My Macbook Pro",
    "uploadDate" : ISODate("2011-07-29T07:57:29.599Z"),
    "length" : 419575,
    "chunkSize" : 262144,
    "md5" : "f9d4aed29e59b409701f3c6c75796320"
}
```

The query returns a document that shows the filename, type, and caption of the uploaded image. These are the fields that we explicitly set while storing the file. It also has the size of the file (`length`), time of upload (`uploadDate`), size of each chunk (`chunkSize`), and the MD5 hash of the file. These fields are set by MongoDB itself.

Now, let's take a look at chunks:

```
>db.fs.chunks.find({files_id:ObjectId("4e3246db5981ae0902010000")})
{ "_id" : ObjectId("4e3267e95981ae1602020000"),
"files_id" : ObjectId("4e3246db5981ae0902010000"),
"n" : 0,
"data" : BinData(2,"AAAEAP/Y/+FG0kV4aWYAAElJKgAIAAAACAAPAQIABgAAA….
```

`chunks` will have one or more documents (depending on file size) associated with a file. The `files_id` field refers to the `_id` of the document in files. `n` shows the position of the chunk in the set of chunks (if `n` is zero then it is the first chunk). And `data` obviously stores the file content.

 By default, both `chunks` and `files` reside under the namespace `fs` of a database.

Have a go hero – perform multiple file uploads in GridFS

Extend the earlier example to handle multiple file uploads. Modify the image uploader to accept up to five separate images and store them all in GridFS.

Serving files from GridFS

We have seen how we can store files in GridFS. Now it is time to learn how we can read them back from it! The next example will show us how to do that.

Time for action – serving images from GridFS

We are going to build two simple PHP pages, the first one will list all the images stored in the database in an HTML table. Clicking on any item on this list will take us to the second script that will output the image in the browser:

1. Open a new file in the text editor and add the following PHP/HTML code to it:

```php
<?php
  require 'dbconnection.php';
  $mongo = DBConnection::instantiate();
  $gridFS = $mongo->database->getGridFS();
  $objects = $gridFS->find();
?>
<html xmlns="http://www.w3.org/1999/xhtml" xml:lang="en">
  <head>
    <title>Uploaded Images</title>
    <link rel="stylesheet" type="text/css"
      href="styles.css"/>
  </head>
  <body>
    <div id="contentarea">
      <div id="innercontentarea">
        <h1>Uploaded Images</h1>
        <table class="table-list" cellspacing="0"
          cellpadding="0">
          <thead>
            <tr>
              <th width="40%">Caption</th>
              <th width="30%">Filename</th>
              <th width="*">Size</th>
            </tr>
          </thead>
          <tbody>
            <?php while($object = $objects->getNext()): ?>
              <tr>
                <td>
                  <?php echo $object->file['caption'];?>
                </td>
                <td>
                  <a href="image.php?id=
                    <?php echo $object->file['_id'];?>">
                    <?php echo $object->file['filename'];?>
                  </a>
                </td>
                <td >
                  <?php echo ceil($object->file['length'] /
                    1024).' KB';?>
                </td>
```

```
        </tr>
      <?php endwhile;?>
      </tbody>
    </table>
   </div>
  </div>
 </body>
</html>
```

2. Save the file as `list.php`.

3. Create another PHP script named `image.php` and add the following code to it:

```php
<?php
$id = $_GET['id'];
require 'dbconnection.php';
$mongo = DBConnection::instantiate();
$gridFS = $mongo->database->getGridFS();
//query the file object
$object = $gridFS->findOne(array('_id' => new MongoId($id)));
 //set content-type header, output in browser
header('Content-type: '.$object->file['filetype']);
echo $object->getBytes();
?>
```

4. Open the `list.php` file in a browser. Click on any of the links under the **Filename** column to load the image in browser:

Uploaded Images

Caption	Filename	Size
My Macbook Pro	05082009264.jpg	410 KB
Me @ water rafting!	rafting.jpg	1182 KB
Trying something new	20022010474.jpg	486 KB
Heating up the racetrack	racetrack.jpg	274 KB
Chilling at the beach	beach.jpg	60 KB

What just happened?

In step 1 of the last example, we created a script named `list.php` that queries the database to get all the file objects. The `find()` method invoked on the `MongoGridFS` object returns a `MongoGridFSCursor` object. It behaves in the same way as the `MongoCursor` object does. We iterated over the cursor to list all the files stored in the database. Each object in the cursor is a `MongoGridFSFile` object, which represents a file stored in the database. We can access various metadata fields of the file by accessing the `file` property of the `MongoGridFSFile` object:

```php
<?php while($object = $objects->getNext()): ?>
  <tr>
    <td><?php echo $object->file['caption']; ?></td>
    <td>
      <a href="image.php?id=<?php echo $object->file['_id'];?>">
        <?php echo $object->file['filename']; ?>
      </a>
    </td>
    <td >
      <?php echo ceil($object->file['length'] / 1024).' KB'; ?>
    </td>
  </tr>
<?php endwhile;?>
```

In step 2, we created another script called `image.php`. It receives the `_id` of the file through the HTTP GET parameter, and queries the database with it. The `findOne()` method returns a `MongoGridFSFile` object representing the image we are trying to open. Since this script is supposed to output an image, we set the `Content-type` header as the type of the file (image/jpeg or image/png or any other format). Next, we output the contents of the file by calling the `getBytes()` method on the `MongoGridFSFile` object. `getBytes()` returns the contents of the file as a string of bytes:

```php
header('Content-type: '.$object->file['filetype']);
echo $object->getBytes();
```

Use getBytes() with care

Be careful when you use `getBytes()`. This will load the entire content of the file into memory. If the file is too big to fit in the memory, it will lead to critical problems. As of this writing, the PHP driver for Mongo does not provide any built-in method for partially reading GridFS files.

Updating metdata of a file

It is also possible to update the metadata of a file by calling the `update()` method on a `MongoGridFS` object. The `update()` method of `MongoGridFS` works much the same way as that of the `MongoCollection` (actually, `MongoGridFS` extends the `MongoCollection` class):

```
$gridFS = $mongo->selectDB('myfiles')->getGridFS();
//change the caption of the file 'beach.jpeg'
$gridFS->update(array('filename' => 'beach.jpeg'),
  array('$set' => array('caption' =>
  'Me @ the beach')));
```

 You can also update the contents of a file by modifying the binary data stored in the associated documents in the `chunks` collection. But you have to be very careful not to corrupt the integrity of the file as a whole (for example, if you are messing with the content of a video file stored in GridFS, you might accidentally drop frames in it). You should rather upload a new version of the file instead, and store the version information as file metadata.

Deleting files

We can delete files by calling the `remove()` method on a `MongoGridFS` object, which works the same as `remove()` of `MongoCollection`:

```
$mongo     = new Mongo();
$database = $mongo->selectDB('myfiles');
$gridFS    = $database->getGridFS();
//remove all files of PNG format
$gridFS->remove(array('filetype' => 'image/png'));
```

The thing you should know about `remove()` is that it does not alert you when it fails. To verify whether the file deletion was actually successful, you can call the `lastError()` method on MongoDB object, right after calling `remove()` and see if it returns any error message:

```
$mongo     = new Mongo();
$database = $mongo->selectDB('myfiles');
$gridFS    = $database->getGridFS();
//remove all files of PNG format
$gridFS->remove(array('filetype' => 'image/png'));
$error = $database->lastError();
if(isset($error['err'])) {
  echo 'Files deleted.';
} else {
  echo 'Error deleting files '.$error['err'];
}
```

Have a go hero – create an image gallery with GridFS

Your task is to create a gallery of thumbnail size images. Whenever an image is uploaded, create a thumbnail version of it and store it along with the original image (You can use the GD library that comes built-in with PHP5 installations for image processing). Build a page that displays the thumbnails. When the user clicks on one of them, load the full-sized image in a new window.

Reading files in chunks

In the earlier example, we used the `getBytes()` method of the `MongoGridFSFile` class to read the contents of a file. We learned that there is a potential problem with this approach, `getBytes()` attempts to load the entire content of the file into memory. Reading large files in this way may affect performance negatively. But there is a way to get around this problem. As we know that in GridFS a file's contents are split into chunks, we could use the PHP driver to read and output the data of each chunk individually, thus avoiding dumping the entire content into memory. In the next example we are going to see how we can do that.

Time for action – reading images in chunks

We are going to make some changes in our earlier example. When serving an image file from GridFS to the browser, we are going to read the image in chunks, instead of loading the entire file in memory. Let's see how we can do that:

1. Create a new PHP file in your text editor and add the following lines of code to it:

```php
<?php
  $id = $_GET['id'];
  require 'dbconnection.php';
  $mongo   = DBConnection::instantiate();
  $gridFS  = $mongo->database->getGridFS();
  $object  = $gridFS->findOne(array('_id' => new MongoId($id)));
  //find the chunks for this file
  $chunks = $mongo->database->fs->chunks->find(array('files_id'
    => $object->file['_id']))
    ->sort(array('n' => 1));
  header('Content-type: '.$object->file['filetype']);
  //output the data in chunks
  foreach($chunks as $chunk){
    echo $chunk['data']->bin;
  }
```

2. Save the file as `stream.php`.

3. Open the `list.php` file. Find the following line in it:

   ```
   <a href="image.php?id=<?php echo $object->file['_id'];?>">
   ```

   Change the line to:

   ```
   <a href="stream.php?id=<?php echo $object->file['_id'];?>">
   ```

4. Open the `list.php` file in the browser. Click on the file with the largest size and watch it load in the browser:

What just happened?

We modified the `list.php` script that we created for the earlier example, to hyperlink the names shown under the **Filename** column of the HTML table to the `stream.php` file instead of the `image.php` file. `stream.php` is functionally the same as `image.php`. It outputs the image in the browser, except it outputs the image in chunks. After it loads the file metadata from `files`, it queries `chunks` with the `_id` of the file to get all the file chunks, ordered by their position (the n field):

```
$object = $gridFS->findOne(array('_id' => new MongoId($id)));
//find the chunks for this file
$chunks = $mongo->database->fs->chunks->find(array('files_id' =>
  $object->file['_id']))
  ->sort(array('n' => 1));
```

It sets the `Content-type` appropriately (as the type of the file itself) and outputs the binary data stored in each chunk individually. It reuses the same piece of memory over and over, and thus keeps the memory consumption lower than the previous implementation `image.php`.

```
header('Content-type: '.$object->file['filetype']);
//output the data in chunks
foreach($chunks as $chunk){
  echo $chunk['data']->bin;
}
```

Benchmarking the scripts

Benchmark the `stream.php` script against `image.php` to verify changes in performance. Use the `memory_get_peak_usage()` function to measure the memory consumption of the scripts and compare them with each other.

When should you not use GridFS

One of the major selling points of MongoDB is scalability. It has been designed with features that are supposed to help your application scale out. If you are developing your application to be highly scalable, and your use cases fit into one of those advantages of GridFS we discussed earlier in this chapter, you may consider it as your asset storage backend. But for a website that experiences small to medium traffic, serving files over GridFS rather than the filesystem is an overkill. As Martin Fowler rightly says, *"Premature optimization is the root of all evil."*

Also, benchmarks show that for serving small static files (JavaScript, CSS, and so on, on your website), using Apache or Nginx web server over the filesystem is faster than GridFS (Chris Heald has a very informative post on his blog available at `http://www.coffeepowered.net/2010/02/17/serving-files-out-of-gridfs/`). So you should stick to the filesystem if you only need to serve small files over HTTP.

Summary

We have covered enough about GridFS to give you a good understanding of it. We covered:

- What GridFS is, the rationale behind it
- The GridFS specification, advantages of using GridFS over a traditional filesystem
- How we can store files in GridFS using PHP, how to read them back, how to update their metadata, and how to delete them

We also discussed limitations of GridFS and situations where using the traditional filesystem is preferable. In the next chapter, we will learn about a cool feature of MongoDB, Geo-spatial indexing, and how we can use it to build location-aware web applications with it.

8
Building Location-aware Web Applications with MongoDB and PHP

Location-aware websites are one of the hottest trends in the present day web development scenario. A location-aware web application takes the user's geographic location as an input, and renders output to that user (or provides some sort of service to him) based on his location. Take Foursquare for example, a hugely popular social networking website that lets you "explore" interesting venues around your location, gives you badges when you "check in" at a venue, shows where your friends are checking in, and so on. Applications like this require databases that have special capabilities for storing, querying, and comparing geographic position parameters (latitude, longitude, and so on). MongoDB has Geospatial Indexing, which makes it efficiently perform location-based queries. In this chapter, we are going to work with geospatial indexing and learn how to use it to develop location-aware applications with PHP.

So in this chapter, we will:

- Cover a little background on geolocation
- Learn how to detect the current location of a user
- Learn how to build geospatial indexing
- Learn how to locate items near a user's location using geospatial indexing
- Learn about geospatial haystack indexing

The practical examples in this chapter are going to use a lot of JavaScript. So I suggest you brush up your JavaScript skills before continuing!

A geolocation primer

The term **geolocation** refers to the act of locating the geographic position of a person, a place, or any place of interest. The geographic position of the object is determined mainly by the latitude and longitude of the object, sometimes its height from sea level is also taken into account. In this section, we are going to learn about different techniques that location-based applications use to determine a user's location. You may skip this section if you are already familiar with them, or if you just cannot wait to get started coding!

Methods to determine location

There are several ways to locate the geographic position of a computing device. Let's briefly learn about the most effective ones among them:

- **Global Positioning System (GPS)**: Nowadays, tech savvy people carry GPS-enabled smartphones in their pockets. Devices like these act as GPS receivers; they constantly exchange information with GPS satellites orbiting the Earth and calculate their geographic position. This process is known as **trilateration**. This is perhaps the most accurate way to determine location, as of today.

- **Cellphone tracking**: Each cellphone has a Cell ID assigned to it that uniquely identifies it in a particular cellular network. In a process known as **cellular triangulation**, three base stations (cellphone towers) are used to correctly identify the latitude and longitude of the cellphone identified by the Cell ID. This method is more accurate in urban areas, where there are more cellphone towers close to each other, than in rural areas.

- **IP address**: Internet service providers are given blocks of IP addresses based on a country/city/region. When a user visits a website, the website could take a look at his IP address and consult an database that stores location data against IP addresses (it might be either an internal database or provided by a third-party service) to get the location of the user. Accuracy of this approach depends on the accuracy of the database itself. Also, if the user is behind a proxy server, the application will see the IP address of the proxy server, which could be located in a different region than the user.

- **Wi-Fi MAC address tracking**: A Wi-Fi access point has a MAC (Media Access Control) address assigned to it, which is globally unique. Some location-based services use this to identify the location of the Wi-Fi router, and therefore, the location of users on that Wi-Fi LAN. In principle, it works in the same way IP address-based geolocation does. Google has an API that gives location information (latitude, longitude, and so on) when provided with a MAC address.

If you are curious to learn more about how geolocation works, *How Stuff Works* has a comprehensive article on it available at http://electronics.howstuffworks.com/everyday-tech/location-tracking.htm.

Pop Quiz – locating a smartphone

1. Suppose you are the proud owner of a high-end, cutting-edge smartphone. Which of the following techniques could potentially be used to detect its geographic location?

   a. GPS

   b. Cell ID

   c. Its IP address (when connected to the Internet)

   d. All of the above

Detecting the location of a web page visitor

When building a location-aware web application, the first part of the problem to be solved is to get the location of the user visiting the web page. We have covered geolocation techniques in the previous section, now it is time to see them in action.

The W3C Geolocation API

We are going to use the W3C Geolocation API for locating the visitors to our web page. The W3C Geolocation API provides a high-level interface for web developers to implement geolocation features in an application. The API takes care of detecting the location using one or more methods (GPS, Cell ID, IP address). The developers do not have to worry about what is going on under the hood; they only need to focus on the geographic information returned by the API! You can read the whole specification online at http://www.w3.org/TR/geolocation-API/.

Browsers that support geolocation

The following table lists the browsers that support the W3C Geolocation API:

Browser	Version
Google Chrome	5.0+
Mozilla Firefox	3.5+
Internet Explorer	9.0+
Safari	5.0+
Opera	10.6+
iPhone	3.1+
Android	2.0+
Blackberry	6.0+

Make sure you use one of these browsers when you try the practical examples in this chapter.

Time for action – detecting location with W3C API

In this section, we are going to build a web page that detects the location of a visitor using the Geolocation API. The API will detect the latitude and longitude of the user who loads the page in his browser. We are going use that information on a map, rendered dynamically using the Google Maps API:

1. Fire up your text editor and create a new HTML file named `location.html`. Put the following code in it:

```
<!DOCTYPE html PUBLIC "-//W3C//DTD XHTML 1.0 Transitional//EN"
  "http://www.w3.org/TR/xhtml1/DTD/xhtml1-transitional.dtd">
  <html xmlns="http://www.w3.org/1999/xhtml" xml:lang="en"
  lang="en">
    <head>
      <meta http-equiv="Content-Type" content="text/html;
      charset=utf-8"/>
      <link rel="stylesheet" href="styles.css"/>
      <style type="text/css" media="screen">
        div#map {
          width:450px;
          height: 400px;
        }
      </style>
      <title>Locating your position</title>
    </head>
```

```
<body>
  <div id="contentarea">
    <div id="innercontentarea">
      <h2>Locating your position</h2>
      <div id="map"></div>
    </div>
  </div>
  <script type="text/javascript"
    src="http://maps.googleapis.com/maps/api/js?sensor=false">
  </script>
  <script type="text/javascript" src="geolocation.js">
  </script>
</body>
</html>
```

2. Create another file named `geolocation.js` and put the following JavaScript code in it:

```
var mapContainer = document.getElementById('map');
var map;
function init() {
  //Google map settings (zoom level, map type etc.)
  var mapOptions = {zoom: 16,
    disableDefaultUI: true,
    mapTypeId: google.maps.MapTypeId.ROADMAP};
  //map will be drawn inside the mapContainer
  map = new google.maps.Map(mapContainer, mapOptions);
  detectLocation();
}
function detectLocation(){
  var options = { enableHighAccuracy: true,
    maximumAge: 1000, timeout: 30000};
  //check if the browser supports geolocation
  if (window.navigator.geolocation) {
    //get current position
    window.navigator.geolocation.getCurrentPosition(
      drawLocationOnMap,
      handleGeoloacteError,
      options);
  } else {
    alert("Sorry, your browser doesn't seem to support
      geolocation :-(");
  }
}
```

```
//callback function of getCurrentPosition(), pinpoints location
//on Google map
function drawLocationOnMap(position) {
  //get latitude/longitude from Position object
  var lat = position.coords.latitude;
  var lon = position.coords.longitude;
  var msg = "You are here: Latitude "+lat+", Longitude "+lon;
  //mark current location on Google map
  var pos = new google.maps.LatLng(lat, lon);
  var infoBox = new google.maps.InfoWindow({map: map,
    position:pos,
    content: msg});
  map.setCenter(pos);
  return;
}
function handleGeoloacteError() {
  alert("Sorry, couldn't get your geolocation :-(");
}
window.onload = init;
```

3. Load the `location.html` page in your browser. When the browser asks for permission to allow the page to access your location, click **Yes/OK/Allow**:

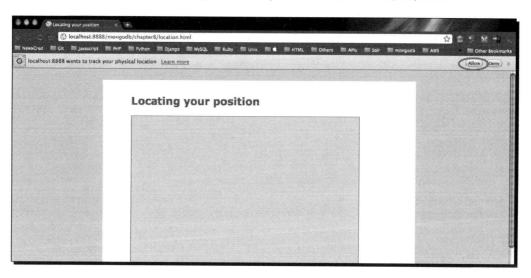

4. Once you allow the page to access your location, it renders a map that shows your current location on it, along with the geographic coordinates:

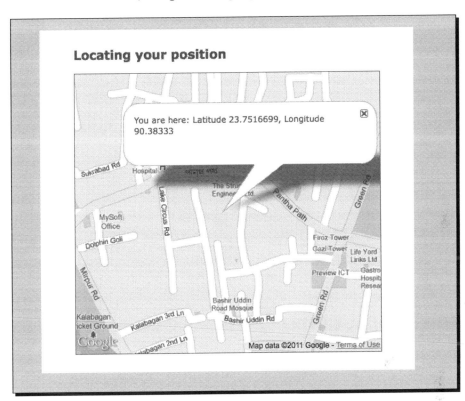

What just happened?

We built a web page and added JavaScript code that detects the latitude and longitude of the user who loads the page in his browser. The API needs the user's permission to get his geographic information. So when the page loads, it prompts the user to specify whether or not he will allow the page to get his location. If the user agrees, the JavaScript code executes and gets his geographic coordinates using the W3C Geolocation API. Then it renders a small map using the Google Maps API, and highlights the user's location on the map.

The Geolocation object

The `Geolocation` object implements the W3C Geolocation API. The JavaScript engine uses this object to obtain geographic information of the computer or phone on which the browser is running. `Geolocation` is a property of the Browser object (`window.navigator`), accessed as `window.navigator.geolocation`. In our example, we detect if the browser has geolocation capabilities by accessing this object, and notify the user if the browser fails the test:

```
//check if the browser supports geolocation
if (window.navigator.geolocation) {
  window.navigator.geolocation.getCurrentPosition(
    drawLocationOnMap,
    handleGeoloacteError,
    options);
} else {
  alert("Sorry, your browser doesn't seem to support geolocation.");
}
```

The getCurrentPosition() method

The location information is obtained invoking the `getCurrentPosition()` method on the `Geolocation` object.

```
getCurrentPostition(callbackOnSuccess, [callbackOnFailure, options])
```

The argument `callbackOnSuccess` is a reference to a callback function. It is executed when the `getCurrentPosition()` method successfully determines the geolocation. This is a mandatory argument. `callbackOnFailure` is an optional argument, a callback function for handling failure to get the geolocation. `options` represents the `PositionOptions` object, which specifies optional configuration parameters to the method. The `PositionOptions` object has the following properties:

- `enableHighAccuracy`: Tells the API to try its best to get the exact current position. It is set to `false` by default. When set to `true`, the API response tends to be slower.

- `maximumAge`: If API responses are cached, this setting specifies that the API will not use the cached responses older than `maximumAge` milliseconds.

- `timeout`: The timeout value in milliseconds to receive the API response.

In our example, we used the `drawLocationOnMap()` method as a `callbackOnSuccess` function, which draws a map and pinpoints the location on it (we will walkthrough it shortly). The `handleGeoloacteError()` method notifies the user of any error while getting the position:

```
window.navigator.geolocation.getCurrentPosition(
  drawLocationOnMap,
  handleGeoloacteError,
  options);
```

Drawing the map using the Google Maps API

The Google Maps API is a popular JavaScript API for drawing maps on a web page. This API has methods to highlight objects on the rendered map. We can access the API methods by adding the following script tag in the web page (as we did in the location.html file):

```
<script type="text/javascript"
src="http://maps.googleapis.com/maps/api/js?sensor=false"></script>
```

 If you are on a GPS-enabled device, set the sensor parameter to true, as follows:
<script type="text/javascript"
src="http://maps.googleapis.com/maps/api/js?sensor=true"></script>

When the script is loaded, we can initiate the map drawing by instantiating the google.maps.Map object. The Map object takes a DOM object as its first parameter; the map will be rendered inside this DOM. It also takes an optional JSON object that specifies configurations for the map (zoom level, map type, and so on):

```
var mapContainer = document.getElementById('map');
var mapOptions = {zoom: 16,
  disableDefaultUI: true,
  mapTypeId: google.maps.MapTypeId.ROADMAP};
map = new google.maps.Map(mapContainer, mapOptions);
```

Now, let's focus on the drawLocationOnMap() function in the geolocation.js file, which is the callback function of the getCurrentPosition() method. As we know, this method gets called when the W3C API successfully locates the position; it receives a Position object as its argument. This object holds all the geolocation data returned by the API. The Position object holds a reference to the Coordinates object (accessed by the property coords). The Coordinates object contains geographical coordinates such as latitude, longitude, altitude, and so on of the location:

```
function drawLocationOnMap(position) {
  var lat = position.coords.latitude;
  var lon = position.coords.longitude;
  var msg = "You are here: Latitude "+lat+", Longitude "+lon;
  .................................................................................
}
```

After we get the latitude and longitude values of the coordinate, we set it as the center of the map. We also display an information box with a message saying, **You are here** on the map!

```
function drawLocationOnMap(position) {
  var lat = position.coords.latitude;
  var lon = position.coords.longitude;
  var msg = "You are here: Latitude "+lat+", Longitude "+lon;
  var pos = new google.maps.LatLng(lat, lon);
  var infoBox = new google.maps.InfoWindow({map: map,
    position:pos,
    content: msg});
  map.setCenter(pos);
  return;
}
```

Get to know Google Maps API

We are going to use the Google Maps API in the upcoming examples as well. You might consider familiarizing yourself with it by reading some of its online documentation at `http://code.google.com/apis/maps/documentation/javascript/basics.html`.

Geospatial indexing

We can now turn our attention to the main topic of this chapter—geospatial indexing. A geospatial index is a special kind of index, designed specifically with location queries in mind, so you can perform queries like "Give me the closest *n* objects to my location". Geospatial indexing essentially turns your collection into a two-dimensional map. Each point of interest on that map (each document in the collection) is assigned a special value named `geohash`. **Geohashing** divides the coordinate system into hierarchical buckets of grids; the whole map gets divided into smaller quadrants. When you look for objects nearest to a point `(x,y)` on the map, MongoDB calculates the geohash of `(x,y)` and returns the points with the same geohash. I am not going to delve into much detail here on how it works, but if you are interested, I recommend you read MongoDB in Flatland (found at `http://www.snailinaturtleneck.com/blog/2011/06/08/mongo-in-flatland/`), an elaborate yet simple demonstration of how geospatial indexing works in MongoDB.

Indexes are generally applied on fields to make field lookups faster. We will cover indexing in more detail in the next chapter.

Time for action – creating geospatial indexes

Let's see how we can build the geospatial index on a MongoDB collection:

1. Launch the mongo interactive shell. Switch to a new database namespace called geolocation:

    ```
    $ ./mongodb/bin/mongo
    MongoDB shell version: 1.8.1

    connecting to: test
    > use geolocation
    switched to db geolocation
    >
    ```

2. Insert a few documents in a collection named map. Each document must contain an embedded document with two fields, latitude and longitude:

    ```
    > db.map.insert({coordinate: {latitude:23.2342987,
      longitude:90.20348}})
    > db.map.insert({coordinate: {latitude:23.3459835,
      longitude:90.92348}})
    > db.map.insert({coordinate: {latitude:23.6743521,
      longitude:90.30458}})
    ```

3. Create the geospatial index for the map collection by issuing the following command:

    ```
    >db.map.ensureIndex({coordinate: '2d'})
    ```

4. Enter the next command to check if the index was created:

    ```
    > db.system.indexes.find()
    { "name" : "_id_", "ns" : "geolocation.map", "key" : { "_id" : 1
    }, "v" : 0 }
    { "_id" : ObjectId("4e46af48ffd7d5fd0a4d1e41"), "ns" :
    "geolocation.map", "key" : {      "coordinate" : "2d" }, "name" : "
    coordinate _" }
    ```

What just happened?

We created a MongoDB collection named geocollection in a database named map. We manually inserted documents into the collection, each document contains some random latitude and longitude values in an embedded document named coordinate:

```
> db.map.findOne()
{
  "_id" : ObjectId("4e46ae9bffd7d5fd0a4d1e3e"),
  "coordinate" : {
```

```
    "latitude" : 23.2342987,
    "longitude" : 90.20348
  }
}
```

After that, we built the geospatial index on the latitude/longitude pairs by calling the `ensureIndex()` method on the collection:

db.map.ensureIndex({coordinate: "2d"})

Next, we invoked the `system.indexes.find()` method that lists the indexes in the database. The index we created should be in that list:

```
> db.system.indexes.find()
{ "name" : "_id_", "ns" : "geolocation.map", "key" : { "_id" : 1 }, "v" :
0 }
{ "_id" : ObjectId("4e46af48ffd7d5fd0a4d1e41"), "ns" : "geolocation.map",
"key" : {     "coordinate" : "2d" }, "name" : " coordinate _" }
```

Geospatial indexing – Important things to know

There are a few of things you must know about geospatial indexing:

- There can be only one geospatial index for a MongoDB collection. You cannot have more than one geospatial index for a collection.

- The index must be created for an embedded document or an array field of the document. If you build the index for an array field, the first two elements of the array will be considered as the (x,y) coordinate:

  ```
  >db.map.insert({coordinate: [23.3459835, 90.92348]})
  >db.map.ensureIndex({coordinate: "2d"})
  ```

- Ordering is important when you are storing coordinates. If you store them in the order (y,x) rather than (x,y), you will have to query the collection with (y,x).

Use arrays to store coordinates

When storing coordinates in a geospatially indexed field, arrays are preferable to embedded objects. This is because an array preserves the order of items in it. No matter what programming language you are using to interact with MongoDB, this comes in very handy when you do queries.

Performing location queries

We learned how to build geospatial indexes in MongoDB. Now it is time to learn how we can perform location queries on the indexed field. We will use some of the JavaScript code that we wrote in the earlier section to get the current location of the user. After we get the location coordinates of the user, we will query MongoDB with them to get points of interest near that location.

Time for action – finding restaurants near your location

In this example, we will build a web page that shows restaurants near the user's location. Similar to the earlier example, we will get the current location with the W3C Geolocation API, and mark it on a map rendered by the Google Maps API. Once the page is loaded and the location is marked on the map, we will perform an AJAX request to query MongoDB with the coordinates and get the location of the nearby restaurants (we will insert some sample data into the collection before hand):

1. Launch the mongo shell and switch to the `geolocation` database:

```
$./mongodb/bin/mongo
MongoDB shell version: 1.8.1
connecting to: test
> use geolocation
switched to db geolocation
```

2. Manually insert some sample data into a collection named `restaurants` (the location coordinates of the fictional restaurants should be close to your location):

```
> db.restaurants.insert({name:"McDowells", serves: "Fast Food",
"location": [23.755235, 90.375739]})
> db.restaurants.insert({name:" Bucksters Coffee", serves: "Fast
Food", "location": [23.755339, 90.375408]})
> db.restaurants.insert({name:"Dinkin Donuts", serves: "Fast
Food", "location": [23.752538, 90.382792]})
```

Use the Foursquare API for sample data

You can use the REST API of Foursquare (which also uses MongoDB by the way!) to get geographic coordinates of eateries in your area for using as sample data for this example. Use the Explore Venues method of the API to get the list of locations near you: `https://developer.foursquare.com/docs/venues/explore.html`.

3. Build the geospatial index with the following command:

```
> db.restaurants.ensureIndex({location:"2d"})
```

4. Create an HTML file named `restaurants.html` and add the following code to it:

```html
<html xmlns="http://www.w3.org/1999/xhtml" xml:lang="en"
  lang="en">
  <head>
    <meta http-equiv="Content-Type" content="text/html;
      charset=utf-8"/>
    <link rel="stylesheet" href="styles.css"/>
    <style type="text/css" media="screen">
      div#map {
        width:450px;
        height: 400px;
      }
    </style>
    <title>Restaurants near me</title>
  </head>
  <body>
    <div id="contentarea">
      <div id="innercontentarea">
        <h2>Restaurants near me</h2>
        <div id="map"></div>
        <br/>
      </div>
    </div>
    <script type="text/javascript"
      src="http://maps.googleapis.com/maps/api/js?sensor=false">
    </script>
    <script type="text/javascript"
      src="http://ajax.googleapis.com/
      ajax/libs/jquery/1.6.2/jquery.min.js">
    </script>
    <script type="text/javascript" src="restaurants.js">
    </script>
  </body>
</html>
```

5. Create a JavaScript file called `restaurants.js` and put the following code in it:

```javascript
var mapContainer = document.getElementById('map');
var map;
function init() {
  //Google map settings (map type, zoom level etc.)
  var mapOptions = {zoom: 14,
```

```
        disableDefaultUI: true,
        mapTypeId: google.maps.MapTypeId.ROADMAP};
     //draw the map insidet the mapContainer DOM
     map = new google.maps.Map(mapContainer, mapOptions);
     detectLocation();
}
function detectLocation(){
     var options = { enableHighAccuracy: true, maximumAge: 1000,
        timeout: 30000};
     //check if the browser supports geolocation
     if (window.navigator.geolocation) {
        //get the current position of user
        window.navigator.geolocation.getCurrentPosition(
           markMyLocation,
           handleGeoloacteError,
           options);
     } else {
        alert("Sorry, your browser doesn't seem to support
           geolocation");
     }
}
function markMyLocation(position) {
     //latitude, longitude of current location
     var lat = position.coords.latitude;
     var lon = position.coords.longitude;
     var msg = "You are here";
     var pos = new google.maps.LatLng(lat, lon);
     map.setCenter(pos);
     var infoBox = new google.maps.InfoWindow({map: map,
        position:pos,
        content: msg});
     //draw a Google Map Marker on current location
     var myMarker = new google.maps.Marker({map: map,
        position: pos});
     getNearByRestaurants(lat, lon);
     return;
}
function handleGeoloacteError() {
     alert("Sorry, couldn't get your geolocation :-(");
}
function getNearByRestaurants(lat, lon) {
     //Send an Ajax request to get nearby restaurants
```

```
      $.ajax({
        url      : 'query.php?lat='+lat+'&lon='+lon
        ,dataType : 'json'
        ,success  : ajaxSuccess
      });
    }
    function ajaxSuccess(data){
      //callback function for Ajax, marks each nearbu restaurant
      //on Google map
      data.forEach(function(restaurant){
        var pos = new google.maps.LatLng(restaurant.latitude,
          restaurant.longitude);
        var marker = new google.maps.Marker({map: map,
          position: pos});
      });
    }
    window.onload = init;
```

6. Create a PHP file named `query.php` and put the following code in it:

```php
<?php
    $lat = (float)$_GET['lat'];
    $lon = (float)$_GET['lon'];
    $mongo = new Mongo();
    $collection = $mongo->selectDB('geolocation')
      ->selectCollection('restaurants');
    //query the collection with given latitude and longitude
    $query = array('location' => array('$near' => array($lat,
      $lon)));
    $cursor = $collection->find($query);
    $response = array();
    while($doc = $cursor->getNext()) {
      $obj = array(
        'name' => $doc['name'],
        'serves'=> $doc['serves'],
        'latitude' => $doc['location'][0],
        'longitude' => $doc['location'][1]
      );
      array_push($response, $obj);
    }
    //convert the array in JSON and send back to client
    echo json_encode($response);
```

7. Run `restaurants.html` in your browser, once your location is identified the nearby restaurants in the database will be marked on the map:

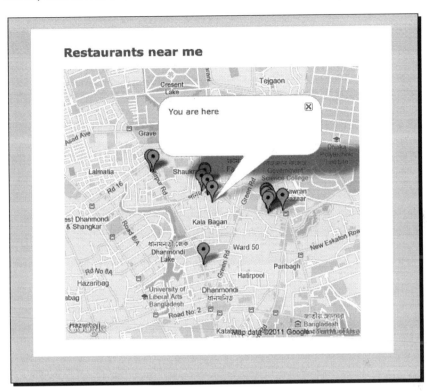

What just happened?

In steps 1 and 2, we inserted some sample data (names and geographic coordinates of some fictional eateries) into a collection named `restaurants`. In step 3, we built the geospatial index on the collection:

```
> db.restaurants.ensureIndex({location:"2d"})
```

After that, we wrote a couple of HTML and JavaScript files that render a Google map centered to your current location. The code is almost the same as our earlier example; we just added some AJAX functionality to it. The callback method of the `Geolocation.getCurrentPosition()` method marks your current location on the map and then calls the `getNearByRestaurants()` method with the latitude/longitude of your location.

The `getNearByRestaurants()` method uses the ubiquitous JQuery library to perform an AJAX request. It sends the latitude and longitude as HTTP parameters and receives a JSON response, containing information about any nearby restaurants.

```
function getNearByRestaurants(lat, lon) {
    $.ajax({
       url       : 'query.php?lat='+lat+'&lon='+lon
       ,dataType : 'json'
       ,success  : ajaxSuccess
    });
}
```

The callback method of the AJAX call, marks the location of the restaurants on the rendered Google map:

```
function ajaxSuccess(data){
    data.forEach(function(restaurant){
       var pos = new google.maps.LatLng(restaurant.latitude,
          restaurant.longitude);
       var marker = new google.maps.Marker({map: map,
          position: pos});
    });
}
```

Now, let's take a look at the code in the `query.php` script that performs the location lookup in MongoDB. The code is pretty much straightforward except when querying the restaurants collection with the coordinates. We used the `$near` operator so that it looks for nearby points instead of an exact match:

```
$query = array('location' => array('$near' => array($lat, $lon)));
$cursor = $collection->find($query);
```

The coordinates returned by the query are automatically sorted by their distance from the query coordinate. Once we get the data from the database, we encode them in JSON format and send the data to the script making the AJAX call.

The geoNear() command

An alternative to using the `find()` command with the `$near` operator for geolocation queries, is using the `geoNear()` command. It has the added benefit of returning the distance of each item in the result set from the specified point. It comes in handy when you are debugging:

```
> db.runCommand({geoNear: 'restaurants', near:
[23.75174102,90.383315705], num: 2})
{
   "ns" : "geolocation.restaurants",
```

```
"near" : "110100100000000010111000000110111111001010111110111",
"results" : [
  {
    "dis" : 0.0009566879712264728,
    "obj" : {
      "_id" : ObjectId("4e4921045981ae03020a0000"),
      "name" : "Dinkin Donuts",
      "serves" : "Donuts",
      "location" : [
        23.752538,
        90.382792
      ]
    }
  },
  {
    "dis" : 0.001794195350846737,
    "obj" : {
      "_id" : ObjectId("4e4921045981ae03020b0000"),
      "name" : "The Kebab Palace",
      "serves" : "Mid-eastern Cuisine",
      "location" : [
        23.753012,
        90.382051
      ]
    }
  }
],
"stats" : {
  "time" : 0,
  "btreelocs" : 15,
  "nscanned" : 15,
  "objectsLoaded" : 7,
  "avgDistance" : 0.001375441661036605,
  "maxDistance" : 0.001794195350846737
},
"ok" : 1
}
```

The `num` parameter in the query limits the number of items in the result set (works like the `limit()`). The `dis` field in each result of the set shows the distance of the point from the query coordinate. The `stats` field contains some helpful data such as average distance, maximum distance, and so on. The equivalent command in PHP will be as follows:

```
$db->command(array('geoNear' => 'restaurants',
    'near' => array(23.75174102,90.383315705),
    'num' => 2));
```

Bounded queries

Suppose you have drawn an imaginary circle with your current position as the centre. Now you want all restaurants within that circle. Is that possible to do in MongoDB? The answer is yes. The following query returns all restaurants in a circle of radius 10 around the point (23.42342, 90.23423):

```
$center = array(23.42342,90.23423);
$radius = 10;
$collection->find(array('location' => array('$within' =>
                                    array('$center' =>
                                        array($center,
                                        $radius)
                                    )
                                )
                        )
                );
```

Notice that we used the `$within` operator instead of the `$near` operator, and passed the coordinate and radius as the `$center` parameter. This is an example of a bounded query; we are looking for items with in a geometrical shape on the map. The shape does not have to be a circle; it could also be a box or a polygon. Visit the related page in the MongoDB online documentation to learn more about it `http://www.mongodb.org/display/DOCS/Geospatial+Indexing#GeospatialIndexing-BoundsQueries`.

Geospatial haystack indexing

Sometimes querying on the geographic coordinates is not enough, you may need to specify some additional criteria. For example, we may need to search for nearby restaurants that serve pizza. This is what geospatial haystack indexing is good for. This is a bucket-based geospatial index, tuned for small-region latitude/longitude queries where some extra criteria are also specified. We will learn how to build and use this index through our next practical example.

Time for action – finding nearby restaurants that serve burgers

We are going to refine our earlier example to look for nearby eateries that serve burgers and display them on the map. Let's see how we can do that:

1. In the `mongo` shell, enter the following commands to build a geospatial haystack index for the location and `serves` field of the `restaurants` collection:

```
> use geolocation
switched to db geolocation
> db.restaurants.ensureIndex({location:"geoHaystack",
serves:1},{bucketSize : 1})
```

2. Create a file named `haystack.html` and put the following code in it:

```html
<html xmlns="http://www.w3.org/1999/xhtml" xml:lang="en"
  lang="en">
  <head>
    <meta http-equiv="Content-Type" content="text/html;
      charset=utf-8"/>
    <link rel="stylesheet" href="styles.css"/>
    <style type="text/css" media="screen">
      div#map {
        width:450px;
        height: 400px;
      }
    </style>
    <title>Burger place near me</title>
  </head>
  <body>
    <div id="contentarea">
      <div id="innercontentarea">
        <h2>Burger place near me</h2>
        <div id="map"></div>
        <br/>
      </div>
    </div>
    <script type="text/javascript"
      src="http://maps.googleapis.com/maps/api/js?sensor=false">
    </script>
    <script type="text/javascript"
      src="http://ajax.googleapis.com/ajax/libs/jquery/
      1.6.2/jquery.min.js">
    </script>
    <script type="text/javascript" src="haystack.js"></script>
  </body>
</html>
```

3. Create a JavaScript file named `haystack.js` with the following code:

```javascript
var mapContainer = document.getElementById('map');
var map;
function init() {
  var mapOptions = {zoom: 15,
    disableDefaultUI: true,
    mapTypeId: google.maps.MapTypeId.ROADMAP};
  map = new google.maps.Map(mapContainer, mapOptions);
  detectLocation();
}
function detectLocation(){
  var options = { enableHighAccuracy: true, maximumAge: 1000,
    timeout: 30000};
  //check if the browser supports geolocation
  if (window.navigator.geolocation) {
    window.navigator.geolocation.getCurrentPosition(
      markMyLocation,
      handleGeoloacteError,
      options);
  } else {
    alert("Sorry, your browser doesn't seem to support
      geolocation");
  }
}
function markMyLocation(position) {
  var lat = position.coords.latitude;
  var lon = position.coords.longitude;
  var msg = "You are here";
  var pos = new google.maps.LatLng(lat, lon);
  map.setCenter(pos);
  var infoBox = new google.maps.InfoWindow({map: map,
    position:pos,
    content: msg});
  var myMarker = new google.maps.Marker({map: map,
    position: pos});
  getNearByRestaurants(lat, lon);
  return;
}

function handleGeoloacteError() {
  alert("Sorry, couldn't get your geolocation :-(");
}
function getNearByRestaurants(lat, lon) {
  $.ajax({
    url     : 'haystack.php?lat='+lat+'&lon='+lon
    ,dataType : 'json'
```

```
        ,success   : ajaxSuccess
    });
}
function ajaxSuccess(data){
    data.forEach(function(restaurant){
        var pos = new google.maps.LatLng(restaurant.latitude,
            restaurant.longitude);
        var marker = new google.maps.Marker({map: map,
            position: pos });
        var infoBox = new google.maps.InfoWindow({map: map,
            position: pos,
            content: restaurant.name});
    });
}
window.onload = init;
```

4. Create a PHP script named `haystack.php` and add the following code in it:

```php
<?php
    $lat = (float)$_GET['lat'];
    $lon = (float)$_GET['lon'];
    $mongo = new Mongo();
    $db = $mongo->selectDB('geolocation');
    //perform a search on the haystack index with the lat/long and
    //where serves == Burger
    $command = array('geoSearch' => 'restaurants',
        'near' => array($lat, $lon),
        'search' => array('serves' => 'Burger'),
        'maxDistance' => 3);
    $response = $db->command($command);
    $jsonResponse = array();
    foreach($response['results'] as $result) {
        $obj = array(
            'name' => $result['name'],
            'serves'=> $result['serves'],
            'latitude' => $result['location'][0],
            'longitude' => $result['location'][1]
        );
    array_push($jsonResponse, $obj);
}
echo json_encode($jsonResponse);
```

5. Open the `haystack.html` file in your browser. If there are any restaurants that serve burgers they will be marked on the map, as shown in the following screenshot:

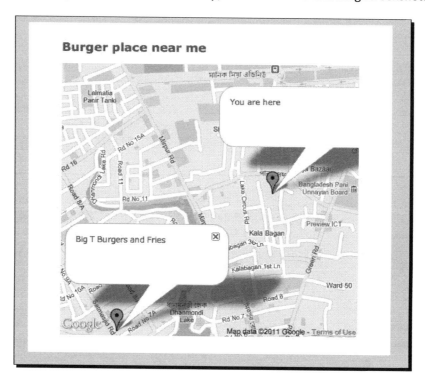

What just happened?

In step 1, we built the geospatial haystack index on the `location` and `serves` fields of the `restaurants` collection by issuing the following command in the mongo shell:

```
> db.restaurants.ensureIndex({location:"geoHaystack", serves: 1},
{bucketSize : 1})
```

The index of the location field is of type `geoHaystack` (as opposed to `2d` in a regular geo index). We also passed `{serves: 1}` to the `ensureIndex()` command to specify that we are going to search on the `serves` field of the collection. The `bucketSize` parameter is a mandatory one; it determines the granularity of the bucket index. A value of `1` for bucket size means that coordinates within 1 degree of latitude or longitude will be stored in the same bucket.

The HTML and JavaScript code for this example are almost the same. In the JavaScript code, we changed the AJAX URL in the `getNearByRestaurants()` method to make requests to the `haystack.php` script instead of the `query.php` script. Also, we changed the `ajaxSuccess` callback to add the information window showing the names of the burger places:

```
function ajaxSuccess(data){
  data.forEach(function(restaurant){
    var pos = new google.maps.LatLng(restaurant.latitude,
      restaurant.longitude);
    var marker = new google.maps.Marker({map: map,
      position: pos });
    var infoBox = new google.maps.InfoWindow({map: map,
      position: pos,
      content: restaurant.name});
  });
}
```

In the `haystack.php` file, we queried the database with the following command:

```
$command = array('geoSearch' => 'restaurants',
  'near' => array($lat, $lon),
  'search' => array('serves' => 'Burger'),
  'maxDistance' => 1);
$response = $db->command($command);
```

The `geoSearch` parameter is a query on the haystack index of the `restaurants` collection. The `near` and `search` operators represent the query coordinate and the restaurant type respectively. Setting the `maxDistance` parameter (also a mandatory one) to 3 means to get all burger places in the area with a given maximum area of 3 degrees of latitude and longitude.

Summary

Let's see what we have covered in this chapter:

- We learned about geolocation and ways to get the geographic coordinates of a computing device
- We learned how to use the W3C Geolocation API to get the latitude and longitude of a user visiting a website
- We learned about MongoDB geospatial indexing, how it works, and how can we build it for a collection
- We learned how to get nearby objects of interest on the map by querying a geospatially-indexed collection
- We learned about geospatial haystack indexing, and how to use it to perform location queries that require querying on additional criteria of objects

In the next chapter, we are going to learn how to improve query performance, security, and the data durability of MongoDB.

9
Improving Security and Performance

Up until now, we have covered MongoDB from an application developer's point of view. But when we are ready to deploy the application on the production server, we have to pay attention to a few things other than ensuring that the application works the way we want it to. For instance, we want the queries to be fast enough so that it does not slow the website down. We have to make sure the database is safe and secure as we do not want some malicious user getting control of the database. In this chapter, we are going to touch all of these topics. So this is going to be a little more theoretical than other chapters.

So, in this chapter we will learn:

- How to improve query performance using indexes
- How to use built-in tools for profiling and optimizing queries
- How to add user authentication and improve the security of a MongoDB server
- How to improve durability of data in MongoDB

Enhancing query performance using indexes

If you have worked with a relational database such as MySQL before, indexes should not be new to you. In MongoDB, an index is a special data structure (A B-Tree in computer science terms) that holds information about the values of specific fields of the documents in a collection. When we query the collection on these fields, MongoDB looks into this data structure to quickly sort through and order the documents.

We covered geospatial indexes in the previous chapter. The geospatial index is a special kind of an index (implemented by encoding geohash values on top of B-Tree structures) designed for location-based queries. In this chapter, we will focus on general purpose indexes.

To understand how indexing benefits query performance, consider a collection of movies:

```
> db.movies.find()
{ "_id" : ObjectId("4db439153ec7b6fd1c9093ec"), "name" : "Source Code",
  "genre" : "sci-fi", "year" : 2011 }
{ "_id" : ObjectId("4db439df3ec7b6fd1c9093ed"), "name" : "The Dark
  Knight", "genre" : "action", "year" : 2008 }
{ "_id" : ObjectId("4db439f33ec7b6fd1c9093ee"), "name" : "Megamind",
  "genre" : "animation", "year" : 2010 }
{ "_id" : ObjectId("4db439f33ec7b6fd1c9093ef"), "name" : "Paranormal
  Activity", "genre" : "horror", "year" : 2009 }
{ "_id" : ObjectId("4db439f43ec7b6fd1c9093f0"), "name" : "Hangover 2",
  "genre" : "comedy", "year" : 2011 }
```

Now, let's assume that we need to find all the science fiction movies. We can do that simply by querying on the genre field.

```
> db.movies.find({genre: "sci-fi"})
{ "_id" : ObjectId("4db439153ec7b6fd1c9093ec"), "name" : "Source Code",
  "genre" : "sci-fi", "year" : 2011 }
```

When we issued that command, MongoDB looked through every document in the collection and checked the value of the genre field. If the collection had a larger number of documents, it would take longer for the query to complete! This is where indexing helps. If the collection has an index on the genre field, MongoDB will check the index first instead of the collection, and randomly access the documents that matched the criteria.

Time for action – creating an index on a MongoDB collection

Let's see how we can build an index on a field of a MongoDB collection using the mongo interactive shell.

1. Launch the mongo interactive shell and switch to a database named testdb:

```
$ ./mongodb/bin/mongo
MongoDB shell version: 1.8.1
connecting to: test
> use testdb
switched to db testdb
>
```

2. Insert information about some of your favorite movies in a collection named `movies`:

```
> db.movies.insert({name: "The Matrix", genre:"sci-fi", year:
1998})
> db.movies.insert({name: "Lord of the Rings", genre:"fantasy",
  year: 2002})
> db.movies.insert({name: "Saving Private Ryan", genre: "war",
  year: 1997})
> db.movies.insert({name: "Goodwill Hunting", genre: "drama",
  year: 1995})
> db.movies.insert({name: "The Dark Knight", genre: "action",
  year: 2008})
> db.movies.insert({name: "Inception", genre: "sci-fi", year:
2010})
```

3. Enter the following command to create an index on the `genre` field:

```
> db.movies.ensureIndex({genre:1})
```

4. Use the next command to list all the indexes in the `movies` collection:

```
> db.movies.getIndexes()
[
  {
    "name" : "_id_",
    "ns" : "testdb.movies",
    "key" : {
      "_id" : 1
    },
    "v" : 0
  },
  {
    "_id" : ObjectId("4e5772551f4be29af4a55ae9"),
    "ns" : "testdb.movies",
    "key" : {
      "genre" : 1
    },
    "name" : "genre_1",
    "v" : 0
  }
]
>
```

What just happened?

The example is quite simple. We entered some sample data into a collection and built an index on its genre field.

```
> db.movies.ensureIndex({genre:1})
```

The ensureIndex() method, invoked on the movies collection, creates an index, on the genre field (as specified by the {genre:1} JSON argument to the method).

We can see what indexes are in the collection by calling the getIndexes() method. When we did that for the movies collection, we saw the index on the genre field in the output list.

```
> db.movies.getIndexes()
[
{
  "name" : "_id_",
  "ns" : "testdb.movies",
  "key" : {
    "_id" : 1
  },
  "v" : 0
},
{
  "_id" : ObjectId("4e5772551f4be29af4a55ae9"),
  "ns" : "testdb.movies",
  "key" : {
    "genre" : 1
  },
  "name" : "genre_1",
  "v" : 0
}
]
```

The second document in the array ,returned by getIndexes(), shows information on the index we just created. The key field of this document specifies the field of the collection that we created the index on. The name field shows the name of the index, which is genre_1 in this case. The index is given this name by default, but we could also explicitly specify it as an optional argument to ensureIndex().

```
> db.movies.ensureIndex({genre:1},{name: "genre_index"})
```

The last command will create an index on the `genre` field and name it `genre_index`.

Finally, the `_id`, `ns`, and `v` fields specify the ObjectId, namespace, and version of the index respectively.

 To get information about indexes created for all the collections in a database, use the `db.system.indexes.find()` command.

The _id index

If you look at the output of `getIndexes()`, you will notice there is an index on the `_id` field, even though we did not create this index explicitly.

```
> db.movies.getIndexes()
[
  {
    "name" : "_id_",
    "ns" : "testdb.movies",
    "key" : {
      "_id" : 1
    },
    "v" : 0
  },
```

The `_id` index gets created automatically, every time we create a collection, except for capped collections. The values of `_id` fields are unique for each document and invariant. Lookups using the `_id` field always tend to be fast.

Unique indexes

Unique indexes work like the UNIQUE KEY in MySQL. It ensures that no two documents in a collection will have the same value for the indexed field. The following command creates a unique index on the `name` field of the `movies` collection:

```
> db.movies.ensureIndex({name:1}, {unique:1})
```

If we try to insert two documents with the same value for the uniquely indexed field, we will get an error. Also, if we insert a document that is missing the value for the uniquely indexed field, MongoDB will insert a `null` value for that value. Thus, we will not be able have two documents in the collection missing the `unique` field.

```
//this document has a null value for the name field
>db.movies.insert({genre:'romance', year:1997})
//this will result in an error
>db.movies.insert({genre:'romance', year:1997})
```

If the field in question has non-unique values across the collection, we will not be able to create a unique index for it. To get around this, we can add the `dropDups` option. For example, the next command will create a unique index on the `name` field. If there are multiple documents with the same value for name, only the first such document will be indexed and the rest of them will be dropped. Obviously, we need to be mindful about the possible data loss when applying such an operation.

```
> db.movies.ensureIndex({name:1}, {unique:1, dropDups: true})
```

Compound keys indexes

In MongoDB, you can create an index on multiple fields of a document. This is known as a **compound keys index**. The next command creates a compound index on genre and year fields of movies:

```
> db.movies.ensureIndex({genre: 1, year: -1})
```

The numbers associated with key names (`1` and `-1`) in the command specify the direction of the index. `1` specifies direction in the ascending order, while `-1` in the descending order. Direction is very important in compound indexes when you need to perform sorting and range queries. For example, the business logic may require showing recently released movies appear first in the UI, and the movies should be alphabetically ordered by their genres. So, it makes sense to create a compound index on the `year` field in descending order, and on the `genre` field in ascending order. For single-key indexes or random access retrievals, ordering does not matter much (unless the queries involve reversing the result set order).

Furthermore, when you have a compound index on several fields, you can use it to query on a subset of fields. For example, suppose there is a compound index on fields `x`, `y`, and `z` of the documents in a collection. This index can be used to query on:

- `x`
- `x, y`
- `x, y,` and `z`

So, if you have a compound index on `x`, `y`, and `z`, you don't need a single key index on `x` (or a compound keys index on `x, y`). However, if we do a query on `y, z` or `y` only, the compound index may not be used unless we explicitly hint the query planner to do so using the `hint()` command (which we will cover later in this chapter).

Indexing embedded document fields

Indexes can be applied on any type of fields, including an embedded document. For example, let's say we have an additional meta field in our `movies` collection, storing the duration of the movie and the name of the studio:

```
> db.movies.insert({name: "Thor", genre: "action", year: 2011, meta:
{duration_minutes: 115, studio: "Paramount"}})
```

We can create an index on the meta field as follows:

```
> db.movies.ensureIndex({meta: 1})
```

We could do equality or range queries on the fields of the embedded document:

```
> db.movies.find({meta: {duration_minutes: 115, studio: "Paramount"}})
{ "_id" : ObjectId("4e58bf4c3eadcfa57f69447b"), "name" : "Thor", "genre"
 : "action", "year" : 2011, "meta" : { "duration_minutes" : 115,
 "studio" : "Paramount" } }

> db.movies.find({meta: {$gte :{duration_minutes: 115}}})
{ "_id" : ObjectId("4e58bf4c3eadcfa57f69447b"), "name" : "Thor", "genre"
 : "action", "year" : 2011, "meta" : { "duration_minutes" : 115,
 "studio" : "Paramount" } }
```

Alternatively, we could use Dot notation to reach into the embedded documents and create compound key indexes on their fields.

```
> db.movies.ensureIndex({"meta.duration_minutes": 1, "meta.studio": 1})
> db.movies.find({"meta.duration_minutes": 115})
```

There is an important difference between creating an index on a nested document and creating an index on a specific field of the nested document. In the first one, we have to specify the query parameters in the same order as they appear in the embedded document.

```
//this query will return an object
> db.movies.find({meta: {duration_minutes: 115, studio: "Paramount"}})
//but this query will not
> db.movies.find({meta: {studio: "Paramount", duration_minutes: 115}})
```

This is not the case when you use the dot notation; you can specify the query parameter in any order:

```
> db.movies.find({"meta.studio": "Paramount", "meta.duration_minutes":
115})
```

Indexing array fields

Indexes can also be built on array fields. For example, suppose the documents in the `movies` collection have an array field named `tags`:

```
> db.movies.insert({name: "Iron Man 2", genre: "action", year: 2010,
   tags: ['superhero', 'marvel', 'comics', 'scifi']})
```

If we build an index on this array field, MongoDB will index each element of the array:

```
> db.movies.ensureIndex({tags: 1})
> db.movies.find({tags: 'superhero'})
```

Deleting indexes

The index on a field of a collection can be deleted using the `dropIndex()` method.

```
> db.movies.dropIndex({tags:1})
{ "nIndexesWas" : 7, "ok" : 1 }
```

The last command drops the index on the `tags` field of the `movies` collection. If we need to delete all the indexes for the collection, we could use the `dropIndexes()` command instead:

```
> db.movies.dropIndexes()
{
  "nIndexesWas" : 6,
  "msg" : "non-_id indexes dropped for collection",
  "ok" : 1
}
```

The maximum allowed size for a key to be indexed is around 800 bytes. Any document having a key greater than this size will be stored, but the key will not be indexed.

When indexing cannot be used

Indexing will not work in any of the following situations:

- Queries involving negation operators, such as `$ne`, `$not`, and so on
- Queries using arithmetic operations, such as `$mod`
- Queries involving most regular expressions.
- JavaScript expressions used in a `$where` statement
- JavaScript code in MapReduce jobs; the query engine is not able to see through the mapping functions

Indexing guidelines

Indexes definitely help boost query performance, but that does not mean we can keep creating indexes and not worry about it ever. An indexing operation has its own cost, so we should give it some thought before building an index for a large dataset. Also, we should be smart about choosing the keys so that we can reap the benefits of indexing. Let's take a look at some basic guidelines on indexing.

Choose the keys wisely

We should try to figure out what keys are going to be used in most queries, and build indexes for them. MongoDB uses only one index per query. So having a combined key index is more effective than having multiple single key indexes. The direction of the indexes should match the sorting behavior of your queries. For instance, if the documents have a `created_at` field, and we need the latest created objects to appear at the start of the result set, the index for `created_at` should be in descending order.

Keep an eye on the index size

MongoDB tries to fit the indexes in RAM. If the index gets too big, part of it will get swapped out to the disk. This will cause the queries to get slower, and this is why we should keep an eye on the size of the index. The following command gives us the size of the index in bytes:

```
>db.movies.totalIndexSize()
65637
```

If the size gets too big to fit in RAM, we should try to find out if there are indexes not being used as much as the others, and drop them.

 Recently, people are turning to **Solid State Drives** (**SSD**) instead of magnetic **Hard Disk Drives** (HDD) for use as a secondary memory. SSDs are blazingly fast compared to HDDs and give significant performance boost when used in database server machines. However, their reliability is still an issue. Have a solid back-up and restore plan if you use them.

Avoid using low-selectivity single key indexes

When creating an index, we should choose a field that has high-selectivity, that is, a field that has more distinct values for the documents in a collection compared to other fields. Say for example, our `movies` collection has a Boolean field `in_theater` that could either be `true` or `false`. This is a low-selectivity key, so creating an index on it is not going to be of much help, rather it will be taking up space. Such a low-selectivity single key is to be avoided, and should be made part of a compound index instead (depending on the query).

Be aware of indexing costs

Indexing incurs extra overhead on `insert`/`update`/`delete` operations. Every time we create, update, or delete a document in the collection, the index needs to be updated accordingly. This is why we should think about the read-write ratio of the collection before building indexes on it. A read-heavy collection definitely benefits from having indexes. But if it is write-heavy, we should carefully weigh the indexing overhead during writes with whatever we hope to gain from adding the index.

On a live database, run indexing in the background

Building indexes for a large dataset takes time. Also, the database gets locked down during the creation of the index and no read or writes are allowed to happen. If your database is live on a production website, creating indexes will block other operations. To get around this, indexes should be built in the background.

```
> db.movies.ensureIndex({genre: 1}, {background: true})
```

In this mode, other operations on the data will not be blocked while the index is being built. The only catch is that the index takes a longer time to be created than in the usual foreground mode.

Pop quiz – the indexing MCQ test

1. What data structure is used for storing indexes in MongoDB?

    a. Stack

    b. Priority Queue

    c. B-tree

    d. Heap

2. What is the maximum allowed size for a key to be indexed?

    a. 1 MB

    b. 1 KB

    c. 800 Bytes

    d. None of the above

3. Which of the following use cases is not suitable for having indexes on a collection?

    a. Write heavy operations

    b. Map/Reduce jobs

    c. Regular expression queries

    d. All of the above

Have a go hero – implement search in the blogging application

Remember the simple blogging application that we built in the earlier chapters? We need to implement a search feature for this application. Users will type in keywords and hit a search button, and the application will present a list of relevant articles. How would you go about implementing this? What fields should you have the indexes on? Brainstorm about it.

Optimizing queries

In this section, we are going to look at some tools provided by MongoDB for analyzing individual queries, and learn how to use their output for optimization.

Explaining queries using explain()

The `explain()` method is used to explain a query, giving us useful information about how the query was performed, which we could use to fine-tune the query itself. It is invoked on a cursor, and it returns a document holding pieces of data about the query.

```
> db.movies.find({name: 'Inception'}).explain()
{
  "cursor" : "BtreeCursor genre_1",
  "nscanned" : 3,
  "nscannedObjects" : 3,
  "n" : 3,
  "millis" : 0,
  "nYields" : 0,
  "nChunkSkips" : 0,
  "isMultiKey" : false,
  "indexOnly" : false,
  "indexBounds" : {
    "genre" : [
      [
        "action",
        "action"
      ]
    ]
  }
}
>
```

Let's take a look at some of the important information returned by `explain()`:

- `cursor`: The value for this field could either be a `BasicCursor` or a `BtreeCursor`. If it is the second, it means the query has used an index. Since the `genre` field was indexed, the value is obviously `BtreeCursor` in this case.

- `nscanned`: It returns the number of items scanned through the collection by the query.

- `n`: It returns the number of documents returned by the query.

- `millis`: It returns the number of milliseconds it took for the database to execute the query.

Optimization rules

We can employ the following rules for optimizing queries using the output of `explain()`:

- The number of items scanned (`nscanned`) should be close to the number of documents returned (`n`). If the query is scanning a large number of documents and returning a small number of them, we should fine-tune the indexing on the fields.

- The number of milliseconds to perform the query (`millis`) should be very small.

Have a go hero – compare outputs of explain() for indexed and non-indexed queries

Run two separate queries, one on an indexed field and the other on a non-indexed field. Compare the outputs of `explain()` for both queries, note the differences in `nscanned`, `n`, and `millis`.

Using hint()

The `hint()` method can be used to explicitly direct MongoDB to use a certain index. Let's say we are querying on multiple fields and only some of those fields are indexed. We can supply the indexed field as a JSON argument to `hint()` and force MongoDB to use the index.

```
//hint the query planner to use the genre index
> db.movies.find({name: 'Inception', genre: 'sci-fi'}).hint({genre:1})
```

In most situations, using `hint()` will be unnecessary, because the MongoDB query optimizer is quite smart about choosing which index to use. When a query is run for the first time, the optimizer attempts multiple query plans concurrently. It uses the plan that finishes first and suspends the others. This query plan is used in all future queries using the same keys.

[
Force a table scan

You can use the `hint ()` method to force a table scan even when you are querying an indexed field.

> db.movies.find({genre: 'sci-fi'}).hint({$natural:1})
]

Profiling queries

MongoDB ships with a built-in database profiler tool. It comes in handy for analyzing different database operations.

Profiling is turned off by default. It is turned on by running the `setProfilingLevel()` command in the mongo interactive shell. Profiling is database-specific.

```
> use testdb
switched to db testdb

> db.setProfilingLevel(1, 100)
{ "was" : 0, "slowms" : 10, "ok" : 1 }
```

These commands tell MongoDB to profile any query slower than 100 milliseconds on the database `testdb`. The profiling data is stored in the `system.profile` collection of the database.

```
> db.system.profile.find()
{ "ts" : ISODate("2011-08-28T13:51:12.725Z"), "info" : "query
  testdb.movies reslen:257 nscanned:7344  query: { query: { genre:
  \"action\" }}  nreturned:1 110ms", "millis" : 110 }
```

Understanding the output

The following are some of the important fields stored in the `system.profile` documents:

- `ts`: It is the timestamp when the profiling occurred
- `millis`: Specifies the time took to perform the operation in milliseconds
- `info`: Gives detailed information about the operation and could be either `query`, `update`, or `insert`
    - `ntoreturn`: It returns the number of objects requested by the client to return from the query
    - `query`: It returns the details of the query specification
    - `nscanned`: It returns the number of objects scanned while executing the operation

○   `reslen`: It returns the length of objects in the query result, specified in bytes

○   `nreturned`: The number of objects returned from the query

○   `upsert`: This indicates an `upsert` operation

Visit the following page for database profiling on MongoDB documentation to get more information about output fields: http://www.mongodb.org/display/ DOCS/Database+Profiler#DatabaseProfiler-UnderstandingtheOutput.

Optimization rules

Looking at the output of the profiling information, we can apply some general optimization rules:

•   When querying documents, `nscanned` should not be much larger than `nreturned` (for reasons explained earlier in this chapter). If so, we should consider building indexes on the query fields (this also applies for `update`/`upsert` operations).

•   If the size of objects returned by the query (`reslen`) is too big, performance will suffer. We should send a second parameter to `find()` to return only the fields that we need.

Securing MongoDB

MongoDB provides a basic user authentication mechanism for authorizing users accessing the database. In this section, we are going to learn how to add user authentication, adding/removing users to/from databases, and connecting to MongoDB with PHP in authenticated mode.

Time for action – adding user authentication in MongoDB

In this example, we will start the MongoDB server in authentication mode, and then add an admin user to the database. We will use this admin user account to create users for specific databases.

1.   Launch the `monogd` process in authentication mode by passing in the `--auth` flag:

```
$ ./mongodb/bin/mongod --auth

Sat Aug 27 23:11:56 [initandlisten] MongoDB starting : pid=603
   port=27017 dbpath=/data/db/ 32-bit
```

2. Launch the mongo shell and switch to `admin` database:

```
$ ./mongodb/bin/mongo
MongoDB shell version: 1.8.1
connecting to: test
> use admin
switched to db admin
>
```

3. Add a user named `dbadmin` to the `admin` database and set an arbitrary password:

```
> db.addUser('dbadmin', 'mysecretpass')
{
    "user" : "dbadmin",
    "readOnly" : false,
    "pwd" : "ca75881da377b1f792f82ce374cb2c0f"
}
```

4. Authenticate yourself as the just created `admin` user using the following command:

```
> db.auth('dbadmin', 'mysecretpass')
1
```

6. Switch to a different database named `testdb`. Add the user `testuser` for this database:

```
> use testdb
switched to db testdb
> db.addUser('testuser', 'abcd1234')
{
    "user" : "testuser",
    "readOnly" : false,
    "pwd" : "c930e938bc4479b5544cac839211c9d8"
}
```

7. Issue the next command to list all the users of the current database:

```
> db.system.users.find()
{
    "_id" : ObjectId("4e593b8ae088769ac5295593"),
    "user" : "testuser",
    "readOnly" : false, "pwd" : "c930e938bc4479b5544cac839211c9d8"
}
```

What just happened?

In the previous example, we demonstrated how to turn authentication on in the MongoDB server and create user accounts with administrative privileges over the whole server and/or a certain database. To turn authentication on, the `mongod` server process has to be started with the `--auth` flag:

```
$ ./mongodb/bin/mongod --auth
Sat Aug 27 23:11:56 [initandlisten] MongoDB starting : pid=603
   port=27017 dbpath=/data/db/ 32-bit
```

After that, we launched the mongo shell client and switched to the `admin` database. This is a special database for doing administrative tasks.

```
$ ./mongodb/bin/mongo
MongoDB shell version: 1.8.1
connecting to: test
> use admin
switched to db admin
>
```

Creating an admin user

An admin user is one who has administrative privileges over the entire database server. To create an admin, we have to be in the `admin` database and use the `addUser()` method, as follows:

```
> use admin
switched to db admin
> db.addUser('dbadmin', 'mysecretpass')
{
   "user" : "dbadmin",
   "readOnly" : false,
   "pwd" : "ca75881da377b1f792f82ce374cb2c0f"
}
```

This command creates an admin `user` named `dbadmin` and sets the password as `mysecretpass`. Once created, we have to authenticate as the admin user using the `auth()` method to perform further administrative tasks:

```
> db.auth('dbadmin', 'mysecretpass')
1
```

An admin user can create/remove database-specific users, and has read-write access to all databases on the server.

Creating regular user

As an admin user, we can create regular users, the ones having read/write access on a single database. To do so, we have to authenticate as admin, switch to a new database, and use the `addUser()` method again to create a user account for that namespace.

```
> use testdb
switched to db testdb
> db.addUser('testuser', 'abcd1234')
{
   "_id" : ObjectId("4e593b8ae088769ac5295593"),
   "user" : "testuser",
   "readOnly" : false,
   "pwd" : "c930e938bc4479b5544cac839211c9d8"
}
> db.auth('testuser', 'abcd1234')
1
>
```

We could also create a read-only user for a database:

```
> db.addUser('readonlyuser', 'abc123', true)
{
   "user" : "readonlyuser",
   "readOnly" : true,
   "pwd" : "bb15dce2e51f865353f0e7d8527f52f0"
}
>
```

Viewing, changing, and deleting user accounts

To list all the users in a database, use the following command:

```
> db.system.users.find()
{ "_id" : ObjectId("4e593b8ae088769ac5295593"), "user" : "testuser",
  "readOnly" : false, "pwd" : "c930e938bc4479b5544cac839211c9d8" }
{ "_id" : ObjectId("4e5950cde088769ac5295595"), "user" : "readonlyuser",
  "readOnly" : true, "pwd" : "bb15dce2e51f865353f0e7d8527f52f0" }
```

To change the password of an existing user, use the following command:

```
> db.addUser('testuser', 'newpassword')
{
  "_id" : ObjectId("4e593b8ae088769ac5295593"),
  "user" : "testuser",
  "readOnly" : false,
  "pwd" : "4b710c355d07736ea06795dfcd5f8c1c"
}
```

Since the `testuser` account already exists, the command will set its password to `newpassword`.

Finally, to remove a user account, use the following command:

```
> db.removeUser('testuser')
```

This will delete the `testuser` account from the namespace.

User authentication through PHP driver

To authenticate users when connecting to the server using the PHP driver, we have to pass the username and password as optional arguments to the `Mongo()` constructor. Consider the following code snippet:

```php
<?php
  $user = 'testuser';
  $password = 'abcd1234';
  $host = 'localhost';
  $port = 27017;
  $database = 'testdb';
  $connectionString = sprintf('mongodb://%s:%d/%s', $host, $port,
    $database);
  try{
    $dbConnection = new Mongo($connectionString,
      array('username' => $user, 'password' => $password));
    echo 'Connected to database!';
  } catch(MongoConnectionException $e) {
  exit($e->getMessage());
  }
```

The first argument to the constructor is the connection string, in the format `mongodb://<hostname>:<port>/<databasename>`. We sent the username and password as optional arguments.

Have a go hero – modify DBConnection class to add user authentication

Modify the `DBConnection` class defined in the `dbconnection.php` file that we created in earlier chapters to add user authentication.

Filtering user input

Developers building applications on top of relational databases have to take special care to guard against the dreaded SQL Injection. Since in MongoDB queries are not built from strings, we do not have to worry about that. That being said, we should be cautious about accepting user input, and filter them in the following situations:

- We should be careful about running server-side JavaScript (code supplied by the `MongoCode()` class in the PHP driver). The use of `$where` statements in a query comes to mind as an example. We should avoid concatenating user-supplied input to build JavaScipt code as arguments to `$where`. This will be similar to being vulnerable to SQL injection attacks.

- In situations where the keys of the BSON objects will be user-supplied, we should not allow any key having the dollar (`$`) or dot (`.`) sign in it, since these are part of special query operations. We could either remove these characters from key names, or use their full width Unicode equivalents.

For more detailed information about how to handle such cases, visit this page at the MongoDB official documentation site: `http://www.mongodb.org/display/DOCS/Do+I +Have+to+Worry+About+SQL+Injection`.

Running MongoDB server in a secure environment

The user authentication scheme in MongoDB is very basic and not so secure against sophisticated attacks. This is why it is recommended that a production MongoDB server should be deployed in a trusted environment. You may consider the following measures for ensuring such an environment:

- The server can be deployed behind a firewall

- Rather than listening to all available IP addresses on a machine (by default), the server should be configured to listen on a specific IP (specified using the `bind_ip` configuration option)

- The TCP ports utilized by the server should be configured so that only trusted machines can access them.

Ensuring data durability

One of coolest features of MongoDB that we discussed and used in earlier chapters, is its support for fast asynchronous writes. MongoDB achieves this speed by using memory-mapped files. A memory-mapped file is a data structure that represents a file in main memory the same way it is stored on the disk. Processes accessing such a file can treat it as a part of memory, speeding up the I/O performance. MongoDB uses memory-mapped files to perform disk I/O operations. When a document is loaded in the application, MongoDB transparently loads it from the disk to memory. Any writes to the document results in writing to the appropriate address in memory. MongoDB flushes the data in memory back to the disk every 60 seconds (which is the default interval between two successive flushes. It is configurable through the `--syncdelay` command-line option).

The problem with this approach is that if the system crashes even 1 millisecond before the flush, we will lose all the data since the last flush. The impressive write speed comes at the cost of durability. Fortunately, MongoDB provides us with ways to get around this problem. In this section, we are going to learn what can we do to improve the durability of data.

Journaling

Recent releases of MongoDB (version 1.7.5 and greater) provide a feature named **Journaling**. All the operations on data are recorded in special journal files. If the system ever crashes, the records from the journals are played back when the `mongod` process restarts, to restore the corrupted databases.

To enable journaling, we have to start the server with the `--journal` switch:

```
$ ./mongodb/bin/mongod --journal
```

 Since MongoDB 2.0 journaling is turned on by default in 64 bit versions, the default journaling could be turned off by sending the `--nojournal` flag.

When journaling is on, MongoDB creates a directory named `journal` under the `dbpath` (`/data/db by default`). This is where all the journaled files will reside. These files are all rotated, so we don't have to worry about them eating up disk space. If the server is shut down cleanly, all the files will be cleaned up. If the server crashes, the `mongod` process uses these files to replay the write operations. After it has finished the recovery process, it will start accepting connections from clients. Time to recover depends on the volume of journaled data.

Performance

When journaling is turned on, read performance is not affected, but write operations will incur the journaling overhead (journaling is a write-ahead operation, where changes to data are logged in the journal before they actually take place). However, MongoDB's official documentation says the overhead is too small to influence the writes, and claims to have minimized the speed gap between journaled and nonjournaled writes in the most recent releases.

Adrian Hills has done some benchmarking on MongoDB journaling and published the results in his personal blog: `http://www.adathedev.co.uk/2011/03/mongodb-journaling-performance-single.html`.

Measure journal overhead with journalLatencytest

To measure how long it takes your volume to write to the disk, use the `journalLatencyTest` command.

> use admin

> db.runCommand('journalLatencyTest')

Using fsync

If you want to make sure that your data makes it to the disk, you can use the `fsync` command in mongo shell.

```
> use admin
> db.runCommand({fsync:1})
```

`fsync` puts the write operations on hold until the data is written to the disk at the next flush. The read operations however, will not be blocked. We should use this command as sparingly as possible. We definitely don't want to use it on every insert, as it will slow down the write operations.

Doing fsync at insertion

The MongoDB-PHP driver allows us to force the data to be synced to disk at the time of insertion. This is done by setting the optional `fsync` option to TRUE in the `MongoCollection::insert()` method.

```
$collection->insert(array('user' => 'joe',
  'email' => 'joe@example.com'), array('fsync' => TRUE))
```

When doing an `fsync` insert, a safe insert is implied. (This means insert will not be asynchronous and program control waits for a server response.)

Replication

We could also use replication to ensure the durability of data. In a replicated setup, the database is hosted on multiple nodes instead of one. One of the nodes act as a master and all the write operations take place in this node. Other nodes are known as slaves and used for reads. The changes to data are asynchronously copied over from the master to the slave(s).

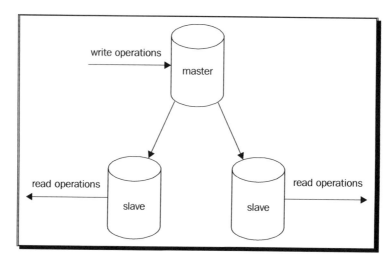

If the master crashes, we would still be able to read from the slaves. We can configure one of the slaves to act as master until the crashed master comes back up. Ideally, journaling should be turned on at the master node to ensure safe recovery of data.

Another way to ensure multi-server data durability is replica sets. A **Replica Set** essentially acts just like a master-slave replication cluster (it has a master node and one or more slave nodes) except the roles of the nodes are not fixed. When the master node (called a primary node in replica set context) goes down, the slave nodes (also known as secondary nodes) automatically elect a new master. Each node has a predefined priority and when the primary goes down, the node with the highest priority is elected as the new primary. In case of a tie, the node with the most recent version of data is elected. The developer does not have to be concerned about all this since it all happens automatically.

Features, such as replication and replica sets (and sharding) are excellent tools for ensuring data durability as well as improving scalability, a major selling point of MongoDB as a database server. Setting up and using these features is too advanced to be covered in a beginner's guide. But if you are interested, there are a lot of blog posts, books, and other kinds of content available covering those topics. You can start from this page at the MongoDB official documentation site: `http://www.mongodb.org/display/DOCS/Replication`.

Pop quiz – flushing data to disk

1. What is the default interval between data flushes to disk in MongoDB?

    a. 1 second

    b. 0.1 second

    c. 1 minute

    d. 1 millisecond

2. What happens when the `fsync` flag is set to TRUE during insertion?

    a. Program control continues to the next statement (asynchronous insert)

    b. MongoDB checks for data integrity, such as uniqueness of `_id`

    c. Data is flushed to disk

    d. All of the above

Summary

Let's review what we covered in this chapter:

- We learned how to enhance query performance by creating indexes on appropriate fields
- How to use the MongoDB database profiler, explain and hint tools to analyze, and optimize queries.
- Enabling user authentication in MongoDB, adding/removing user accounts, and using user authentication through the MongoDB-PHP driver
- Using the journaling feature to improve data durability

We also covered when indexes are not a good idea, when and why we should filter user input for security reasons, and what is the speed-durability trade-off when journaling is turned on. In the next chapter, we will learn about tools for administering a MongoDB server.

10
Easy MongoDB Administration with RockMongo and phpMoAdmin

We have been using the **mongo** interactive shell quite heavily for querying MongoDB, inserting data, building indexes, and so on. This is because getting comfortable with using the JavaScript query language in the shell is very important for a developer working with MongoDB, even though he would be using PHP (or the programming language of his choice) most of the time for talking to the database. However, when it comes to being productive, many people prefer using graphical user interface (GUI) tools (I am saying many people, not all people, because there are those of us who prefer the command line!). There are quite a few GUI tools available for administering MongoDB, developed and supported by third-party developers. But we are going to focus on the ones built with PHP – **RockMongo** and **phpMoAdmin**. The obvious benefit of using PHP based admin GUIs is that we can deploy them on the existing **LAMP** (**Linux-Apache-MongoDB-PHP**) stack, and don't have to install any additional software to support them. In this chapter, we are going to cover how to install and run both RockMongo and phpMoAdmin on a computer; how to use them to query, insert, update, and delete documents; how to import or export data; how to retrieve server stats; and so on. Finally, we will compare these two tools based on their features and try to identify the more suitable one.

Specifically, in this chapter, we will discuss the following topics:

- Downloading and installing RockMongo on the computer
- Using RockMongo to query, save, and delete documents
- Importing and exporting data using RockMongo, getting server/database stats

- Installing phpMoAdmin on the machine; querying databases, saving, and deleting documents, using data import/export tools, getting server stats

- Comparing features of RockMongo and phpMoAdmin

Administering MongoDB with RockMongo

RockMongo is a GUI tool for browsing and administering MongoDB and written in PHP 5. It is basically a web application running on top of Apache (or any web server that supports PHP 5) that lets you manage databases hosted on a MongoDB server. It is an open source project (BSD license), hosted on Google Code (`http://code.google.com/p/rock-php/`) and has released stable versions.

Time for action – installing RockMongo on your computer

In this section, we will learn how to download, configure, and run RockMongo on a computer. The following instructions are not platform specific, and you can run them either on a Windows or a UNIX machine:

1. Download the latest stable version of RockMongo (marked as *Featured*) from the **Downloads** page of the project website `http://code.google.com/p/rock-php/downloads/list`:

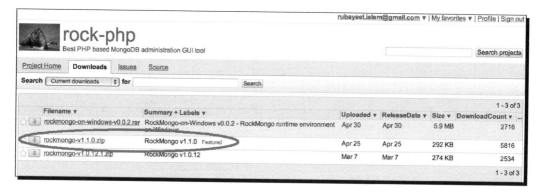

2. Unzip the downloaded zip file and rename the unzipped directory as `rockmongo`.

3. Move the `rockmongo` directory under the document root (the `htdocs` folder in case you are using Apache) of your web server.

4. Open the `config.php` file under `rockmongo` in your text editor and set the `$MONGO["servers"][$i]["mongo_auth"]` variable to `true`.

```
$MONGO["servers"][$i]["mongo_auth"] = true;
```

5. Launch the web browser and visit the `index.php` file of the app. You will see the **Log-in** page of RockMongo:

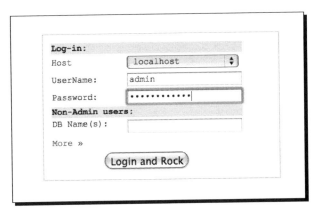

6. Type in the **Username** and **Password** of the admin user of your MongoDB server, and click the **Login and Rock** button. You will be redirected to the landing page as shown in the following screenshot (in case you don't have an admin user, keep the `mongo_auth` settings to `false` in step 5 and use `admin` as the default username and password).

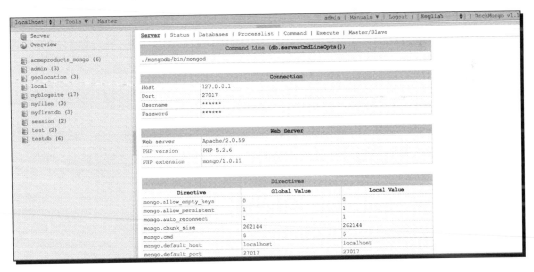

What just happened?

We downloaded the latest stable version of RockMongo as a zipped file from Google code, unzipped the package, and deployed it on the web server running on your machine. We changed the `config.php` file so that only admin users in MongoDB are allowed access to RockMongo. We achieved this by switching the `mongo_auth` flag to `true`:

```
$MONGO["servers"][$i]["mongo_auth"] = true;
```

By default, `mongo_auth` is set to `false`, and we can use `admin` as the default username and password. We can change these default values by changing the `control_users` flag:

```
//one of control users [USERNAME]=PASSWORD, works only if
//mongo_auth=false
$MONGO["servers"][$i]["control_users"]["admin"] = "mysecretpass";
```

The `config.php` file contains global configurations for the entire app; we can set the host, port, and connection timeout values for the MongoDB server. We can also configure RockMongo so that it shows only the databases that we want it to show, and hides others. The configuration file is quite well commented, so users can easily figure out how to achieve these changes.

After logging into RockMongo, we arrived at a landing page that lists all the databases hosted on the server in the left sidebar. The content area on the right shows server settings (host, port, and so on), web server name, PHP version, and runtime directives. If we click on the **Databases** link on the top of the content area, it shows a table listing all the databases, along with some additional information such as number of collections per database, index size, total number of objects, and so on. A new database can be created by clicking on the **Create new Database** link at the top of the table.

Exploring data with RockMongo

Clicking on a database name on the left sidebar expands it and shows all the collections in the database. We can create a new collection by clicking on the **Create** link on the expanded tree in the left pane. Clicking on a collection name shows all the documents in a paginated list in that collection in the content area to the right.

Querying

We can query documents by writing the query expression in the text area at the top of content panel and then hitting the **Submit Query** button. Query expressions can be written either in JSON format or in PHP array format. This could be a little inconvenient for those who don't like typing query expressions in the command line, since this does not give them any point and click alternative for achieving the task, as GUI tools are supposed to do. The documents returned by the query are displayed below the text area in a paginated list:

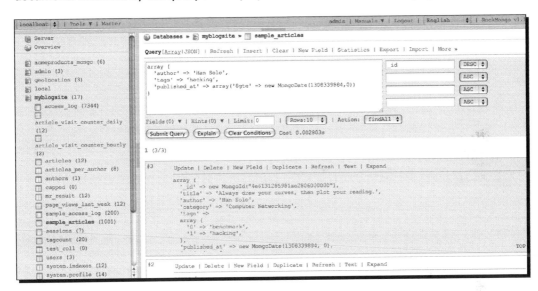

The textboxes to the right of the text area are used for sorting the results; we can specify the fields on which to sort in the textboxes, and select the desired order (ascending or descending) from the drop-down menu. The textbox labeled **Limit** is used to limit the query. Finally, the **Fields** menu can be used to specify a subset of fields to be returned by the query.

Updating, deleting, and creating documents

Documents returned by the query can be individually updated by clicking on the **Update** link on top of each document. Clicking the link opens the associated document (either in PHP or JSON format) in a text area of a new page, where the user can make changes to the document and click on the **Save** button to apply the changes. We can add a new field to a single document by clicking on the **New Field** link associated with it. It shows a pop-up box where we can specify the name, data type, and value of the field.

We can also perform bulk updates by writing the query for selecting documents to be updated in the query text area and choosing **modify** from the **Action** drop-down menu (default is **findAll**). This will open a second text area, below the one we are using, where we can write the expression for updating each document. Once we have done that, we can apply the bulk edit by clicking on the **Submit Query** button:

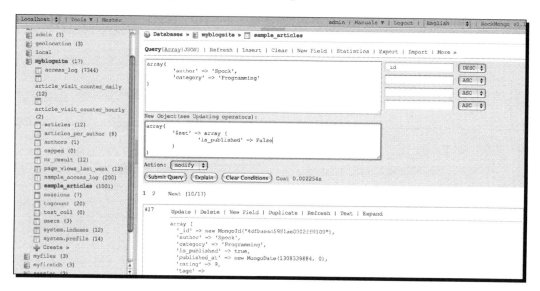

In the previous screenshot, we are querying all documents in the `sample_articles` collection having Spock as the author and Programming as category and setting their `is_published` flag to `false`.

We can delete individual records by clicking on the **Delete** link on top of each document shown in the paginated list. We can also perform bulk deletes much in the same way we do bulk updates (specifying the query and selecting **remove** from the **Action** drop-down menu).

To insert documents, we have to click on the **Insert** link at the top of the content panel. It takes us to a new page showing a big text area. Here we can type in the new document in PHP array syntax or JSON and insert it by clicking the **Save button**.

Importing and exporting data

Data importing and exporting options are important features for any database administration tool. We need them for creating backups or migrating data. RockMongo allows us to export data in one or more collections in JSON format. When exploring a database, clicking on the **Export** link at the top of the page takes us to the data export page:

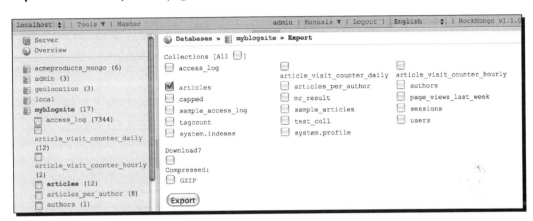

We can select the collections whose data we want to export by ticking the checkboxes next to their names (or we could select the checkbox labeled **All** and dump the entire database). If the **Download?** option is selected, RockMongo will write the exported data in a JSON file, which will be downloaded automatically on to the computer. Selecting the GZIP option compresses the downloadable file; this comes in handy when exporting a large dataset.

The import interface is pretty simple and shows a form with a file upload field. We just need to select the JSON file containing the data and hit the **Import** button. We will get a success message if the data is imported without any glitches.

> When exporting/importing large amounts of data, RockMongo may run out of memory and execution time allotted per PHP script. To get around this, set the `max_execution_time` and `memory_limit` directives in `php.ini` to higher values.

Viewing stats

To get different stats about the server running on the machine, click on the **Server** link at the top of the left sidebar, and then click on **Stats** on the resulting page in the content area:

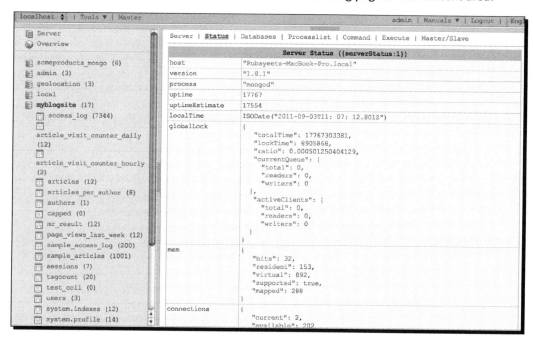

This page shows some useful information about the server, such as uptime, memory consumption, number of open connections, network activity, and so on. We can also view what operations are running on the server in real time by clicking on the **Processlist** link at the top.

Miscellaneous

We can view the users authorized for a particular database by clicking on the database name on the left sidebar and then clicking on the **More | Authentication** link in the top-right corner of the content area. The page will display the currently authorized users for the database in a table. We can add new users by clicking on the **Add User** link and filling out the form.

To see what indexes there are for a collection, click on the collection name on the left sidebar and click on the **More | Indexes** link at the top of the content panel. We can view existing indexes, add new ones, or drop them individually from using the links shown in the landing page.

RockMongo also has support for GridFS. The `files` and `chunks` collections can be browsed just like regular collections, except when we are browsing `files` we will see **Download** and **Chunks** links on top of each document. Clicking on the former will download the stored file on the computer, while clicking on the latter will display the associated `chunks` documents for that file.

We can also run MapReduce jobs on RockMongo. While on the database view, clicking on the **Execute** link at the top of content area takes us to a page showing a text area where we can define the JavaScript map, reduce, and finalize functions. Hitting the **Execute Code** button will run the defined functions on the database and the response will be printed at the bottom.

Using phpMoAdmin to administer MongoDB

phpMoAdmin is a GUI tool for administering MongoDB databases. It is built with PHP and runs on Apache. phpMoAdmin is built using a stripped-down version of Vork, a high-performance PHP web framework. It is very light-weight, and the entire app is contained within a 95 Kilobyte file. Like RockMongo, this is also open sourced (GPLv3 FOSS License), and hosted on Github (`https://github.com/MongoDB-Rox/phpMoAdmin-MongoDB-Admin-Tool-for-PHP`).

Time for action – installing phpMoAdmin on your computer

In this example, we will see how to download and install phpMoAdmin on your computer. The following instructions can be run either on a Windows or a Unix platform:

1. Download the phpMoAdmin app from its official website: `http://www.phpmoadmin.com/file/phpmoadmin.zip`.

2. Unzip the zipped file to extract the `moadmin.php` script.

3. Create a new directory named `phpmoadmin` inside the document root directory of your web server (the `htdocs` folder in case you are running Apache). Copy and paste the `moadmin.php` script to this new directory.

4. Open the `moadmin.php` file in your text editor and uncomment the following line

   `$accessControl = array('scott' => 'tiger');`

5. Launch the web browser and visit the `phpmoadmin/moadmin.php` page, type in `scott` and `tiger` as username and password. You will be redirected to the default landing page of the app:

What just happened?

Installing phpMoAdmin on the computer is very simple, as we saw in the last example. We downloaded the single script app and copied it to the document root folder of our local web server in its own directory. We configured the script and turned on user authentication (turned off in phpMoAdmin by default) by uncommenting the following line:

```
$accessControl = array('scott' => 'tiger');
```

We can modify this line to change the default password, and/or add as many users as we like.

```
$accessControl = array('admin' => 'mysecretpass',
   'scott' => 'tiger');
```

Finally, we launched the app by running the script on the browser. After providing the username and password, we were redirected to the landing page of the app. By default, the admin database is selected as the database to be explored.

Viewing databases and collections

The databases hosted on the MongoDB server are listed as options in the drop-down box in the top-left corner of the page. The collections in the database are listed under the drop-down box. By default admin is selected as the database, and none of its collections are shown (since it is a system database). To switch to a different database, we have to choose one from the drop-down and hit the **Change database** button:

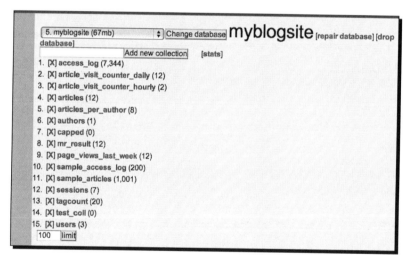

Querying documents

When we click on a collection shown in the list, the page reloads with all the documents in the database. We can write queries in PHP array syntax or JSON format in the text area that appears once we click on the **[query]** link. The result of the query can be sorted by selecting a sort key and order from the drop-down boxes that appear when the **sort** link is clicked. An interesting feature of phpMoAdmin is the *search* feature. We can choose a field name from the drop-down menu in the top-left corner (this appears when the **[search]** link is clicked) and specify the value in the textbox next to it. After that we can launch a search by clicking on the **Search** link. This comes in very handy when quickly looking for documents. We can also perform a search by entering wildcards (*), JSON objects, or regular expressions in the search box. Although the search box can search on only one field, we can narrow the scope of the search by adding query expressions in the text area below (this appears when the **[query]** link is clicked):

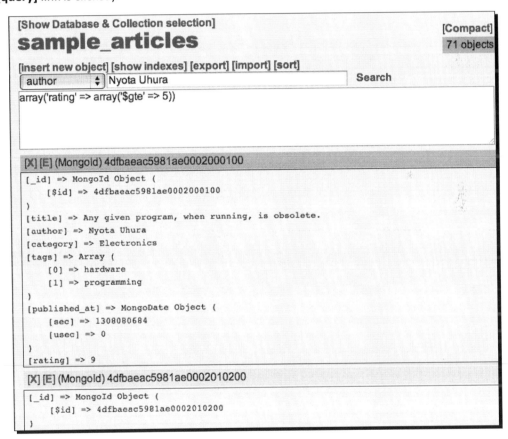

The previous screenshot shows how to perform a search where we are looking for documents in the **sample_articles** collection with Nyota Uhura as the author with a rating greater or equal to 5.

Saving and deleting objects

Every document shown in the result set has two links, X and E in the top-left corner. Clicking on the former deletes the document (after confirmation from the user); clicking on the latter opens the document in a text area in PHP array syntax where we can modify it and save it by hitting the **Save Changes** button. We can also create new documents by clicking on the **insert new object** link, writing the document in PHP array syntax in the text area, and clicking on the **Save changes** button.

Importing and exporting data

phpMoAdmin is quite impressive when it comes to importing or exporting data. It allows us to export the data returned by a query, as well as to export the whole collection. In the case of importing, it lets us specify what to do when duplicate objects are encountered. Both import and export use the JSON format:

[Show Database & Collection selection]

sample_articles

- **Export full results of this query (ignoring limit and skip clauses)**
- **Export exactly the results visible on this page**

Import
(Choose File) No file chosen
(•)Insert: skips over duplicate records
( )Save: overwrites duplicate records
( )Update: overwrites only records that currently exist (skips new objects)
( )Batch-Insert: Halt upon reaching first duplicate record (may result in partial dataset)
(Import records into this collection)

Unfortunately, there is no option to export an entire database.

Viewing stats

To see server stats, we can click on the **[Show databases & Collection selection]** link at the top, choose the intended database from the drop-down box, and then click on the **stats** link. The information is displayed in the content area of the page in a plain HTML unordered list, which is not very visually useful:

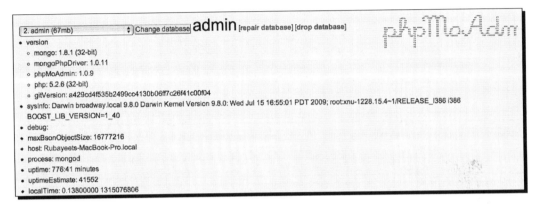

Other features

Here are some other mentionable features of phpMoAdmin:

- The index view (this appears when the **show indexes** link is clicked when browsing a collection) shows us what indexes are in a collection, and lets us create or drop indexes.

- It has GridFS support. GridFS file objects are automatically linked to GridFS chunks.

- Supports multiple themes. Themes can be set by changing the theme constant in the `moadmin.php` file (the choices are classic, trontastic, and swanky-purse), although it hardly serves any purpose from a functionality point of view, as follows:

```
/**
 * Sets the design theme - themes options are: swanky-purse,
 * trontastic and classic
 */
define('THEME', 'classic');
```

RockMongo versus phpMoAdmin

Now that we have played with both RockMongo and phpMoAdmin, let us compare these two GUI tools based on some important factors and try to figure out which one is more suited to our specific needs.

Feature	RockMongo (v1.1.0)	phpMoAdmin (1.1.0)
Installation	Installation is quite easy. Some configuration is needed to turn password-protection on.	Installation is very simple. Just drop the single script app in a directory on the web server and it is ready to go.
Configurability	User can change the default configuration settings by modifying the well-commented `config.php` file.	Not as configurable. User will have to delve deep into the code and tweak the default settings.
User authentication	Supports both app level and database level user authentication. Allows the user to add/remove users on a MongoDB database.	Only app level user authentication. No support for authenticating/adding/removing users defined in MongoDB.
Interface	The UI is very clean and professional looking. The controls on the screen are placed in clearly defined regions; operation results are printed in visually comprehensible form.	Interface is not as good. Doing some of the tasks is not as intuitive as it should be.
Querying	Supports querying in both PHP array and JSON syntax. No visual tool for performing queries; might be inconvenient for some people.	Provides a smart search box that supports querying using text, integers, JSON objects, regular expressions, and so on. Complex queries are done using JSON or PHP array syntax.
Data import and export	Supports importing and exporting of data in JSON format. No option for resolving duplicate objects while importing. Supports export of entire databases.	Importing and exporting are done in JSON format. Allows the user to export the result of a query. User can specify how to resolve duplicate data issues while importing data.

Feature	RockMongo (v1.1.0)	phpMoAdmin (1.1.0)
Server stats display	Supports displaying server stats information in a clearly comprehensible format. User can check what processes are running in the background.	Displays sever stats, but the output is not visually helpful. No support for checking processes running in background.
Managing Indexes	Supports listing, creating, and dropping of indexes on a collection.	Supports listing, creating, and dropping of indexes on a collection.
Map/Reduce	Allows the user to define map and reduce functions in JavaScript and execute them.	No support for running MapReduce through the interface.
GridFS	Files are automatically associated with chunks. Supports downloading of files.	Files and chunks are automatically associated. No support for downloads.

The verdict

If you are looking for a GUI tool to manage MongoDB servers in the production environment, you should go with RockMongo. Its clean and professional looking interface with the ability to control background processes, run Map/Reduce jobs, and so on to makes it an excellent choice for a serious MongoDB administration tool. If you are working on your local machine and just looking for a simple and visual alternative to the `mongo` interactive shell (one that lets you run queries using buttons and drop-down menus!) you might want to go with phpMoAdmin.

Summary

Let's quickly go over what we covered in this chapter:

- We learned how to download and install the RockMongo GUI tool into a LAMP environment and how to configure it to support the MongoDB user authentication system.

- We reviewed how RockMongo can be used to explore databases and collections on a MongoDB server, how documents are queried, created, modified, and deleted, how to perform other administrative tasks such as index management, data import/export, adding user accounts, and so on.

- We learned how to download and install the phpMoAdmin GUI tool.

- We played around with phpMoAdmin and figured out how to create/update/delete documents with it, how to import and export data, and how to use its smart search box to quickly query and view data.

- We drew a comparison between RockMongo and phpMoAdmin based on their features, and attempted to choose the better tool for development and production environments.

This concludes our journey of learning web development with PHP and MongoDB. I hope you enjoyed it as much as I did. I would encourage you to keep learning more about the topics covered in this book using the Internet, master advanced topics, such as scaling with replication and sharding, and build really cool web applications with PHP and MongoDB!

Pop Quiz Answers

Chapter 1, Getting Started with MongoDB

- What is the default port address of MongoDB?

  o **Answer**: 27017

- How does a new database get created in MongoDB?

  o **Answer**: By doing `use <databasename>` first and then doing `db.<collectionname>.insert(<jsondocument>)`

Chapter 2, Building your First MongoDB Powered Web App

- What does this following query do?

  ```
  $movies->find(array('genre' => 'comedy',
    'year' => array('$gt' => 2009, '$lt' => 2011)));
  ```

  o **Answer**: Gets all movies released after the year 2009 and before the year 2011

Chapter 3, Building a Session Manager

- Which session handling callback method gets called when we call the `session_destory()` method in our code?

  o **Answer:** `destroy()`

Chapter 4, Aggregation Queries

- The concept MapReduce has been derived from which programming paradigm?

  o **Answer:** Functional Programming

- When running a MapReduce job in a distributed environment that is, on a cluster of machines, which of the following task a master node is supposed to do?

  o **Answer:** both a. and c.

- Which of the following is a limitation of the `group()` command for running aggregation queries in MongoDB

  o **Answer:** All of the above

Chapter 5, Web Analytics using MongoDB

- Which of the following is a false statement?

  o **Answer:** Documents in a capped collection cannot be modified

- What happens when a capped collection exceeds its pre-allocated size when we are inserting new documents into it?

  o **Answer:** The newly inserted objects automatically replace the oldest ones in the collection

- Sorting by natural order means:

  o **Answer:** The documents that were inserted first will be returned first (First in First Out)

Chapter 7, Handling Large Files with GridFS

- What is the maximum allowed size of BSON objects (MongoDB documents)?

  o **Answer:** 16 MB

- If a 20 MB file is stored in GridFS, how many chunks will it be split into?

  o **Answer:** 80

Chapter 8, Building Location-aware Web Applications with MongoDB and PHP

- Suppose you are the proud owner of a high-end, cutting-edge smartphone. Which of the following techniques could potentially be used to detect its geographic location?

  o **Answer:** All of the above

Chapter 9, Improving Security and Performance

- What data structure is used for storing indexes in MongoDB?

  o **Answer:** B-tree

- What is the maximum allowed size for a key to be indexed?

  o **Answer:** 800 Bytes

- Which of the following use cases is not suitable for having indexes on a collection?

  o **Answer:** All of the above

- What is the default interval between data flushes to disk in MongoDB?

  o **Answer:** 1 minute

- What happens when the `fsync` flag is set to TRUE during insertion?

  o **Answer:** Data is flushed to disk

Index

D

daily sales history of products
  storing, in MongoDB 153-159
dashboard.php file 53
data
  exploring, with RockMongo 244
  exporting 252
  importing 252
data archiving
  about 148
  MongoDB, using for 160
databases
  articles, retrieving from 38-41
  creating 19, 20
  creating, implicitly 35
  creating, in MySQL 150, 152
  safe inserts, performing for 35
  selecting, shortcut approach 35
  viewing 250
data durability
  ensuring 236
  journaling 236
  replication 238
data exchange format, MongoDB 11
data, exploring with RockMongo
  about 244
  documents, creating 245, 246
  documents, deleting 245, 246
  documents, querying 245
  documents, updating 245, 246
data exporting options, RockMongo 247
data importing options, RockMongo 247
date() function 37
dates
  range queries, performing on 50
DBConnection class 83, 107
dbconnnection.php file 107
delete() method 170
destroy() method 79, 84
distinct categories
  listing, of articles 125, 126
distinct() method
  about 125
  using, in mongo shell 127

distinct values
  listing, for fields 125
document-based databases 8
documents
  about 10
  anatomy 10
  conditional queries 44
  counting, with count() method 127
  creating 19, 20, 245, 246
  deleting 245, 246
  deleting, in capped collection 135
  deleting, in MongoDB 58
  fields 104
  grouping, by custom keys 124
  inserting, in MongoDB 30
  querying 245, 251
  querying, in collection 38
  relationships, managing between 63
  returning, in array 43
  structure 104
  updating 245, 246
  updating, in capped collection 135
  updating, in MongoDB 51
domains
  setting, for session cookies 100
drawLocationOnMap() function 199
drawLocationOnMap() method 198
dropIndex() method 224
drop() method 135
Dynomite 8

E

echo statement 36
embedded document fields
  indexing 223
embedded documents
  about 64
  versus referenced documents 69
embedded objects
  querying 69, 70
emit() method 112
ensureIndex() command 214
ensureIndex() method 202, 220
entity metadata
  storing 149

explain() method
about 227
arguments 228
queries, explaining with 227, 228
explain() method, arguments
cursor 228
millis 228
n 228
nscanned 228

F

Facebook 8
features, MongoDB 9, 130
features, phpMoAdmin 253
fields
deleting, with $unset 57
distinct values, listing for 125
renaming, with $rename 57
subset, returning 49
files
about 176
deleting 186
reading in chunks 187
serving, from GridFS 182-185
storing, in GridFS 178, 180
files_id field 176
finalize function 140
find() command 20, 113, 134, 208
find() method 41, 42, 49, 103
findOne() method 41
Flatland 200
Flexible schema feature 130
foreach loop 43
foreign key constraints
dealing with 163
Foursquare 9, 191
Foursquare API
used, for sample data 203
fsync command 237

G

gc method 79, 85
geographic position
determining, of computing device 192
geohashing 200
geolocation 192

Geolocation object
about 198
getCurrentPosition() method 198
geoNear() command 208, 210
geoSearch parameter 215
geospatial index
about 218
creating, on MongoDB collection 201
geospatial indexing
about 200
overview 202
getBytes() method 185
getCollection() method 83
getCurrentPosition() method 198, 199
getIndexes() method 220
getMetadata() method 172
getNearByRestaurants() method 208, 214
getNext() method 41, 43
Global Positioning System. *See* **GPS**
Google 108, 192
Google Maps API
about 199
used, for drawing map 199, 200
google.maps.Map object 199
GPLv3 FOSS License 249
GPS 192
graph-based data-stores 8
GridFS
about 175, 248
advantages, over filesystem 177
files, serving from 182-185
files, storing in 178, 180
images, serving from 183-185
images, uploading to 178, 180
principle 176
group() method
about 120-124
aggregation, performing with 120
optional arguments 120
parameters 120
versus MapReduce 124
group() method, parameters
initial 120
key 120
reduce 120
GUI tool 242

H

handleGeoloacteError() method 198
Hard Disk Drives (HDD) 225
hasNext() method 43
haystack.php file 215
Hbase 8
hint() command 222
hint() method 228
HomeBrew 17
HTTP 74
HTTP request
  about 130
  aspects 131
HTTP session
  about 74
  overview 74
Hypertable 8

I

image gallery
  creating, with GridFS 187
images
  reading, in chunks 187-189
  serving, from GridFS 183-185
  uploading, to GridFS 178, 180
index
  creating, on look up fields 145
  creating, on MongoDB collection 218, 220
  deleting 224
  query performance, enhancing 217, 218
indexing
  cost 226
  don'ts 224
  guidelines 225, 226
indexing costs 226
indexing guidelines 225, 226
index size 225
initialize() static method 83
insert
  timeout, specifying on 36
insert() method 30, 35
installing
  MongoDB, on OS X 17
  PHP driver, for MongoDB 21, 22
  PHP-MongoDB driver, on UNIX 23

IP address 192
isLoggedIn() method 92
iterator_to_array() function 43

J

Java 11
JavaScript 130
JOIN queries 160
journalining
  about 236
  enabling 236
  fsync command, using 237
  performance 237
journalLatencyTest command 237
JSON 11

K

key-value data stores 8

L

LAMP (Linux-Apache-MongoDB-PHP) 241
lastError() method 186
limit() method 50
Linux
  MongoDB, running on 15, 16
listDBs() method 25
location
  detecting, of web page visitor 193
  detecting, with W3C Geolocation API 194-197
location-aware web application 191
location queries
  performing 203-208
login page
  about 93
  creating 93-98
logout page
  about 93
  creating 93-98
logRequest() method 134
log table 149
look up fields
  index, creating on 145

User class
  building 89-92
user generated _id
  setting 37
user input
  filtering 235
username
  comments, getting by 70

V

Views
  about 160
  replacing, with MongoDB 160
Voldemort 8

W

W3C Geolocation API
  about 193
  browsers 194
  location, detecting with 194-197
web analytics 130
web page visitor
  location, detecting 193
while loop 42
Wi-Fi MAC address tracking 192
Windows
  MongoDB, running on 13, 14
  PHP driver, installing for MongoDB 21, 22
write() method 78, 84

Thank you for buying
PHP and MongoDB Web Development
Beginner's Guide

About Packt Publishing

Packt, pronounced 'packed', published its first book "*Mastering phpMyAdmin for Effective MySQL Management*" in April 2004 and subsequently continued to specialize in publishing highly focused books on specific technologies and solutions.

Our books and publications share the experiences of your fellow IT professionals in adapting and customizing today's systems, applications, and frameworks. Our solution based books give you the knowledge and power to customize the software and technologies you're using to get the job done. Packt books are more specific and less general than the IT books you have seen in the past. Our unique business model allows us to bring you more focused information, giving you more of what you need to know, and less of what you don't.

Packt is a modern, yet unique publishing company, which focuses on producing quality, cutting-edge books for communities of developers, administrators, and newbies alike. For more information, please visit our website: www.packtpub.com.

About Packt Open Source

In 2010, Packt launched two new brands, Packt Open Source and Packt Enterprise, in order to continue its focus on specialization. This book is part of the Packt Open Source brand, home to books published on software built around Open Source licences, and offering information to anybody from advanced developers to budding web designers. The Open Source brand also runs Packt's Open Source Royalty Scheme, by which Packt gives a royalty to each Open Source project about whose software a book is sold.

Writing for Packt

We welcome all inquiries from people who are interested in authoring. Book proposals should be sent to author@packtpub.com. If your book idea is still at an early stage and you would like to discuss it first before writing a formal book proposal, contact us; one of our commissioning editors will get in touch with you.

We're not just looking for published authors; if you have strong technical skills but no writing experience, our experienced editors can help you develop a writing career, or simply get some additional reward for your expertise.

PHP and CouchDB Web Development Beginner's Guide

ISBN: 978-1-84951-358-6   Paperback: 282 pages

Get your PHP application from conception to deployment by leveraging CouchDB's robust features.

1. Build and deploy a flexible Social Networking application using PHP and leveraging key features of CouchDB to do the heavy lifting

2. Explore the features and functionality of CouchDB, by taking a deep look into Documents, Views, Replication, and much more.

3. Conceptualize a lightweight PHP framework from scratch and write code that can easily port to other frameworks

Cassandra High Performance Cookbook

ISBN: 978-1-84951-512-2   Paperback: 310 pages

Over 150 recipes to design and optimize large scale Apache Cassandra deployments

1. Get the best out of Cassandra using this efficient recipe bank

2. Configure and tune Cassandra components to enhance performance

3. Deploy Cassandra in various environments and monitor its performance

4. Well illustrated, step-by-step recipes to make all tasks look easy!

Please check **www.PacktPub.com** for information on our titles

PostgreSQL 9 Administration Cookbook: LITE

ISBN: 978-1-849516-42-6 Paperback: 88 pages

Configuration, Monitoring and Maintenance

1. Administer and maintain a healthy database

2. Configure your PostgreSQL database to your needs

3. Monitor your database and learn to diagnose any problems

4. Part of Packt's Cookbook series: Each recipe is a carefully organized sequence of instructions to complete the task as efficiently as possible

PostgreSQL 9.0 High Performance

ISBN: 978-1-84951-030-1 Paperback: 468 pages

Accelerate your PostgreSQL system

1. Learn the right techniques to obtain optimal PostgreSQL database performance, from initial design to routine maintenance

2. Discover the techniques used to scale successful database installations

3. Avoid the common pitfalls that can slow your system down

4. Filled with advice about what you should be doing; how to build experimental databases to explore performance topics, and then move what you've learned into a production database environment

17737753R00155

Made in the USA
Lexington, KY
29 September 2012